DEC 1 4

Rocket and Lightship

Rocket and Lightship

Essays on Literature and Ideas

Adam Kirsch

W. W. Norton & Company
NEW YORK · LONDON

For information about permission to reproduce selections from
this book, write to Permissions, W. W. Norton & Company, Inc.,
500 Fifth Avenue, New York, NY 10110

For information about special discounts for bulk purchases, please contact
W. W. Norton Special Sales at specialsales@wwnorton.com or 800-233-4830

Manufacturing by RR Donnelley, Harrisonburg
Book design by Iris Weinstein
Production manager: Ruth Toda

Library of Congress Cataloging-in-Publication Data

Kirsch, Adam, 1976–
[Essays. Selections]
Rocket and lightship : essays on literature and ideas / Adam Kirsch.
page cm
ISBN 978-0-393-24346-8 (hardcover)
1. Literature and society. 2. Authors. 3. Life in literature. 4. Art and literature.
5. Meaning (Psychology) 6. Pleasure. I. Title. II. Title: Essays on literature and ideas.
PS3611.I77A6 2014
814'.6—dc23

2014020823

W. W. Norton & Company, Inc., 500 Fifth Avenue, New York, N.Y. 10110
www.wwnorton.com

W. W. Norton & Company Ltd., Castle House, 75/76 Wells Street,
London W1T 3QT

1 2 3 4 5 6 7 8 9 0

For Remy

Contents

Preface

o o o

"It is important, therefore, to hold fast to this: that poetry is at bottom a criticism of life." Matthew Arnold's formulation, which he advanced in his essay on Wordsworth and returned to in later essays, has never quite recovered from the beating it took at the hands of T. S. Eliot, who found it a shallow way of thinking about something as fundamentally mysterious as poetry. "At bottom, that is a great way down; the bottom is the bottom. At the bottom of the abyss is what few ever see, and what those cannot bear to look at for long; and it is not a 'criticism of life,'" Eliot replied. Indeed, it is hard to be quite comfortable with the way Arnold goes on to define the "criticism of life" as the "powerful and beautiful application of ideas to life." Application sounds like too external and mechanical a process, and not all the ideas we need are beautiful.

To understand the phrase more broadly, however, may redeem it. All literature, not just poetry, is a criticism of life—but not in the sense of a negative comment or a suggestion for improvement, as Arnold seems to imply. Such criticism is, rather, the record of one mind's response to the experience of being in the world. Each genre of literature has its own methods for representing that experience and interpreting it: poetry uses rhythm and metaphor, fiction uses plot and character. In a broader sense, even genres of writing that are not ordinarily thought of as literary—such as theory, philosophy, politics, history—can also be seen as criticisms of life. For any kind of serious writing is expressive of the writer's experience of being in the world, of his aspirations and expectations and anxieties.

If this is so, then almost any genre of writing can be usefully subjected to literary criticism. For criticism, too, is a kind of literature; the critic expresses his own sense of life through his responses to other minds and sensibilities. This makes criticism, inevitably, a less immediate and powerful form of writing than poetry or fiction, and a more self-conscious one. But since all serious readers engage in this same process of shaping themselves in response to what they read, criticism is also capable of a unique kind of intimacy, and even, despite appearances, vulnerability. For the critic's assertions are always, read truly, only propositions, impressions, requests for assent. This is how it seems to me: does it seem that way to you too?

Thinking of my own work as a critic in this way, I see a basic continuity between writing about poetry, as I have done in the past, and writing more broadly about literature and ideas, as I do in this book. These essays, written over approximately the last eight years, engage with texts at the point where literature intersects with society and history—the point where, I think, criticism eventually has to end up. Begin thinking about, say, the novels of E. M. Forster, and soon enough it becomes clear that Forster's fiction is born from, and limited by, a certain understanding of liberalism. Thinking about Darwinism means wondering what the animalization of humanity means for art and ethics. Examining a writer's Jewishness, as I do in several essays, means exploring his or her most personal being and most public, historical identity.

This way of thinking about criticism rests on the liberal principle that the individual, the individual's experience of life, is prior to all the languages we use to describe it. Different kinds of writing demand different techniques of response, but in every case what interests me is the criticism of life a text expresses. And the way that certain themes and concerns keep coming back from essay to essay in this book suggests that I have tried, at times unconsciously, to express something of my own experience in the form of criticism.

Rocket and Lightship

Art over Biology

∘ ∘ ∘

In his early story "Tonio Kröger," Thomas Mann created a parable of one of the central modern beliefs, which is that the artist is unfit for life. Starting from childhood, everything about Tonio serves to mark him out from the society in which he is fated to live. Dark among blonds, half-Spanish among Germans, an introvert among the sociable—all these are merely symbols of his true estrangement, which is that he is a writer. But his pride in the depth of his feeling and understanding is inseparable from his longing for, and envy of, the ordinary, which is embodied in his boyhood friend Hans Hansen and his teenage love Ingeborg Holm—neither of whom reciprocate or even notice his passion. At the end of the story, Tonio has a vision of these two paired off in happy, fruitful partnership—a destiny he can never share: "To be like you! To begin again, to grow up like you, regular like you, simple and normal and cheerful, in conformity and understanding with God and man, beloved of the innocent and happy." But love and marriage and parenthood are barred to Tonio, because he has an artist's soul: "For some go of necessity astray, because for them there is no such thing as a right path."

In associating art with loneliness, sorrow, and death, Mann was not presenting a new idea but perfecting an old tradition.

Everywhere you look in the art and literature and music of the nineteenth century, you find examples of this same figure, the artist banished from life: in Leopardi, the stunted, ugly, miserable poet; in Flaubert, the novelist too fastidious for bourgeois existence; in Nietzsche, the wanderer upon the earth. What is different about Mann is that, writing in 1903, he has fully assimilated the Darwinian revolution, which taught him to think about life in terms of survival and fitness. In his great novel *Buddenbrooks*, Mann tells the story of a family whose fitness to thrive in modern society declines in tandem with the growth of its interest in ideas and art. Its last representative, Hanno, is a musical prodigy who dies an excruciating death before reaching sexual maturity.

Mann's sense of the perverse glory of the artist's unfitness is one of his legacies from Nietzsche, who wrote in *Human, All Too Human*, under the rubric "Art dangerous for the artist," about the inability of the artist to flourish in a modern, scientific age:

> When art seizes an individual powerfully, it draws him back to the views of those times when art flowered most vigorously. . . . The artist comes more and more to revere sudden excitements, believes in gods and demons, imbues nature with a soul, hates science, becomes unchangeable in his moods like the men of antiquity, and desires the overthrow of all conditions that are not favorable to art. . . . Thus between him and the other men of his period who are the same age a vehement antagonism is finally generated, and a sad end— just as, according to the tales of the ancients, both Homer and Aeschylus finally lived and died in melancholy.

As Nietzsche's reference to the Greeks suggests, the link between artistry and suffering is not a modern invention. What is modern is the sense of the superiority of the artist's inferiority, which is only possible when the artist and the intellectual come to see the values of ordinary life—prosperity, family, happiness—as inherently contemptible. The exhilarating assault on bourgeois values that was modernism, in all the arts and in politics too, rested on the assumption, nurtured through the nineteenth century, that there was nothing enviable about what T. S. Eliot bitterly derided as the cycle of "birth, copulation and death." Art, according to a modern understanding that has not wholly vanished today, is meant to be a criticism of life, especially of life in a materialist, positivist civilization such as our own. If this means that the artist cannot share in civilization's boons, then his suffering will be a badge of honor. (Dictators who sought to protect their people from the infection of "degenerate art" were paying a twisted homage to this principle.)

It is no coincidence that the same era should have given birth to Darwinism and to the aesthetic cult of decadence. The iron law of Darwinian evolution is that everything that exists strives with all its power to reproduce, to extend life into the future, and that every feature of every creature can be explained as an adaptation toward this end. For the artist to deny any connection with the enterprise of life, then, is to assert his freedom from this universal imperative, to reclaim negatively the autonomy that evolution seems to deny to human beings. It is only because we can freely choose our own ends that we can decide not to live for life, but for some other value that we posit. The artist's decision to produce spiritual offspring rather than physical ones is thus allied to the monk's celibacy and the warrior's death for his country, as gestures that deny the empire of mere life.

Darwin himself recognized that the human instinct to produce and admire art posed a challenge to the law of the survival of the fittest. He addressed the subject obliquely in 1871 in *The Descent of Man*, the work in which he advanced the idea of sexual selection as a complement to natural selection. Sexual selection was Darwin's ingenious way of explaining features of the natural world that seemed gratuitously wasteful, in a fashion that the parsimony of evolution ought not to have permitted. The classic example is the peacock's tail: why should the bird devote so much of its energy to producing a totally nonfunctional but amazingly decorative tail? It is the kind of natural splendor that, to earlier generations, might have spoken of the generosity of a Creator. The problem plagued Darwin: "The sight of a feather in the peacock's tail, whenever I gaze at it, makes me sick."

The discovery of sexual selection solved the problem with brilliant economy. Such displays, Darwin realized, were male animals' ways of competing for the favor of the female. By this logic, the tiniest initial preference of the female for a conspicuous male—a peacock with a patterned tail, an elk with enlarged antlers—sparked a continual competition among males to become even more conspicuous. In every generation, a more beautiful peacock would leave more offspring than a homelier one, thus passing on the genes for beauty to his offspring, who would undergo the same kind of selection.

Animals produce beauty on their bodies; humans can also produce it in their artifacts. The natural inference, then, would be that art is a human form of sexual display, a way for people to impress mates with spectacularly redundant creations. There is even an animal precedent for this: the Australian bowerbird, which attracts females by building an incredibly elaborate bower out of grass and twigs, and decorating it with colorful bits and the juice of crushed berries. The bower is a perfect example of an artwork whose explicit purpose is to promote reproduction.

For Darwin, the human sense of beauty was not different in kind from the bird's. "This sense," he remarked in *The Descent of Man*, "has been declared to be peculiar to man," but "when we behold a male bird elaborately displaying his graceful plumes or splendid colors before the female . . . it is impossible to doubt that she admires the beauty of her male partner." Still, Darwin recognized that the human sense of beauty was mediated by "complex ideas and trains of thought," which make it impossible to explain in terms as straightforward as a bird's: "When ... it is said that the lower animals have a sense of beauty, it must not be supposed that such sense is comparable with that of a cultivated man, with his multiform and complex associated ideas."

In particular, Darwin suggests that it is impossible to explain the history or the conventions of any art by the general imperatives of evolution: "Many of the faculties, which have been of inestimable service to man for his progressive advancement, such as the powers of the imagination, wonder, curiosity, an undefined sense of beauty, a tendency to imitation, and the love of excitement or novelty, could hardly fail to lead to capricious changes of customs and fashions." Such changes are "capricious" in the sense that they are unpredictable from first principles. Put more positively, one might say that any given work of art can be discussed critically and historically, but not deduced from the laws of evolution.

This sensible reticence served both art and science well enough for more than a century after Darwin's death. But with the rise of evolutionary psychology, it was only a matter of time before the attempt was made to explain art in Darwinian terms. After all, if ethics and politics can be explained by game theory and reciprocal altruism, there is no reason why aesthetics should be different. In each case, what appears to be a realm of human autonomy can be reduced to the covert expression of biological imperatives.

The first popular effort in this direction was Denis Dutton's much-discussed book *The Art Instinct*. For Dutton, the exposure of the Darwinian origins of art was meant to build a case against the excesses of postmodernism. If human aesthetic preferences—for representation in visual art, tonality in music, and narrative in literature—are the product of hundreds of generations of evolutionary selection, then it follows that art that rejects those preferences is doomed to irrelevance. In this sense, Dutton's Darwinism was aesthetically conservative: "Darwinian aesthetics," he wrote, "can restore the vital place of beauty, skill, and pleasure as high artistic values." Dutton's argument has been reiterated and refined by a number of subsequent writers, who do not necessarily share his aesthetic agenda or his artistic cultivation. But their proliferation suggests that Darwinian aesthetics—and its more empirical cousin, neuroaesthetics—is growing quickly in confidence and appeal.

◦ ◦ ◦

On its face, the notion that the human instinct to make and appreciate art can be explained by evolution seems true, even a truism. We are the products of evolution in the things that make us distinctively human no less than in the things we share with the lower animals. There is no longer any argument, for example, that language is an evolutionary adaptation, which over the course of human prehistory must have paid large dividends in terms of survival and reproduction. This makes theoretical sense—language is the basis of human cooperation and innovation—and the evidence supports it: language is a human universal, appearing in every culture and learned by every individual in the same way at the same phase of life. It is as innate as walking and eating.

Almost the same can be said of art. As Dutton put it: "The universality of art and artistic behaviors, their spontaneous appearance everywhere across the globe . . . and the fact that in most cases they can be easily recognized as artistic across cultures suggest that they derive from a natural, innate source: a universal human psychology." Dutton's own fieldwork among the Sepik River people of New Guinea showed him that the Sepik carvers were automatically identifiable as artists even to an American who is the product of a wholly alien culture: "Sepik criteria of artistic excellence are in principle available to anyone with the time and the will to learn to perceive; they are not monadically sealed in Sepik culture." Again like language, art is universal in the sense that any local expression of it can be "learned" by anyone.

Yet earlier theorists of evolution were reluctant to say that art was an evolutionary adaptation like language, for the simple reason that it does not appear to be evolutionarily adaptive. After all, every moment and every calorie spent carving a canoe, or building a cathedral, or writing a symphony, is one not spent getting food, evading predators, or reproducing. Not only is it not obvious that art and "high culture" help human fitness; as we have seen, there is a long tradition holding that the artist is peculiarly unfit for life, especially family life.

To avoid this contradiction, Stephen Jay Gould suggested that art was not an evolutionary adaptation but what he called a "spandrel"—that is, a showy but accidental by-product of other adaptations that were truly functional. Gould, Dutton writes, "came to regard the whole realm of human cultural conduct and experience as a by-product of a single adaptation: the oversized human brain." Having a large brain was useful to our ancestors, allowing them to plan and forecast, cooperate and invent; and it just so happens that a large brain also allowed them to make art. Steven Pinker suggested something similar, if more disparagingly, when he described the brain as a "toolbox" which, in addition to promoting survival and reproduction, "can be used to assemble Sunday afternoon projects of dubious adaptive significance."

The new Darwinian aesthetics is motivated by a desire to defend the honor of art against this kind of dismissal. In a strictly Darwinian nature, of course, there is no such thing as honor, value, or goodness; there is only success or failure at reproduction. But the very words "success" and "failure," despite themselves, bring an emotive and ethical dimension into the discussion, so impossible is it for human beings to inhabit a valueless world. In the nineteenth century, the idea that fitness for survival was a positive good motivated social Darwinism and eugenics. Proponents of these ideas thought that in some way they were serving progress by promoting the flourishing of the human race, when the basic premise of Darwinism is that there is no such thing as

progress or regress, only differential rates of reproduction. Likewise, it makes no logical sense for us to be emotionally invested
in the question of whether or not art serves our evolutionary
fitness. Still, there is an unmistakable sense in discussions of Darwinian aesthetics that by linking art to fitness, we can secure it
against charges of irrelevance or frivolousness—that mattering
to reproduction is what makes art, or anything, really matter.

It is in this spirit that Brian Boyd, the biographer of Nabokov,
sets out in *Why Lyrics Last* to perform a Darwinian reading of
Shakespeare's sonnets. Boyd begins with the premise that human
beings are pattern-seeking animals: both our physical perceptions and our social interactions are determined by our brain's
innate need to find and make coherent patterns. Art, then, can
be defined as the calisthenics of pattern-finding. "Just as animal
physical play refines performance, flexibility, and efficiency in
key behaviors," Boyd writes, "so human art refines our performance in our key perceptual and cognitive modes, in sight (the
visual arts), sound (music), and social cognition (story). These
three modes of art, I propose, are adaptations . . . they show evidence of special design in humans, design that offers survival and
especially reproductive advantages."

"Special design" is a particularly unfortunate phrase here,
since the whole meaning of Darwinism is that nothing is designed
and nothing is special. But Boyd's point is clear. He is proposing
a direct link between art and fitness: the more art we experience,
the more likely we are to survive and reproduce. Art, in this
model, is like a gym in which "we incrementally fine-tune our
neural wiring through our repeated and focused engagement in
each of the arts."

This is, in fact, simply a restatement in Darwinian language
of an idea that I. A. Richards promoted almost a century ago,
at another moment when the high prestige of the sciences—at
that time, psychology—was giving literature a bad conscience.
In 1925, in his book *Principles of Literary Criticism*, Richards also
proposed a calisthenic theory of literature: the poet's "work is the

ordering of what in most minds is disordered," he instructed, and "the value of what [the poet] accomplished is found always in a more perfect organization which makes more of the possibilities of response and activity available."

If pattern is good for us, and Shakespeare's sonnets contain many patterns, then Shakespeare's sonnets are good for us. Boyd's concern in his book is to prove the minor premise, which is easy to do, and which he does intelligently and well. Like Helen Vendler in her commentaries on Shakespeare's sonnets, Boyd emphasizes the verbal texture of the poems, the play with sounds and images, the parallels and oppositions between different sonnets.

The problem, for Boyd as for Richards before him, is that there is not the slightest plausibility to the claim that art renders us more "organized" or more "fit," and there is considerable evidence to the contrary. To prove that art is directly adaptive, one would have to show that people who write symphonies or listen to symphonies have more children than people who do not. Or else one might devise a neurological test to show that an hour of Wagner renders your reflexes a millisecond or two quicker. If both these ideas are preposterous on their face, it is because our actual experience of art points so far from these conclusions. As Kant taught, the very definition of the aesthetic is that it is disinterested, that it suspends our involvement with practical and goal-oriented life. A truly Darwinian account of art would have to embrace this phenomenological reality, rather than simply positing what its premises compel it to posit, which is that art is ultimately useful because it serves the biological cause of reproductive fitness.

The great irony of *Why Lyrics Last* is that, in Shakespeare's sonnets, Boyd has chosen one of the supreme statements of the inferiority of physical life, and specifically of biological reproduction, to art. This is dramatized in the structure of the sequence, whereby the poet moves from urging his "fair friend" to become a father to boasting that his own poems will be his friend's posterity: "So long as men can breathe or eyes can see, / So long lives this, and this gives life to thee." Boyd is aware of this, of course, and he addresses Shakespeare's treatment of death and immortality, but he does not seem aware of how deeply it undermines his own Darwinian analysis of art. When Shakespeare tells us repeatedly that it is better to write and be written about than to live and have children, he is positing a value directly opposed to biological necessity.

How could such an unfruitful urge as a sonnet ever have evolved, since only what serves life can be selected for by evolution? Boyd hazards an explanation:

> But making intense efforts to secure an "immortal" status, a still longer-term fame, might seem in biological terms a cost without benefit. We could perhaps compare it to the follow-through in a golf swing or tennis stroke. Although what happens to club or racquet after the ball leaves it can no longer affect the ball's flight, those previously committed to the follow-through will be more likely to send their ball farther and straighter. In the same way, perhaps, those committed to the long-term follow-through in time, to works attracting attention down the ages, commit more to the imaginative effort and therefore often secure better short-term results too.

But even Boyd does not seem to really believe this. How could he, knowing as much as he does about the history of art and artists' lives? The whole notion of art as a vocation implies that the "short term" and the "long term" are not aligned— that immortality requires a sacrifice of this life and its rewards. Shakespeare had three children, one surviving grandchild, and no great-grandchildren: he singularly failed to perpetuate his genes. Yet he is regarded as one of the most successful, the most worthwhile, the most consequential men ever to have lived, because his spiritual children have thrived beyond measurement. And once you acknowledge that human beings can and do think about success and failure in this way, the possibility of comprehending art, and all human endeavor, in purely Darwinian terms simply disappears.

o o o

"If even just one of your ancestors had decided to give up having children for his or her art," Mark Pagel points out in *Wired for Culture*, "the consequences for you would be no different than had that ancestor been killed." How is it possible, then, that the human species continues to produce artists? To answer this question, Pagel, a biologist, takes a very different approach from Dutton and Boyd, who are humanists. Dutton and Boyd seek to vindicate art in Darwinian terms, and so they attribute to it fitness-enhancing powers that are clearly beyond its province. Pagel, by contrast, has little to say about actual artworks, and no evident affection for them. Instead, he considers art as part of a larger complex that he calls culture, which he casts as an inherently illogical and therefore dubious phenomenon. "People will risk their health and well-being, their chances to have children, or even their lives for their culture," he observes. "People will treat others well or badly merely as a result of their cultural inheritance."

As this suggests, Pagel is taking advantage of—though he is also perhaps a victim of—the double meaning of the word "culture," conflating its honorific and aesthetic meaning with its descriptive and anthropological one. Culture in the first sense—works of art, music, and literature—is therefore able to justify itself as part of culture in the second sense, the sum total of practices and beliefs that define the particular way of being of a group of people. The first kind of culture gives us paintings, the second gives us patriotism; and while paintings are not obviously adaptive, patriotism is.

Indeed, Pagel argues that "culture became our species' strategy for survival, a biological strategy, not just some bit of fun and amusement on the side." This argument involves the vexed question of "group selection"—that is, the problem of whether evolution can select for traits that benefit a group while being detrimental to an individual. It is easy to see, for instance, how a warrior's willingness to die in battle for his tribe benefits the survival of the tribe. But since it costs the warrior all chance of reproduction, it is not clear what mechanism would allow the gene for self-sacrifice to spread.

Pagel argues that so-called "cooperative altruism" can succeed if each of its participants shares a gene for it. In this way, my death allows copies of my altruism gene to go on living in my neighbors' bodies. (For the same reason, he writes, amoebae are able to cooperate in the service of reproduction, even though only one of many cooperating individuals will actually get the chance to spread its genes.) That is why we have evolved to have warm feelings toward people we consider members of our group, and hostile feelings toward members of other groups: "humans seem to be equipped with emotions that encourage us to treat others in our societies as if they were 'honorary relatives.'" Or, as Pagel puts it in a more revealing passage, "natural selection has duped us with an emotion that encourages group thinking."

But the word "duped" covertly introduces an invalid value judgment into the discussion. Caring about our group can be considered a kind of false consciousness only if there is also a true consciousness, which would entail caring about our own individual genetic prospects. But while discussions of evolution often use metaphors of agency—as when we talk of evolution "selecting for" a trait—for a gene there is no such thing as "caring" one way or another. There is only an endless process of differential reproduction, in which genes that make more copies of themselves outnumber genes that make fewer copies. In other words, it makes literally no sense for a human being to care about her own genes or feel duped if she is made to care about someone else's genes. There is no one, no thing, to be the object of this concern. When we say that we care about our genes, what we really mean is that we care about our selves—but the self is an entity of an entirely different order, a humanly created order with its own priorities and values. It is because he wanted to perpetuate his self that Shakespeare wrote his boasting poems. Selves live by other means than genes do.

Pagel has a utilitarian understanding of art, as a Darwinist aesthetician must. But unlike Boyd, he does not claim that making or experiencing art is immediately helpful to genetic fitness. Rather, the use of the arts is indirect: they promote group cohesion, and the survival of the group in turn promotes the survival of the gene. "Proponents of group selection," he writes, "interpret music, dance, religion, and even laughter as aids to promoting the sense of group membership and mutual well-being that gives rise to . . . self-sacrificial emotions."

In this way of thinking, art is religion is culture is nationalism. This does not encourage Pagel to have any affection for religion, about which he is as crude as any New Atheist ("some of us will get infected despite our desperate attempts to evade these brain parasites"). But it does promote a certain hardheaded respect for the arts, which he refers to as "cultural enhancers": "To prehistoric people, the arts and religion might have been like having a class of performance-enhancing drugs . . . at their fingertips."

Here we are back to the Boyd-Richards model of art as mental calisthenics. Clearly, what Pagel has in mind is some sort of vaguely primordial artistry that would directly cultivate a group mystique: an initiation rite in a painted cave, or war songs chanted before battle. Even Greek tragedies might fall into this category, interpreted loosely enough. But what cannot at all be explained in this way is any art that works to separate the individual from the group—which is to say, most art, and certainly most modern art. A Bach partita does no more to reinforce group affiliation than a Monet landscape; such works cultivate and demand solitude, a temporary secession of the listener or the viewer from any kind of collective experience. And much of the greatest modern art proclaims the value of the individual in direct opposition to the group, ruthlessly interrogating tribe, class, and family sentiment.

Against this obvious truth, Pagel adduces the solidarity-promoting experience of singing hymns ("the words to hymns often have a military quality to them, as in 'Onward, Christian Soldiers'"), and the supposed power of "visual art [to] help us to think and remember more clearly." Once again, Darwinian aesthetics proves unable to offer any recognizable account of what happens when we experience art, much less explain it in evolutionary terms.

○ ○ ○

Darwinian aesthetic principles are also the foundation of *The Age of Insight*, by the Nobel Prize–winning neurobiologist Eric Kandel. But the foundation, in this case, is not made to generate the aesthetic superstructure in a naïvely immediate fashion. Kandel recognizes that between our genes and, say, our enjoyment of a painting there intervene two levels of experience that cannot be paraphrased away in Darwinian language. The first is intellectual: what we see in a painting is determined by our knowledge of art history and artistic convention. The second is neurological: what we see in a painting is determined by the way different parts of our brains respond to visual stimuli.

The Age of Insight can be roughly divided into two parts, each dealing with one of these explanatory schemes. In the first half of the book, Kandel offers the reader a compressed but erudite discussion of the culture of Vienna at the turn of the century, with an emphasis on three painters—Gustav Klimt, Oskar Kokoschka, and Egon Schiele. The decision to focus on this milieu is partly personal: Kandel was born to a Jewish family in Vienna in 1929, and had to flee the country at the age of nine following Hitler's Anschluss. He remains enamored of the city that he left behind, and relishes descriptions of the salons, schools, and museums where the culture of Vienna thrived.

But there is a reason beyond nostalgia that makes Kandel take this period as his case study. He argues that this culture was especially conducive to attempts to delve beneath the surface of things, to explorations of hidden causes. Other historians explain this by reference to the political climate of turn-of-the-century Austria, with its worship of a dying dynasty and its self-conscious refinement cloaking ethnic and economic hatreds. For Kandel, the source of this unmasking impulse is best explained medically and scientifically, as the influence of the Vienna School of Medicine. He is particularly fascinated by Carl von Rokitansky, who "introduced Modernism into biology and medicine" by using symptoms to deduce their underlying physiological causes. As Kandel tells it, this kind of clinical pathology was a precursor to Freud's better-known mental pathology: Freud, too, read the depths from the surfaces, the latent from the manifest. Kandel regards his chosen painters, especially Kokoschka and Schiele, as inheritors of the same tendency, using Expressionist techniques to reveal the inner life of the people they depicted.

In the second half of his book, Kandel turns to his particular area of expertise, reporting on the current state of knowledge about the biology of the brain. He is especially interested in what happens in the brain when we experience a work of art—or, to put it another way, what neurological capacities the artist instinctively exploits or "recruits" when making a picture. "Our perception and enjoyment of art," Kandel writes, "is wholly mediated by the activity of the brain"—which is a truism, since every mental function is mediated by the brain, but perhaps a counterintuitive one.

Amid all the details, illustrations, and technical language, the message of this part of the book eventually emerges.

Perception, Kandel shows, is not a matter of the brain passively receiving information about the outside world. It is, instead, a highly active process, dependent on the particular capacities our brains have evolved. This is not a new idea—Kant, again, explained how our knowledge of phenomena is inevitably structured by the categories of our understanding—but new advances in technology make it possible to map the brain's capacities with amazing precision. Kandel locates the particular structures that allow us to identify faces; he shows how vision responds to light and motion and outline; and he discusses the "mirror neurons" that may be the biological basis for our ability to empathize with others.

All of this is exciting and worth knowing, but it is not clear that it adds anything to our experience or interpretation of art. Neurobiology demonstrates, with increasing refinement, how (or at least where) the brain generates the mind. But it can do this only because the mental experiences that it seeks to explain are already well known—indeed, universal—and so it cannot actually add to the stock of those experiences.

For this reason, Kandel's attempts to link biology to aesthetics produce banalities. The brain has evolved to "respond selectively to images of the human body," which "might be an important factor in the historical dominance of figurative art." What does this say but that people like to look at images of people? "Because of [our] capacity for empathy, we can increase our sense of well-being by looking at a happy face, whereas we can increase our anxiety by looking at an anxious face." What does this mean but that pleasure is pleasant to witness and pain is painful? "Scientific analysis," Kandel writes, "represents a move toward greater objectivity.... This is accomplished in the case of visual art by describing the observer's view of an object not in terms of the subjective impressions that object makes on the senses, but in terms of the brain's specific responses to the object." When it comes to aesthetics, however, the subjective impressions *are* the objective facts, to which we have full access without knowing a thing about neurons. A neurological analysis of our experience of art tells us as little about the meaning of that experience as a chemical analysis of the pigments of a painting would tell us about the painting's meaning.

And the problem with neuroaesthetics goes deeper. For the uniqueness of the aesthetic domain is that it actually destabilizes these truths about what we like and do not like to look at. We take great pleasure in looking at a painting by Géricault or Goya that depicts horrendous suffering, but we are repelled by a painting by Bouguereau that depicts beauty. If, for the last hundred years, we have generally preferred abstract art to figurative art, it cannot be because our brains changed in 1910, as Virginia Woolf said human nature did. Kandel writes that, in keeping with the brain's capacity for empathy and mirroring, "when we interact with the relaxed and grand people depicted in some of Klimt's art, we feel more relaxed and grand ourselves." But isn't the effect of a picture like Klimt's *Adele Bloch-Bauer* or *Judith* actually to make beauty seem alien, hieratic, even intimidating? Can't beauty also lower us in our own esteem, by reminding us of the ways we are not beautiful?

When it comes to the actual problems of aesthetics, neuroaesthetics turns out to offer no real guidance. The proof of this is the number of contradictory explanations Kandel gives for why we are drawn to art. It is because we want mental communion with the subject of a portrait: "when we look at a portrait, we are experiencing for a moment the sitter's emotional life." But it is also because we want mental communion with the creator of the portrait: "Our response to art stems from an irrepressible urge to recreate in our own brains the creative process...through which the artist produced the work." We enjoy representations of the beautiful: "In art as in life, there are few more pleasurable sights than a beautiful human face." But we are also drawn to the expressive distortions of Kokoschka and Schiele: "the exaggerated bodily or facial features or striking use of color or texture activate the amygdala via relatively direct pathways."

Finally, this uncertainty drives Kandel, no less than Boyd and Pagel, back to the first principles of Darwinism, which are remorselessly utilitarian. And once again the connection of those principles to art is asserted rather than demonstrated. The "exercise in reading minds, which portrait painting provides, is perhaps not only pleasurable but also useful, sharpening our ability to infer what other people are thinking and feeling." Or, again: "And that is why we generate, appreciate, and desire art: art improves our understanding of social and emotional cues, which are important for survival." But could the amount of effort that goes into making a painting possibly be justified on these grounds, when each of us gets "exercise" in interpreting faces thousands of times a day? And don't artworks regularly introduce us to faces we love because they are uninterpretable, or because they express things utterly beyond the domain of practical life? And what about landscapes and still lifes and abstract forms—what social cues do we learn from them? And does our experience tell us that people who spend much of their lives looking at art, or reading novels, or listening to string quartets—much less the people who make them—are better adjusted, more socially adept, and more likely to produce many children than those who do not?

The problem with Darwinian aesthetics and neuroaesthetics is not that art is like religion, something divine that can only be violated by bringing it back to the realm of biology. Aesthetics is different, in that the facts it has to work with are terrestrial, this-worldly. They are the feelings and thoughts we have in response to works of art, and the feelings and thoughts that lead us to want to create them in the first place. So it would seem that there is no reason, in principle, why these cannot be illuminated by evolution. But this can only happen if we begin with a full and accurate account of what we are trying to explain.

Today's Darwinists treat the aesthetic as if it were a collection of preferences and practices, each of which can be explained as an adaptation. But the preferences and practices are secondary, made possible only by the fact that the aesthetic itself is a distinct dimension of human experience—not the by-product of something more fundamental, but itself fundamental. This dimension is defined in many ways—by its love of the hypothetical, of order and symbol, of representation for its own sake, of the clarity that comes from suspending the pragmatic; and it has, perhaps, as much in common with theoretical knowledge and contemplation as it does with sensory enjoyment. The "usefulness" of this whole way of being is what must be explained, if there is to be a plausible Darwinian aesthetics. Even if there were, it is hard to see how it would change the way we experience art, any more than knowing the mechanics of the eye makes a difference to the avidity of our sight.

Darwinism at 150

o o o

In the fall of 2009, in the lull between celebrations of Charles Darwin's 200th birthday (on February 12) and the 150th anniversary of the publication of *The Origin of Species* (on November 22), Darwin and Darwinism received the most fitting gift of all. This was the announcement of the discovery of *Ardipithecus ramidus*, a hominid species that lived some 4.4 million years ago, and is the oldest known ancestor of human beings. Ardi, as the fossil skeleton found in Ethiopia was nicknamed, is more than a million years older than Lucy, the specimen of *Australopithecus afarensis* that was the previous record-holder.

Not many lay readers can have delved into the detailed papers on Ardi published in *Science*—"*Ardipithecus ramidus* and the Paleobiology of Early Hominids," or "Taphonomic, Avian, and Small-Vertebrate Indicators of *Ardipithecus ramidus* Habitat." But the newspapers communicated the basic facts about our new ancestor: it stood four feet high and weighed about 120 pounds. It had long arms and feet without arches. And most important, we were assured, *Ardipithecus ramidus* was a morally admirable being.

Male chimpanzees have big, knifelike teeth that they use in combat, to dominate rivals and compete for mates; but *Ardipithecus* males had short teeth, similar to the females', suggesting that they no longer engaged in such violent struggles. "What could cause males to forfeit their ability to aggressively compete with other males?" asks C. O. Lovejoy, one of the lead researchers, in his *Science* paper "Reexamining Human Origins in Light of *Ardipithecus ramidus.*" The answer, he suggests, is that "a major shift in life-history strategy transformed the social structure of early hominids," a shift that included pair-bonding and a greater role for fathers in caring for their offspring. Such "substantially intensified male parental investment," Lovejoy concludes, was "a breakthrough adaptation with anatomical, behavioral, and physiological consequences for early hominids and for all of their descendants, including ourselves."

Ardipithecus, in other words, was a good husband and a good father. It did not take long for this excellent news to spread. In the *Wall Street Journal*, the eminent primatologist Frans de Waal editorialized, under the headline "Our Kinder, Gentler Ancestors," that *Ardipithecus* put "the last nail in the coffin" of the "macho origin myth" which held that humans are "born killers." Chimps may be aggressive, de Waal conceded, but gorillas are quite pacific; and then there is the beloved bonobo, who "seems to enjoy love and peace to a degree that would put any Woodstock veteran to shame." And Ardi seems to prove that our hominid ancestors were more like bonobos than chimps. "Obviously," de Waal concludes, "we are hard-wired to be in tune with the emotions of others, a capacity that evolution should never have favored if exploitation of others were all that mattered."

In this way, some four-and-half-million-year-old teeth refuted the dogma of original sin. The eagerness with which scientists and the media rushed to this pleasant conclusion was in inverse proportion to its logical force. Even if it is true that *Ardipithecus* was a peaceable creature—even if we don't one day discover that, while it didn't fight with its teeth, it was brutal with its hands or feet—it makes no sense at all for us to be proud of or consoled by our descent from such an exemplar. We may have evolved to be "in tune with the emotions of others," as de

Waal writes (and one hardly needed a biologist to tell us that), but this empathy coexists with a capacity for perfect indifference and cruelty to others. On the same day that the *Wall Street Journal* published de Waal's piece, the *New York Times* carried a story about an incident in Guinea, where soldiers supporting the new president killed 157 protestors at a soccer stadium, using guns and knives and fists. No teeth, sharp or blunt, were needed.

The authors of the biblical story of the fall from Eden had no inkling about *Ardipithecus*, or the theory of evolution. Their account of the creation of mankind, long believed by almost everyone in the West, was refuted forever by Darwin. But what they knew about human nature—about our capacity for both good and evil—cannot be refuted by any discovery about our distant ancestors. If *Ardipithecus* had turned out to be the most violent primate known to science, no one would take that as permission for humans to be violent. Conversely, the peaceful- ness of our ancestors does not mean that it is natural for us to be peaceful. To say otherwise is to say that nature is our standard of morality, that what is, or was, is the measure of what should be.

o o o

If Ardi once again confirmed Darwin's theory of the descent of man from the lower animals, it also once again stirred up con- fusions about the ethics of evolution, and the evolution of ethics, that have surrounded Darwinism from the very beginning. The many books published to mark the Darwin anniversary show how impossible it is to separate the science of evolution from its moral implications. The best of these books are not just about Darwin and Darwinism, but about slavery and racism, evidence and superstition, free will and altruism. In the new second edition of *The Cambridge Companion to Darwin*, three chapters are devoted to Darwin's legacy as a scientist, and fifteen to one or another aspect of his influence on morals, religion, and philosophy.

Nothing is more eloquent of this moralization of evolution

than the way it seems impossible for so many writers to separate the logic of Darwinism from the character of Darwin himself. Newton's religious crotchets do not affect the way we understand the theory of gravity, and Einstein's benevolence does not make the theory of relativity any easier to grasp. But as the continuing flood of biographies makes clear, we seem to have a great need for reassurance about the man who gave us the theory of evolution. As Jean Gayon writes in the *Cambridge Companion*, "While it may not be unique, this persistent positioning of new developments in relation to a single, pioneering figure is quite exceptional in the history of modern natural science."

But then, no other discovery of modern science is as intimately momentous as Darwin's. This is not simply because Darwin refuted Genesis, strongly as some obscurantists continue to resent that achievement. In fact, as John Hedley Brooke writes in the *Cambridge Companion*, in an excellent essay on "Darwin and Victorian Christianity," "the damage inflicted by Darwin on open-minded Christian believers can easily be exaggerated." The inaccuracy of the book of Genesis as an account of the creation of the world had been proved generations before Darwin wrote. Geology, not biology, dealt the crucial blow, by proving that the Earth was inconceivably old, and that it had been constantly shaped and reshaped by natural forces. "If only the geologists would let me alone, I could do very well, but those dreadful hammers!" John Ruskin complained. "I hear the clink of them at the end of every cadence of the Bible verses." For others, like George Eliot, reading the biblical criticism of Strauss and Feuerbach was equally effective in demolishing the infallibility of Scripture.

What Darwin did was, in a sense, more profound and far-reaching than any attack on the Bible. By offering a convincing explanation of how species evolve from one another—by means of natural selection acting on spontaneously occurring variations—he closed any route for human beings to escape from the animal kingdom. Humans, after Darwin, became what we know them as today—*Homo sapiens*, one species

among the many to have emerged in the blind and purpose-
less course of evolution.

This animalization of humanity was immediately perceived,
after the publication of *The Origin of Species* in 1859, to present
an enormous challenge not just to religion, but to metaphysics,
epistemology, and ethics—to all traditional ways of thinking
about human being. This was the case even though Darwin
avoided the subject of human evolution in the *Origin*, restrict-
ing himself to one famously evasive sentence: with the theory
of evolution, he suggested, "Light will be thrown on the origin of man and his history." The omission was tactical, as he
readily acknowledged when he addressed the subject head-on
in *The Descent of Man*, twelve years later: "During many years
I collected notes on the origin or descent of man, without any
intention of publishing on the subject, but rather with the determination not to publish, as I thought that I should thus only add
to the prejudices against my views." During his negotiations
over the *Origin* with the publisher John Murray, Darwin asked
a friend whether he ought to reassure Murray that "my Book is
not more unorthodox, than the subject makes inevitable. That
I do not discuss [the] origin of man. That I do not bring in any
discussions about Genesis, etc."

Despite all this diplomacy, however, Darwin was perfectly
aware of the epochal implications of his theory. If he managed to
keep the excitement and defiance of his dethroning of mankind
out of the *Origin*, it was partly because he had already confided
them to his notebooks, twenty years before. While Darwin did
not go public with his theory of evolution until 1858, he established its contours in the 1830s, in the years immediately following his return to England from the *Beagle* voyage. *The Young
Charles Darwin*, by the Oxford naturalist Keith Thomson, is
chiefly valuable as a study of those notebooks, where Darwin first
recorded his theory's verdict on man: "But Man—wonderful
Man . . . he is not a deity, his end under present form will come . . .
he is no exception."

And if man was no exception to the laws of nature, he could

not have anything like a soul. "The soul by consent of all is superadded, animals not got it," Darwin wrote in the hurried, broken prose typical of the notebooks. But "if we let conjecture run wild then animals our fellow brethren . . . from our origin in one common ancestor we may all be netted together." No wonder that Adrian Desmond and James Moore, the current deans of Darwin scholarship, write in *Darwin's Sacred Cause* that "the mental turmoil he suffered is barely graspable, and on reading his spidery scrawl even now one is staggered by his daring."

Both Thomson and Desmond and Moore suggest that Darwin's invalidism—the stomach pains, dizziness, and nausea that afflicted him virtually every day for the second half of his life—was a kind of psychosomatic penance, the revenge of his conscience on his intellect. "In private he became a subversive, feverishly jotting down thoughts for which he knew everyone would condemn him," Thomson writes. "Not surprisingly, therefore, his health started to break down once again."

This kind of post hoc psychoanalysis can be doubted—other biographers have speculated that Darwin's sickness, which didn't begin until after the *Beagle* voyage, was owed to an exotic disease he contracted in South America. Still, there can be no doubt that Darwin's extraordinary caution about revealing his theory of natural selection bespeaks an awareness of how explosive it would be. It took him twenty years to publish on evolution, and even then, it was only because Alfred Russel Wallace threatened to beat him to it.

o o o

The radical implications of Darwin's theory can be summed up in a note that he attached to his copy of the scientific bestseller *Vestiges of the Natural History of Creation*: "Never use the word higher and lower." *Vestiges*, published anonymously in 1844, was the first book to bring the idea of evolution to a wide audience. The author—who was only much later revealed to be Robert

Chambers, a Scottish man of letters—encountered the same kind
of abuse that would later greet Darwin, as he argued that species
are not immutable, but evolve over time. Yet as Richard Milner
writes in *Darwin's Universe*—his idiosyncratic and highly read-
able encyclopedia of all things Darwinian—*Vestiges* couched its
theory of evolution in consolingly theistic terms: its "tone was
reverential, its language respectful and even religious."

Chambers argued that the evolution of species was inevitably progressive, part of a divine plan leading to the creation of
man. "An impulse," he wrote, "was imparted to the forms of life,
advancing them in definite lines, by generation, through grades
of organization terminating in the highest plants and animals."
In his novel *Tancred*, published in 1847, Benjamin Disraeli mocked
the vogue for *Vestiges* by having a society hostess chatter about
a book called *The Revelations of Chaos*: "You know, all is development. The principle is perpetually going on. First, there was
nothing, then there was something; then, I forget the next, I
think there were shells, then fishes; then we came, let me see, did
we come next? Never mind that; we came at last. And the next
change there will be something very superior to us, something
with wings."

It was in response to such teleological thinking that Darwin
reminded himself never to describe evolution in terms of higher
and lower. For what made Darwin's theory of evolution scientifically credible, in a way that those of Chambers and Lamarck
(or, for that matter, his own grandfather, Erasmus Darwin) never
were, was his insistence on the sheer blindness of natural selection. There was nothing purposive about this agency—any animal that survived, insofar as it survived, was as successful in
evolutionary terms as any other. Humans were adapted to one
niche in the ecosystem, barnacles to another, but humans were
higher than barnacles only in a metaphorical sense.

"It is absurd to talk of one animal being higher than another,"
Darwin elaborated in the notebooks. "We consider those, where
the cerebral structure/intellectual faculties most developed, as

highest. A bee doubtless would when the instincts were." Or, as he later wrote, in a markedly anti-*Vestiges* passage of the *Origin*: "Natural selection tends only to make each organic being as perfect as, or slightly more perfect than, the other inhabitants of the same country with which it has to struggle for existence.... Natural selection will not produce absolute perfection, nor do we always meet, as far as we can judge, with this high standard under nature."

By doing away with higher and lower in the order of nature, however, Darwin seemingly threatened to do away with them altogether—first of all, in the moral sphere. If man is an animal, by what warrant does he demand of himself a more-than-animal standard of conduct? The first reviewers of *The Origin of Species* certainly recognized this tendency of the book, hard as Darwin tried to conceal it. The geologist Adam Sedgwick, after attacking Darwin's facts and inductive method, finished his review in the *Spectator* this way: "I cannot conclude without expressing my detestation of the theory, because of its unflinching materialism ... because it utterly repudiates final causes, and thereby indicates a demoralized understanding...." Darwin's allies said much the same thing, though of course they praised the humiliating materialism that Sedgwick feared. Thomas Huxley, the scientist and polemicist who was nicknamed "Darwin's Bulldog," wrote: "It is as if nature herself had foreseen the arrogance of man, and with Roman severity had provided that his intellect, by its very triumphs, should call into prominence the slaves, admonishing the conqueror that he is but dust."

To some of Darwin's contemporaries, the world he described, without higher or lower, could only be a hell. Nietzsche's parable of the death of God directly echoes Darwin's note: "Are we not perpetually falling? Backward, sideways, forward, in all directions? Is there any up or down left?" Nietzsche's major complaint about Darwin, which fuels the polemic with Darwinism that runs through his books, is that Darwin himself did not sufficiently appreciate the vertigo of a directionless universe.

Darwinism cut us loose from all moral absolutes, yet somehow Darwin went on acting as if Christian morality still held. In *The Will to Power*, Nietzsche observes "to what extent Christian presuppositions and interpretations still live on under the formulas 'nature,' 'progress,' 'perfectibility,' 'Darwinism'. . . That absurd trust in the course of things, in 'life,' in the 'instinct of life,' that comfortable resignation that comes from the faith that if everyone only does his duty all will be well—this kind of thing is meaningful only by supposing a direction of things *sub specie boni*."

Ironically, what Nietzsche attacked here under the name of Darwinism—the belief in progress and perfectibility, in evolution as a "direction of things *sub specie boni*"—is exactly what Darwin rejected. The *Vestiges*, or the philosophical evolutionism of Herbert Spencer, came closer to what Nietzsche derided, in another aphorism, as "the New Testament and the original Christian community—apparent as complete bêtise in the Englishmen, Darwin and Wallace."

In fact, Darwin was capable of as total a rejection of Christianity as Nietzsche himself, though he seldom said so in public. In his brief *Autobiography*, he complained of the cruelty of the theology of damnation: "I can indeed hardly see how anyone ought to wish Christianity to be true; for if so the plain language of the text seems to show that the men who do not believe, and this would include my Father, Brother and almost all my best friends, will be everlastingly punished. And this is a damnable doctrine." (When the *Autobiography*, originally written for private circulation, was published, Darwin's pious widow Emma insisted on deleting this passage.) Still more profoundly, Darwin denied, in a letter to a stranger who had asked for his religious opinions, that human beings were capable of knowing anything at all about the divine: "But then arises the doubt—can the mind of man, which has, as I fully believe, been developed from a mind as low as that possessed by the lower animals, be trusted when it draws such grand conclusions?"

This is the really destabilizing result of Darwinism—not just its moral, but its epistemological implications. Darwin, who read Kant and refers to him in *The Descent of Man*, provided a biological basis for the idea that human cognition and perception were intrinsically limited, able to grasp only appearances, never things in themselves. To a scientist, whose work was devoted to ascertaining the nature of reality, this was a truly humbling realization. In Darwin's quiet question, the whole logic of Nietzsche's perspectivism can be found in embryo: "for the sake of the survival of beings like ourselves such judgments must be believed to be true; though they might, of course, be false judgments for all that," as he put it in *Beyond Good and Evil*.

How is it, then, that Darwin could appear to Nietzsche not as a comrade in arms, but as a meek, respectable Christian? To put the question another way: how did Darwin, who in 1859 seemed to be challenging the very basis of religion and morals, end up being buried in Westminster Abbey, Britain's foremost Christian shrine? *Darwin's Armada,* by the Australian historian Iain McCalman, opens with the scene at the Abbey, on April 26, 1882, a week after Darwin's death. The queen and the prime minister, the evangelical Gladstone, stayed away, but the pallbearers included "two dukes and an earl," the American Ambassador James Russell Lowell, and the president of the Royal Society. Darwin had wanted a quiet burial in Downe, the secluded Kent village where he spent his last forty years, but the Victorian Establishment positively demanded the chance to honor him. "We owe it to posterity to place his remains in Westminster Abbey, among the illustrious dead," editorialized one newspaper. One day, his face would be on the ten-pound note.

In America, such an official endorsement of Darwin would be hard to imagine—too many of us are still too affronted by his theory and its implications. Yet one side effect of the controversy over Darwinism is our continuing interest in Darwin himself. The man has become a symbol, not just of the theory of evolution, but of the enlightened mind, and his partisans can be as pugnacious as his enemies. One of the entries in Milner's *Encyclopedia*, "Darwin Fish," describes the "bumper sticker wars" in which atheists created a parody of the Christian fish symbol, equipping it with legs and replacing the Greek word with Darwin's name. Nietzsche called himself the Anti-Christ, but in this (not wholly tongue-in-cheek) battle, it is Darwin who replaces "Jesus Christ, Son of God, Savior" as the icon of a worldview.

In the same spirit, *One Beetle Too Many*, an illustrated book about Darwin's life, offers enlightened parents a fable with which to arm their children against superstition and conformity. The title alludes to a comic episode in Darwin's *Autobiography*: "Once, out on a beetling expedition, he found under the bark of a tree two beetles he had never seen before," Kathryn Lasky writes. "Within seconds a third strange beetle crawled out, and Charles, lacking a free hand, quickly popped one beetle into his mouth and scooped up the third one." It is odd that a book meant for children omits the conclusion of this story as Darwin tells it: "Alas! it ejected some intensely acrid fluid, which burnt my tongue so that I was forced to spit the beetle out, which was lost, as was the third one."

Maybe this gross-out ending was felt to undermine Lasky's message, which comes across in the book's first sentence: "No one ever said 'Don't touch!' in the house where Charles Darwin grew up." Cleverly, *One Beetle Too Many* links children's natural resentment of the adults who say "don't touch" with a more principled resentment of religious authorities who would put ideas off-limits. The villain of the book is Robert Fitzroy, the captain of the *Beagle*, who is introduced this way: "He had spent most of his life at sea, and his favorite book to read on his travels was the Bible. Over and over he read the stories of the Creation, and while the world beyond his ship constantly changed, these comforting stories did not." No wonder such an authoritarian dullard also believes in "the 'great chain of being,'" in which "every creature, from beetles to children, know[s] its place." The sympathies of the book, and the reader, are of course with the naughty, questing, democratic Darwin: Lasky dedicates the book "in celebration of children, whose boundless curiosity gives them a right to know their history on the Earth."

Unfortunately, the need for a clear-cut bad guy leads Lasky to do less than justice to Fitzroy. It is true that, in middle age, he became a religious reactionary and a foe of Darwinism. In 1860, at a meeting of the British Association for the Advancement of Science, where the *Origins* sparked an intellectual brawl, Fitzroy made an appearance, brandishing a Bible and attacking Darwin's "attempt to substitute human conjecture and human institutions for the explicit revelation which the Almighty has himself made in that book."

But at the time of the *Beagle* voyage—which began in 1831, when Fitzroy was twenty-six years old and Darwin twenty-two, and lasted five years—things were very different. As Thomson shows in *The Young Charles Darwin*, Fitzroy was a "scientist manqué," who gave Darwin his own copy of Charles Lyell's *Principles of Geology*—the cutting-edge work that demonstrated the immense age and constant variability of the earth, thus giving Darwin the deep-time perspective that was crucial to the theory of evolution. And at the time, Darwin himself was quite a conventional Christian; as he later recalled, "I did not then in the least doubt the strict and literal truth of every word in the Bible." One of the best-known passages of *The Voyage of the Beagle* compares the ingenious hunting tactics of the Australian ant and the European ant, and draws a strictly creationist moral: "Now what would the sceptic say to this? Would any two workmen ever have hit on so beautiful, so simple, and yet so artificial a contrivance? It cannot be thought so: one Hand has surely worked throughout the universe."

The inference that a work must have a workman was taken directly from William Paley, whose book *Natural Theology; or, Evidences of the Existence and Attributes of the Deity, Collected from the Appearances of Nature*, made the argument from design a mainstay of Christian apologetics in the early nineteenth century. As a clergyman-in-training at Cambridge, Darwin had studied Paley and been won over: "I do not think I hardly ever admired a book more than Paley's *Natural Theology*. I could almost formerly have said it by heart," he recalled long afterward.

But as this suggests, Darwin's faith was more an intellectual matter than a spiritual one. His degree of interest in Christianity can be gauged by a charmingly ingenuous letter he wrote to his sister Caroline when he was seventeen: "I have tried to follow your advice about the Bible, what part of the Bible do you like best? I like the Gospels. Do you know which of them is generally reckoned the best?" This is not the tone of a man for whom the loss of faith would be a crisis—as it was for Nietzsche, the Lutheran pastor's son. Revealingly, when Darwin did begin to doubt the truth of the Gospels, what he longed for was not a sign of grace, but a new discovery of "old letters between distinguished Romans, and manuscripts . . . at Pompeii or elsewhere, which [would have] confirmed in the most striking manner all that was written in the Gospels."

Christianity, for Darwin, was a failed hypothesis. "Disbelief crept over me at a very slow rate, but was at last complete," he wrote. "The rate was so slow that I felt no distress." He recognized that many people continued to feel a kind of religious awe in the presence of nature, but he could not accept the emotion of reverence as a valid proof that there was something to revere: "The state of mind which grand scenes formerly excited in me, and which was intimately connected with a belief in God, did not essentially differ from that which is often called the sense of sublimity; and however difficult it may be to explain the genesis of this sense, it can hardly be advanced as an argument for the existence of God, any more than the powerful though vague and similar feelings excited by music." Perhaps it is not a coincidence that, with age, Darwin also lost his taste for music and poetry.

The only argument for a divinity—though not for the biblical God—that continued to exert some attraction for Darwin was the old Paleyan one. As late as 1879, he acknowledged "the extreme difficulty or rather impossibility of conceiving this immense and wonderful universe ... as the result of blind chance or necessity. When thus reflecting, I feel compelled to look to a First Cause ... and I deserve to be called a Theist." Yet Darwin also recognized that his own theory, by showing the evolution of man to be the result of a mindless process, rendered this very intuition unreliable: "The old argument from design in Nature, as given by Paley, which formerly seemed to me so conclusive, fails, now that the law of natural selection has been discovered."

o o o

In this way, Darwin acknowledges that he had helped to kill God—and he does so without elation or despair, only his usual confident modesty. This modesty is part of what makes Darwin so attractive, but it also presents a certain challenge for the biographer. For the truth is that Charles Darwin's story, with one major exception, is not dramatic. That exception is the *Beagle* voyage, the round-the-world odyssey in which Darwin lived out every child's dreams: he saw tropical islands, climbed volcanoes, survived an earthquake, sailed through storms, talked with native peoples, and on and on.

Darwin's experiences on the *Beagle*, and the book he wrote about them, were the envy and inspiration of a younger generation of naturalists. As McCalman shows, the three scientists who became Darwin's most important allies in the evolution debate—Joseph Hooker, Thomas Huxley, and Alfred Wallace—all undertook similar voyages, in direct emulation of Darwin. As a student, McCalman writes, Hooker "was so excited by [*The Voyage of the Beagle*] that he slept with the proofs under his pillow, so he could rip through them in the early morning before lectures."

As Darwin said, "The voyage of the *Beagle* has been by far the most important event in my life, and has determined my whole career." He might have added that it was practically the only event in his life. His childhood was ordinary, and no one thought him destined for greatness; as Thomson writes, "In trying to find adjectives to describe the young Darwin . . . 'self-absorbed' most often comes to mind, followed by 'immature.'" The headmaster of his grammar school "called me very unjustly a 'poco curante,'" he recalled, "and as I did not understand what he meant, it seemed to me a fearful reproach." He went to medical school in Edinburgh but dropped out, and at Cambridge he did not try for honors.

Nor is there anything outwardly remarkable about Darwin's life after the *Beagle*. He spent the six years following his return in London, making scientific contacts and building his reputation, but the intellectual drama of his thinking about evolution was confined to his notebooks. He began to settle, in his early thirties, into his lifelong pattern of illness: "By 1839," Thomson writes, "he was increasingly distressed by abdominal pain, flatulence, constipation, nausea, and headaches." He dealt with his frequent prostration by sticking to a rigid work schedule and shunning virtually all professional and social contact. His wife Emma—she was also his first cousin, and a friend since childhood—acted as his nurse, while also bearing ten children. Darwin's way of life was fixed when he moved to the village of Downe in 1842—chosen, Thomson writes, because it was "sufficiently distant from the nearest railway station . . . to discourage casual visitors."

The move marks the effective end of Darwin's *Autobiography*: "My chief enjoyment and sole employment throughout life has been scientific work, and the excitement from such work makes me for the time forget, or quite drives away, my daily discomfort. I have therefore nothing to record during the rest of my life, except the publication of my several books." This must be a discouraging sentence for biographers, and they try to cope with it in various ways. Thomson, like Darwin himself, ends the story in 1842, allowing him to cover the *Beagle* and the discovery of evolution, and omit the many subsequent years of barnacle dissection and hydropathic cures.

At the same time, Thomson tries to heighten the drama of Darwin's development by exaggerating his early mediocrity: "But that could have been the childhood of a dozen men whose later life turned to banking, racing horses, embezzlement, or the church," he writes of the teenage Darwin. "If it is not asking too much of a fifteen-year-old, where was the intellectual?" Thomson is not asking too much, but he is asking it of the wrong person. For Darwin was never an "intellectual," a person interested in ideas for their own sake. (Huxley is much closer to the type, both in his love of verbal combat and his penchant for self-dramatization.) He was a scientist, interested in particular problems that could be solved through observation and induction. Darwin was certainly aware of the momentous implications of the theory of evolution, but he did not devote his life to wrestling with them. Instead, he spent years at a time studying the taxonomy of barnacles, the formation of coral reefs, and dimorphic plants—"I do not think anything in my scientific life has given me so much satisfaction as making out the meaning of the structures of these plants," he wrote. That is why, despite all the attempts of biographers, his life mostly lacks the kind of representative drama that can make a writer's or artist's life the complement of his work.

McCalman takes yet another approach to the biographer's problem: not only does he narrow his focus to Darwin's *Beagle* years, he makes Darwin just one of a quartet of subjects. Along with the *Beagle*, McCalman tells the adventures of the *Erebus*, which took Joseph Hooker on a four-year voyage to Antarctica; the *Rattlesnake*, on which Huxley surveyed Australia and New Guinea; and the various voyages of Wallace, which included long sojourns in the Amazon jungle and the Malay archipelago. It was from Malaysia that Wallace, in 1858, dispatched to Darwin his paper "On the Tendency of Varieties to Depart Indefinitely from the Original Type"—the paper in which he independently formulated the idea of natural selection, on which Darwin had been working for twenty years.

The last part of McCalman's book deals with the crisis of conscience that Wallace's paper provoked in Darwin. "I always thought it very possible that I might be forestalled," he wrote Hooker, "but I fancied that I had grand enough soul not to care; but I found myself mistaken and punished." Clearly, both men could justly claim credit: Darwin had the idea first and developed it further, but Wallace was the first to present it to the scientific world in a paper. And the fate of that paper was in Darwin's hands. "I should be extremely glad now to publish a sketch of my general views in about a dozen pages or so," Darwin wrote Lyell. "But I cannot persuade myself that I can do so honorably. ... I would far rather burn my whole book than that [Wallace] or any man should think that I had behaved in a paltry spirit."

The compromise that followed can be seen either as the mutual self-sacrifice of true gentlemen—which is how both Darwin and Wallace saw it—or as an example, in McCalman's words, of "the arrogance and manipulation of class power." Lyell and Hooker, who were leading figures in Britain's scientific establishment, arranged to have Wallace's paper read at a meeting of the Linnaean Society. As McCalman notes, this is something Wallace, an outsider living half a world away, could never have achieved on his own. At the same time, they made sure that the Society heard an extract from a sketch of the theory of evolution that Darwin had written in 1844, but never published—thus making his priority clear. What's more, thanks to the long delay in communicating with Malaysia, all this took place before Wallace heard a word from Darwin in response to his initial letter.

Here, as at many other moments, McCalman's group portrait allows us to see how pervasive class was in the world of Victorian science. Darwin was a rich man, who could devote himself to science without having to worry about making a living. He studied at Cambridge, where his mentors were the nation's leading scientists. They arranged for him to be offered the post of naturalist on the *Beagle*, and he could afford to take it without a salary. Indeed, it was made clear to Darwin that Fitzroy "wants a man . . . more as a companion than a mere collector and would not take anyone however good a Naturalist who was not recommended to him likewise as a gentleman."

Wallace, on the other hand, was precisely a "mere collector," who freelanced his way around the world by collecting exotic specimens to sell to rich dilettantes back home. As the son of a downwardly mobile lawyer who went bankrupt, and whose death forced his widow to become a domestic servant, Wallace had almost no formal education. He taught himself everything he knew about science, attending Mechanics' Institute lectures and reading in public libraries. He particularly admired the *Voyage of the Beagle*—"so free from all labour, affectation, or egotism," he told a friend; and reading the *Vestiges*, in McCalman's words, was "probably the single most important intellectual experience of Wallace's life." He seems like a scientific Jude Fawley—never more so than when, during his return from a four-year expedition through the Amazon jungle, his ship caught fire and sank, destroying his entire collection.

Such a setback might have broken other men, yet it was only after this disaster that Wallace went to Malaysia and had his evolutionary epiphany. When you measure the distance they had to travel and the obstacles in their path, Wallace's discovery of evolution is actually more remarkable than Darwin's. Yet Wallace, whether out of class deference or intellectual respect or both, accepted his place as Darwin's subordinate. "As to Charles Darwin, I know exactly our relative positions, and my great inferiority to him," he wrote, nicely balancing the intellectual and social implications. "I compare myself to a Guerrilla chief, very well for a skirmish or for a flank movement and even able to sketch out a plan of campaign, but reckless of communications and careless about Commissariat: while Darwin is the great General, who can maneuever the largest army, and by attending to his base operations and forgetting no detail of discipline, arms or supplies, leads on his forces to victory."

o o o

Despite what the bearers of "Darwin fish" might like to think, Darwin's "victory" was nothing like those of Copernicus or Galileo. He was no lonely fighter against entrenched religious bigotry. In fact, the opposition Darwin feared most, during the decades he spent gathering evidence in defense of his theory, was not that of the Church, but that of his fellow scientists. The fanciful evolutionary theories of Lamarck and Chambers had made evolution itself sound like a crank subject—like ufology today, perhaps—and Darwin was very concerned that he would be treated accordingly.

A letter Darwin wrote in 1844 has him making what sounds like a fearful admission: "I am almost convinced (quite contrary to opinion I started with) that species are not (it is like confessing a murder) immutable." This is often quoted, since it makes evolution sound like a heresy that has to be hidden from the Inquisition—a truly "dangerous idea," in Daniel Dennett's phrase. But the recipient of this letter was the botanist Joseph Hooker, and the only thing Darwin was afraid of was that Hooker would think he was not a serious scientist. The "murder" image is jocular hyperbole, in keeping with the rest of the letter: "You will now groan, and think to yourself 'on what a man have I been wasting my time in writing to.'"

In the event, the controversy over Darwin's theory gave way, with surprising speed, to total acceptance. Older scientists, who had an intellectual and professional investment in the immutability of species, attacked the *Origin*; but the younger generation rallied to it, just as Darwin had hoped. In 1864, Darwin won the Copley Medal of the Royal Society, Britain's highest scientific honor—though, as Huxley angrily noted, the Society was too timid to mention evolution in its citation. Even the first, violent opposition to the idea that man was descended from apes soon dissipated. In 1871, just twelve years after he refused to discuss humans in the *Origin*, Darwin published *The Descent of Man*, setting out the case for our primate ancestry at great length: "Now the case wears a wholly different aspect," he noted in the introduction.

Darwin's "victory" came quickly; what took a long time to figure out—we are still at it today—is what that victory meant. Looking at the history of ideas in the century after Darwin, it is easy to make the case that it meant a moral disaster. Darwinism gave rise to social Darwinism, which meant ruthless laissez-faire; to eugenics, which meant sterilization of the poor and sick; to biological racism, which culminated in Nazi race-war. Today's Darwinists are very conscious of that history, which is one reason why they focus so strenuously on the evolution of altruism and cooperation. In his 1975 book *Sociobiology*, Edward O. Wilson argued for the *"genetic evolution of ethics,"* writing that "ethical philosophers intuit the deontological canons of morality by consulting the emotive centers of their own hypothalamic-limbic system."

Here, too, the debate over Darwinism colors the writing of Darwin's life. In *Darwin's Sacred Cause*, Adrian Desmond and James Moore propose that the theory of evolution was important to Darwin primarily as a weapon in the fight for social justice. To most of his admirers, they write, Darwin appears as "a tough-minded scientist doing good empirical research. . . . a detached, objective researcher, the model of the successful scientist." But they dismiss this view as a "caricature." In truth, "Darwin's starting point [was] his abhorrence of racial servitude and brutality, his hatred of the slavers' desire, as he jotted, to 'make the black man [an]other kind.'" They even go so far as to say that, by proving the common ancestry of all human races, Darwin "saved the blacks."

That Darwin was a foe of slavery is no revelation; he made his views very clear in his books and letters. But Desmond and Moore show, thanks to their extensive mastery of the period, just how central slavery and racism were to Darwin's intellectual milieu. He was born into the abolitionist camp: his paternal grandfather, Erasmus Darwin, assailed slavery in his poems, and his maternal grandfather, Josiah Wedgwood, was a major backer of Thomas Clarkson, the pioneering antislavery activist. The Wedgwood pottery works manufactured the famous cameo depicting a chained slave, with the motto "Am I Not a Man and a Brother?" which became the badge of the British abolitionists.

Thus it is not surprising that slavery, rather than the Bible, was responsible for one of Darwin's few open conflicts with Captain Fitzroy aboard the *Beagle*. Darwin's Whig traditions set him on a collision course with Fitzroy, a Tory nobleman, who automatically sided with planters against their slaves. As Darwin remembered in his *Autobiography*:

> early in the voyage at Bahia, in Brazil, [Fitzroy] defended and praised slavery, which I abominated, and told me that he had just visited a great slave-owner, who had called up many of his slaves and asked them whether they were happy, and whether they wished to be free, and all answered "No." I then asked him, perhaps with a sneer, whether he thought that the answer of slaves in the presence of their master was worth anything? This made him excessively angry, and he said that as I doubted his word we could not live any longer together.

Fitzroy quickly apologized for his overreaction—a sign, perhaps, of the emotional instability that eventually led to his suicide—and the friendship resumed. But it is telling that Darwin was willing to jeopardize his relationship with his sponsor and cabinmate by standing up for his antislavery views. Near the end of the journey, when he left Brazil for the last time, Darwin wrote: "I thank God, I shall never again visit a slave-country."

The challenge for Desmond and Moore is to show that

Darwin's science was not just compatible with, but actually "shaped" by, his antislavery beliefs. During the years when Darwin was pondering evolution, they show, biologists on both sides of the Atlantic were debating the question of the origin of human races. The old, Christian, and (one might think) self-evident view was that all humans belonged to the same species. This meant that Europeans and the Africans they enslaved shared common ancestors—if not Adam and Eve, then some other small group.

The antislavery implications of this idea were clear, as the slogan "Am I Not a Man and a Brother?" shows. That is why, as the struggle over slavery in the United States moved toward open warfare, defenders of the institution—Southerners and their English sympathizers—began to challenge the notion of common descent, arguing that the human races were separately created. Desmond and Moore introduce us to many now-forgotten racist theorists, such as J. C. Nott, who wrote in the Louisiana-based *DeBow's Review* that mankind was a genus, comprising a number of separate species.

Nott's intellectual stature can be judged from his comment that "all the ... articles I have written on *niggerology* have been eagerly sought for at the South." But to Darwin's dismay, even Louis Agassiz, the most famous scientist in America, was converted to the doctrine of plural origins. In 1850, Agassiz attended the meeting of the American Association for the Advancement of Science in Charleston, South Carolina, and delivered a speech in which he "confirmed that human races were locked to their zoological provinces. They were aboriginal creations, rooted to the spot," and "could be ranked 'scientifically,'" with Africans at the bottom. This belief was the foundation of what was becoming known, shamefully, as the American School of anthropology.

Such sentiments prompted Darwin to write, in Latin, "Oh for shame Agassiz!"—which is the title of a chapter in *Darwin's Sacred Cause*. For Darwin, of course, the notion of separate creation of the races was absurd, because the notion of creation itself was absurd. All races of humans were descended from the same ancestor—much as all varieties of pigeons, no matter how dramatic their outward differences, were descended from the common rock pigeon (as Darwin was even then proving). *The Origin of Species* conclusively refuted the "American School," which made abolitionists welcome it—Harriet Martineau said it gave her "unspeakable satisfaction." The Harvard scientist Asa Gray, Darwin's leading American disciple, also acknowledged the racial implications of the *Origin*, much more uneasily: "Here lines converge as they recede into the geological ages, and point to conclusions which, upon the theory, are inevitable, but hardly welcome. The very first step backward makes the Negro and the Hottentot our blood-relations."

Darwin's theory of evolution proved that all men were related, and in this sense, as Desmond and Moore write, the "notion of 'brotherhood' grounded his evolutionary enterprise." But even so, there are two important reasons why evolution cannot be viewed, as Desmond and Moore would like, as Darwin's contribution to the "sacred cause" of anti-slavery. The first is that, clearly, Darwin himself did not think of it that way. Darwin's hatred of slavery and race-prejudice is consistent throughout his life—in his *Autobiography*, he made a point of noting that, as a medical student, he took taxidermy lessons from a "negro," and that "he was a very pleasant and intelligent man."

But as Desmond and Moore admit, Darwin was by no means an activist, and certainly did not intend *The Origin of Species* as a political statement. If he had, he would have made sure to include a chapter on human races in the book, appearing as it did on the brink of the American Civil War, just when the slavery debate was at its height. Yet Darwin refused to touch the issue; as he wrote to Wallace, "I think I shall avoid the whole subject" of mankind, which was "too surrounded with prejudices." For Desmond and Moore, who argue that Darwin's anti-racism was the motor of his science, this decision appears inexplicable: "the *raison d'être* of much of Darwin's work was to be concealed... *Hamlet* was to be performed without the prince."

To Darwin it did not look that way, however, because no moral cause—no matter how important to him personally—was the raison d'être of his work. He was a scientist, and he worked to establish the truth, regardless of where it might lead. Indeed, as Desmond and Moore note, Darwin was not especially worried by the prospect that the human races might be different species: "they would still be 'descended from common stock,'" as Darwin jotted in his copy of the racist bestseller *Types of Mankind*, "so it will 'come back' to the same thing."

Here we can see the second, much more important reason why evolution cannot be taken as Darwin's blow against slavery. The way Darwin proved the unity of the races was not to show that all men are created in the image of God. It was to show that all men are animals, products of the same "common stock" as birds and beasts. As Desmond and Moore write, the common descent of Europeans and Africans was just one of "millions upon millions of brotherly 'common descents' going back through history ... mice and men, amoebas and mushrooms."

The implications of this are not as reassuring as Desmond and Moore appear to think. For if our common descent with other animals does not stop us from exploiting and killing them—and who would think twice about picking a mushroom?—then there is no obvious reason why our common descent with other human beings should be morally determinative. The first step up our ancestral tree shows that we are all related; that is why, as Desmond and Moore note, Darwin's antislavery views put him in the same camp with evangelical Christians, and made him the foe of racist "scientists." But the second step, and every step thereafter, shows that genetic relationship is morally meaningless—which is why the evangelical Christians recognized Darwin, after the *Origin*, as a mortal enemy.

There was a basic tension, if not an enmity, between Darwin's moral views and his scientific conclusions. In one of his early evolution notebooks, he observed: "When two races of men meet, they act precisely like two species of animals—they fight, eat each other, bring disease to each other, etc." Darwin did not believe that it was right for men to do this; he was acutely sensitive to human suffering, perhaps because he endured so much of it himself. But because he believed that such competition, resulting in the survival of the fittest, was natural, he also did not really believe it could be prevented. As Desmond and Moore note with chagrin, he goes on to write that "the race with the 'best fitted organization, or . . . intellect'" will inevitably triumph, just as the whites decimated the Aborigines in Australia.

This unresolved tension can be seen most clearly in *The Descent of Man*, where Darwin wrestles, unsuccessfully, with the problem of reinstating ethics in the evolutionary worldview. On the one hand, Darwin argues—in terms similar to those used by evolutionary biologists today—that human beings have evolved to be social creatures. The "so-called moral sense is aboriginally derived from the social instincts, for both relate at first exclusively to the community," he writes. Evolution has given man "some degree of instinctive love and sympathy for his fellows," and "a tendency to be faithful to his comrades." And it is plausible that these instincts and tendencies would be an advantage in the struggle for survival, since they would have encouraged small groups of primitive humans—who were most likely genetically related—to work together.

But is there any evolutionary reason why our social instincts should be extended to all human beings? Does it convey any survival advantage to care about people we are not related to, will never meet, and whom it may even be profitable to harm—the way Darwin, and other English abolitionists, cared about African slaves? Here *The Descent of Man* becomes notably imprecise:

> But as love, sympathy and self-command become
> strengthened by habit, and as the power of reason-
> ing becomes clearer, so that man can value justly
> the judgments of his fellows, he will feel himself
> impelled, apart from any transitory pleasure or

pain, to certain lines of conduct. He might then
declare—not that any barbarian or uncultivated
man could thus think—I am the supreme judge
of my own conduct, and in the words of Kant, I
will not in my own person violate the dignity of
humanity.

At the crucial moment, the language slips into the passive
voice, and value judgments—implicit in words like "clearer,"
"justly," "uncultivated"—make an unexplained entrance. From
cavemen to Kant—this is the evolution, the moral and intellectual evolution, which Darwin is supposed to be explaining;
instead, he presents it as something both automatic and self-
evidently desirable. The language of evolution has given way to
the language of progress.

When Desmond and Moore quote Darwin's notebook entry
about races of men fighting like species of animals, they are
moved to an unusual censoriousness: "his science was becoming emotionally confused and ideologically messy." But if it is
emotional and ideological to observe that humans, and groups of
humans, fight one another, surely it is just as emotional and ideological to say that they should not fight one another, as Desmond
and Moore—and all of us—believe. This paradox brings into
view the basic problem with all attempts to naturalize human
behavior. It is human nature to be violent and competitive, and
it is human nature to be compassionate and cooperative. Unlike
the animals, we are aware that such alternatives exist, and have
no choice but to choose between them, not just once and for all,
but every time we act.

And for making such choices, the language of evolution is
perfectly useless. Evolution can tell us—or try to tell us—how
we became what we are; it cannot tell us what we should be, or
even what we want to be. Darwin believed, as we have seen, that
the theory of evolution implied the radical imperfection of our

senses and intelligence. Yet he still devoted his life to the pursuit of truth, for its own sake; as he wrote, "I believe there exists, and I feel within me, an instinct for truth, or knowledge or discovery, of something the same nature as the instinct of virtue, and that our having such an instinct is reason enough for scientific researches without any practical results *ever* ensuing from them."

Darwin's instinct for truth—or, as it might more accurately be called, his love of truth—is what led him to formulate the theory of evolution. His instinct of virtue, or love of goodness, is what led him to abhor slavery. The faith he lived by was that these two loves would lead, ultimately, to the same conclusion. A century and a half into the Darwinian age, we live by that same faith, because we have no other choice.

Francis Fukuyama
and the Beginning of History

o o o

It is possible that Francis Fukuyama does not take unmixed pleasure in his fame as the author of *The End of History and the Last Man*. Ever since Fukuyama published that book in 1992—indeed, ever since he published the article on which the book was based, in the *National Interest*, in 1989—he has been umbilically joined to the phrase "the end of history." Since then, he has written books on big, complex subjects, from the decline of trust in American society to the future of genetic engineering, and he has participated in countless policy debates. Yet on the cover of his book *The Origins of Political Order*, he is once again identified as "the author of *The End of History and the Last Man*."

Will this book—a 500-page survey of the growth of states "from prehuman times to the French Revolution"—finally be the one to emancipate Fukuyama from the end of history? The question is justified not simply by the size, scope, and ambition of the project, but above all by its emphasis on origins. If the end of the Cold War represented the end of history, Fukuyama's new book starts over at the beginning, with the emergence of the first states out of kin-based tribes more than 3,000 years ago. In the introduction, Fukuyama explains that his purpose in *The Origins of Political Order* is to offer a new theory of political development, to supersede the one that his mentor Samuel Huntington advanced in his 1968 book *Political Order in Changing Societies*.

But it is hard to avoid thinking that Fukuyama is after even bigger game. After all, he emerged in his first book as a proud Hegelian—more, as a rehabilitator of Hegel, in an age that had lost patience with all grand theories of historical progress. "The twentieth century, it is safe to say, has made all of us into deep historical pessimists," Fukuyama wrote. But the events of 1989 made it possible once again to believe that history was marching in the direction of freedom, that liberal democracy would prove to be the solution of mankind's long experiment in politics. This or that tyranny might win a temporary reprieve, but the ultimate judgment was sealed. The concluding metaphor of *The End of History* made Fukuyama's view clear:

> Rather than a thousand shoots blossoming into as many different flowering plants, mankind will come to seem like a long wagon train strung out along a road. Some wagons will be pulling into town sharply and crisply, while others will be bivouacked back in the desert, or else stuck in ruts in the final pass over the mountains. . . . The apparent differences in the situations of the wagons will not be seen as reflecting permanent and necessary differences between the people riding in the wagons, but simply a product of their different positions along the road.

The title of *The Origins of Political Order* seems to promise the backstory to this consummation, the *arche* to history's *telos*. This might well sound like a hubristic project, requiring a kind of universal synthesis that few historians since Toynbee or Spengler have attempted, or wanted to attempt; and Fukuyama, of course, is not a historian. If he undertakes to discuss everything from Chinese Legalism to the Indian caste system to Ottoman eunuchs to French tax farmers, it is not with the pretense to knowing everything about everything. Fukuyama confesses to relying "almost exclusively on secondary sources," some of them, as the bibliography shows, rather antiquated. Nor, of course, does even such a wide range of topics come close to exhausting "the origins of political order": for every civilization Fukuyama treats, half a dozen go unmentioned. Most strikingly, he has almost nothing to say about the Roman Empire, which since Machiavelli and Vico has been the classic case study for thinking about the rise of states.

Still, Fukuyama's project is quite in the spirit of Hegel, who made clear that the writing of universal history does not require giving an account of everything that has ever happened to mankind, a manifestly impossible task. Rather, he explained in the introduction to *The Philosophy of History*, "The History of the world is none other than the progress of the consciousness of Freedom; a progress whose development [is] according to the necessity of its nature." It is this story of progressive enlightenment that the universal historian has to tell.

In the past, Fukuyama has felt that that story was best and most succinctly explained by Alexandre Kojève, the Franco-Russian philosopher whose seminars on Hegel, given in Paris in the 1930s, exerted a huge influence on subsequent political thinkers. (When Fukuyama talks about Hegel, he acknowledged in *The End of History*, he is really talking about "Hegel-as-interpreted-by-Kojève.") It was Kojève who proposed that History came to an end with the French Revolution and the rise of Napoleon—for the sake of convenience, say in 1806, the year of the Battle of Jena and the publication of Hegel's *Phenomenology of Spirit*. By that time, humanity had discovered that the ideal state was a liberal republic in which each citizen recognized every other citizen as equal, thus ending the age-old struggle between masters and slaves that was the engine of historical progress.

Hegel knew, of course, that such a state did not prevail everywhere, or perhaps anywhere, on Earth in 1806. But this was merely a factual matter, not a philosophical one, Kojève explained: "Hegel ... knew full well that the State was not yet realized in deed in all its perfection. He only asserted that the *germ* of this State was present in the World and that the necessary and sufficient conditions for its growth were in existence. Now, can we with certainty deny the presence of such a germ and such conditions in our World?" It took a great deal of confidence for Kojève to ask such a question in 1938, when many people would have been quite willing to deny it. But when Fukuyama returned to the question in the early 1990s, fascism and communism—the twentieth century's major challengers to liberal democracy—had been defeated and discredited, and the "germ" of freedom was sending out new shoots.

Even in 1992, however, it was possible to point to many parts of the world where liberalism had not prevailed. And in the first pages of his new book, Fukuyama acknowledges that the tide of freedom may seem to have retreated in the last decade. True, he writes, there has been a "democratic recession ... around the world in the 2000s," with the post-Soviet states retreating into authoritarianism, communism still enthroned in China, and various kinds of despotism in Iran, Venezuela, and elsewhere. Yet Fukuyama's covered-wagon metaphor has always assumed that there would be laggards on the road to freedom. What matters, from his point of view, is not whether democracy advances or retreats, but whether there are any philosophically plausible alternatives to democracy, in the way that communism once represented such an alternative; and he is confident that there are not. "Very few people around the world," he writes, "openly profess to admire Vladimir Putin's petronationalism, or Hugo Chavez's 'twenty-first-century socialism,' or Mahmoud Ahmadinejad's Islamic Republic. ... China's rapid growth incites envy and interest, but its exact model of authoritarian capitalism is not one that is easily described, much less emulated, by other developing countries."

Such a list exposes the fragility of the Hegelian distinction between History and history: when something like two billion people live under dictatorships, the fact that the idea of democracy goes philosophically unchallenged might seem a little irrelevant. Nor is it actually true that the regimes Fukuyama lists are without their admirers—certainly the Islamic Republic of Iran has plenty of vocal (and well-armed) sympathizers, in Lebanon and beyond. What is true is that these regimes have few defenders among Western and Western-oriented intellectuals. But if intellectual victory is really only victory among the intellectuals, then what Fukuyama is talking about is not so much the end of History as the end of ideology, which Daniel Bell hailed as long ago as 1960.

Still, since ideas do have consequences, the ideological victory of liberalism would be nothing to scorn—if it were really assured. Yet, ironically, *The Origins of Political Order* itself gives reason for doubting this. For in a strange way, without explicitly acknowledging it, Fukuyama has abandoned the central premise of his earlier work, which was the Hegelian necessity of the progress of freedom. It is true that, as before, Fukuyama sees political history as the story of the evolution and spread of liberalism. The strategy of the book is to examine the development, across a range of societies, of what he considers the three pillars of "modern liberal democracy": a strong state, the rule of law, and accountable government. While his choice of historical case studies is unconventional, the trajectory of the book leads him to a very traditional, even Whiggish conclusion: it culminates in an analysis of "England, in which all three dimensions of political development—the state, rule of law, and political accountability—were successfully institutionalized."

The implication is that all the other civilizations Fukuyama discusses are defective Englands—or, to vary the metaphor, that the goal of all countries is "getting to Denmark," where Denmark is shorthand for "a mythical place . . . [that is] stable, democratic, peaceful, prosperous, inclusive, and has extremely low levels of political corruption." One way of reading *The Origins of Political Order* is as a manual on modernization, development, and state-building, the issues that have dominated Fukuyama's work in recent years. They have also, of course, dominated American foreign policy in the post–September 11 era, as the plausibility of building democracy in places like Iraq and Afghanistan became the major question dividing foreign-policy neoconservatives from traditional realists, isolationists, and disillusioned liberals. Fukuyama, once a leading neoconservative, announced his resignation from that school in a 2006 *New York Times Magazine* article, "After Neoconservatism," in which he declared it "very unlikely that history will judge either the [Iraq War] itself or the ideas animating it kindly."

Allusions to this foreign-policy debate can be found at several points in *The Origins of Political Order*, when Fukuyama emphasizes the cultural and geographical obstacles to democratization. "Mountains . . . explain the persistence of tribal forms of organization in many of the world's upland regions," he writes, instancing Afghanistan: "Turks, Mongols, and Persians, followed by the British, Russians, and now the Americans and NATO forces have all tried to subdue and pacify Afghanistan's tribes and to build a centralized state there, with very modest success." Likewise, the persistence of tribalism under the veneer of the modern state is illustrated by Iraq: "As the Americans occupying Iraq's Anbar province after the 2003 invasion discovered, it was easier to control tribal fighters using the traditional authority of the tribal chief than to create new impersonal units that did not take account of underlying social realities."

Such examples, Fukuyama concludes, "should imbue us with a certain degree of humility in the task of institution-building in the contemporary world. Modern institutions cannot simply be transferred to other societies without reference to existing rules and the political force supporting them." There is no arguing with the conclusion. But it does seem significantly at odds with the principle, central to Fukuyama's earlier work, that liberal democracy is the best form of government because it fulfills the universal human desire for recognition.

In *The Origins of Political Order*, Fukuyama makes a considerably weaker claim for democracy: "Once this combination of state, law, and accountability appeared, it proved to be a highly powerful and attractive form of government that subsequently spread to all corners of the world. But we need to remember how historically contingent this emergence was." Contingency and attractiveness have replaced universality and necessity.

What explains this shift, which Fukuyama never explicitly justifies? One answer might be that history—events in Iraq and Afghanistan—has derailed Fukuyama's confidence in History. But the powerful thing about the dialectic, as generations of Marxists knew, is that the mere march of events can never disprove it. Since decades are as moments in the eyes of the Idea— this is one of several ways in which it resembles God—nothing that has happened between 1992 and the present can be taken to disprove the end of History. (Didn't Kojève dismiss everything that happened since 1806 as essentially irrelevant?) By the same token, every outbreak of democracy, no matter how imperiled or fleeting, can be taken as confirmation of Fukuyama's theory— which is why the Arab Spring was invoked, by many commentators, as a vindication of Fukuyama's thesis.

The explanation for Fukuyama's evolution must be sought, rather, in the realm of ideas—in particular, the idea of evolution itself. Briefly put, Darwin has replaced Hegel as Fukuyama's guide to politics. This becomes clear as early as the second chapter of *The Origins of Political Order*, titled "The State of Nature." Fukuyama has never accepted the Hobbesian view of the state of nature as a war of all against all; but the grounds of his rejection have significantly changed. In *The End of History*, he countered Hobbes with Hegel: the Hobbesian view that society is grounded in man's fear of violent death, he argued, was less plausible than the Hegelian view that society arises from man's need to earn recognition from his fellows by dominating them.

In the new book, he again dismisses Hobbes, but this time on Darwinian grounds. Mankind has never consisted of atomized individuals, Fukuyama writes, but even in its most primitive state was organized into small, kin-based bands: "Human sociability is not a historical or cultural acquisition, but something hardwired into human nature." This is because the biological imperative for humans, as for all animals, is the preservation of their genes, which led us to evolve the strategies of "inclusive fitness, kin selection, and reciprocal altruism." So strong is this genetic allegiance that, in most parts of the world, it goes deeper and lasts longer than allegiance to larger groups like nations or states: "From the Melanesian *wantok* to the Arab tribe to the Taiwanese lineage to the Bolivian *ayllu*, complex kinship structures remain the primary locus of social life for many people in the contemporary world, and strongly shape their interaction with modern political institutions."

Yet the effect of using Darwin to disprove Hobbes is actually, it turns out, to confirm Hobbes on another level. There may never have been a war of all individuals against all; but the state of nature was, Fukuyama argues, a war of all extended families against all. (This is already true of chimpanzees, whose violence and status-seeking Fukuyama sees as a primitive form of politics.) The first higher-order social organization, into tribes, was a response to this constant warfare, and the next level of organization, into states, was a way for tribes to gain advantage over one another. Fukuyama illustrates the point by discussing the "warring states" period of Chinese history, the years from 480 to 221 BCE when constant warfare reduced thousands of competing principalities into a single empire. "The chief driver of Chinese state formation," he concludes, "was war and the requirements of war." The title of chapter five, "The Coming of Leviathan," confirms that Fukuyama has taken a Darwinian detour to a Hobbesian conclusion.

War, as Fukuyama understands it, is essentially a matter of Darwinian competition, in which the fittest polities survive. "Political systems evolve in a manner roughly comparable to biological evolution," Fukuyama writes:

> Darwin's theory of evolution is based on two very simple principles, variation and selection. Variation among organisms occurs due to random genetic combinations; those variants that are better adapted to their specific environments have greater reproductive success and therefore propagate themselves at the expense of those less well adapted. In a very long historical perspective, political development has followed the same general pattern: the forms of political organization employed by different groups of human beings have varied, and those forms that were more successful—meaning those that could generate greater military and economic power—displaced those that were less successful.

It is a sign of how powerful the Darwinian worldview has become that Fukuyama could find this metaphor plausible, despite its fundamental defects. None of the principles of the evolution of species apply to states. There is not an oversupply of states relative to available resources, which would produce selection pressure; states do not evolve into different species, but are all individual members of the same species; states do not reproduce. The ability to exert "military and economic power" does not have any clear correlation with a polity's survival in the long term—just look at the way the Mongols destroyed more sophisticated states from Persia to Muscovy to China, and then disappeared in a few generations.

But there are two even more fundamental problems with the Darwinian metaphor. The first is that, like almost every thinker who has tried to apply the evolutionary model to human affairs, Fukuyama cannot avoid thinking of evolution as a matter of the emergence of higher forms out of lower forms. "Strict cultural relativism is at odds with the implications of evolutionary theory," he writes, "since the latter necessitates identifying different levels of social organization and the reason one level gets superseded by another." But at the very heart of Darwinism is the principle that there is no such thing as "levels" or "supersession"; as Darwin adjured himself in one of his marginalia, "Never use the word higher or lower." Human beings are in no ontological sense "higher" than cockroaches—we have simply evolved a different adaptive strategy. In the same way, regarded simply as strategies for survival, no human polity is higher or lower than another, only (temporarily) more or less successful.

If this conclusion is hard to accept, that is because of the second problem with Darwinism as a guide to human affairs: human beings are a species in which the only genetic value, reproduction, is contested by moral and intellectual values which we posit for ourselves. It is not hard for us to imagine situations in which truthfulness, fidelity, or piety can take precedence over the instinct to reproduce, or even to survive—celibacy is a human institution, as is martyrdom. Nietzsche, who was a great antagonist of Darwin, formulated the difference between them precisely in terms of the relative emphasis each thinker placed on survival. In *The Will to Power*, Nietzsche observed that, for human beings, the subjective experience of triumph is more important than actual success in the struggle for survival: "Physiologists should think again before positing the 'instinct of preservation' as the cardinal drive in an organic creature. A living thing wants above all to *discharge* its force." And the discharge of force can take forms inimical to the preservation of life.

The application of this Nietzschean idea to politics is anything but abstract. It is nothing but the ability of human beings to sacrifice their own reproductive fitness in the name of an idea that allows states to form in the first place; the allegiance to a state, or to a religion, is a classic example of a human behavior that can be biologically "irrational." Fukuyama is well aware of this conundrum, since he has always been a devoted and insightful Nietzschean—if the first part of the title of *The End of History and the Last Man* comes from Hegel, the second comes from Nietzsche. That is why he insists many times, in *The Origins of Political Order*, that history cannot be understood simply in materialist terms. "Ideas are extremely important to political order," he writes early on.

In fact, much of the book consists of case studies in how and why ideas trump interests. It is biologically axiomatic, for Fukuyama, that people will seek to benefit themselves and their immediate kin. "When impersonal institutions decay," he writes, kin selection and reciprocal altruism "are the forms that always reemerge because they are natural to human beings." For a state to take precedence over such loyalties, it must possess *legitimacy*, one of the two key concepts in *The Origins of Political Order*. The "Mandate of Heaven," which was said to decide between claimants to the imperial throne of China, is one classic metaphor of legitimacy. "The moral distance between an emperor and a powerful warlord is . . . enormous," Fukuyama writes. "The former is a legitimate ruler whose authority is willingly obeyed; the latter is a violent usurper."

But legitimacy does not only serve to control peoples; it also, even more strikingly, controls rulers. Fukuyama rejects the economist Mancur Olson's characterization of early modern European monarchs as "stationary bandits," mere predators of their subjects' resources. It is not historically true that kings taxed their subjects at the highest possible rate, or continually threatened them with violence. In China, the ideology of Confucianism bound rulers to act justly toward their subjects; in Europe, Catholicism and the institution of the rule of law did the same, in Fukuyama's view much more effectively.

Political order arises when the state commands enough legitimacy to trump its subjects' familial loyalties. Conversely, political decay happens when those loyalties reassert themselves at the expense of the state. This leads to the second major theme of Fukuyama's book, *repatrimonialization*. The classic example here is *ancien régime* France, whose aristocrats and financiers literally purchased parts of the state for their own benefit, in the form of tax-farming franchises and heritable offices. It was, Fukuyama writes, an "early prototype of what is today called a rent-seeking society. In such a society, the elites spend all of their time trying to capture public office in order to secure a rent for themselves."

The most interesting parts of *The Origins of Political Order* deal with the various ways different polities have attempted to head off such repatrimonialization, some of them quite exotic. In the Ottoman Empire, the *devshirme* was a levy of Christian youths, in which gifted boys were taken from their homes and trained to be imperial administrators and janissaries; in this way, the sultans created a bureaucratic caste with no family ties. In China, the use of an examination system to recruit mandarins played a similar role. Both can be seen as strategies for producing Platonic guardians, wholly dedicated to the state; in the *Republic*, Socrates even urges that the guardians be told that they had no human parents, which he calls a "noble lie."

Fukuyama's problem is that he, too, finally has no way to understand the forces that make for legitimacy and political order except as "noble lies." This is because, on the Darwinian view of man, only individual and familial advantage can be a genuinely rational motivation; while nationalism, religion, and ideology, the great drivers of state-building and civilization-building, can only appear irrational. Fukuyama tends to treat religion, in particular, in a crudely functionalist manner, as a collective delusion that was useful for driving the consolidation of tribes into states: "Religion solves this collective action problem . . . if I believe that the chief can command the spirits of dead ancestors to reward or punish me, I will be much more likely to respect his word." Again, he writes, "There is no clearer illustration of the importance of ideas to politics than the emergence of an Arab state under the Prophet Muhammad"—meaning, it appears, that in this case the connection of religious belief with political power is especially naked. It is in this sense that we must take Fukuyama's insistence that "ideas matter."

What this really means, however, is that ideas *mattered*. For there is no way that a reader who shares Fukuyama's Darwinian outlook could ever be moved to action by the kind of ideas he is talking about—the deification of a chieftain, or a prophet, or a nation-state. That's why Fukuyama does not so much explain these phenomena as redescribe them in terms of inherited instinct. Two of the "foundations of political development," Fukuyama writes early in the book, are that "human beings have a capacity for abstraction and theory that generates mental models of causality, and a further tendency to posit causation based on invisible or transcendental forces. This is the basis of religious belief. . . . Humans also have a proclivity for norm following that is grounded in the emotions rather than in reason, and consequently a tendency to invest mental models and the rules that flow from them with intrinsic worth."

It's impossible to miss the circularity of these definitions. Like the doctor in Molière who explains that opium causes sleepiness because it has a "dormitive power," Fukuyama attributes the human susceptibility to religion and morality to our "capacity for abstraction" and "proclivity for norm following." The difference between opium and religion, however, is that being able to describe religion in this way means being immune to it, or emancipated from it. Indeed, to be emancipated from such ungrounded "norms" is what it means to live after the end of History.

Another name for this freedom is nihilism—the nihilism of which Nietzsche was the prophet and would-be doctor. What has been really distinctive about Fukuyama's work, from *The End of History* onward, is that he seriously engages with the condition of nihilism, in which he agrees that we live. But while Nietzsche hoped to counter the apathy of the Last Man with the will-to-power of the *Übermensch*, Fukuyama—inheriting the lessons of the twentieth century—cannot look so blithely at the prospect of new "wars of the spirit." His task, rather, has been to look for nonviolent ways of harnessing the human desire for struggle, recognition, and the "discharge of force."

In his book *Trust*, Fukuyama saw work and corporate loyalty as possible solutions: "liberal democracy works because the struggle for recognition that formerly had been carried out on a military, religious, or nationalist plane is now pursued on an economic one," he wrote. *The Great Disruption*, his analysis of post-1960s cultural and social ills, was based on the recognition that "the situation of normlessness . . . is intensely uncomfortable for us," and Fukuyama looked hopefully forward to the spontaneous emergence of new norms and values. *Our Posthuman Future* was a still more powerful and plausible jeremiad against nihilism, perceived this time in biotechnological terms: "biotechnology will cause us in some way to lose our humanity—that is, some essential quality that has always underpinned our sense of who we are and where we are going."

As long as Fukuyama could believe in History as a dialectical process, moving inevitably in the direction of freedom and equal recognition, there was at least one compass point he could rely on. In the Darwinian world of *The Origins of Political Order*, that directionality has vanished, and we are left with contingency and cynicism as the keys to understanding our own past. That this results in a more conventional book than we have come to expect from Fukuyama may only mean that the conventional wisdom is inescapable—much as he, and we, might wish otherwise.

The Last Men:
Houellebecq, Sebald, McEwan

o o o

There aren't many moments in history when it is possible to worry that the world has become too happy for its own good. One such moment came in Europe in the nineteenth century, when the Napoleonic Wars had receded into the distance and the First World War was still hidden over the horizon. For a brief period, it became possible to believe that the West was headed for a condition of permanent peace; that technology, democracy, and globalization were driving a virtuous circle, which no atavistic violence could disrupt.

This vision never came very close to becoming a reality; the nineteenth century was, after all, the era of communism and anarchism, imperialism and scientific racism. It is remarkable, then, to consider how many of the greatest writers of the period were exercised by the possibility that reason, progress, and material well-being—in short, the bourgeois order—might destroy the human spirit. Think of Flaubert's hatred for middle-class philistinism; of Kierkegaard's scorn for temperate, worldly religion; of Dostoevsky's passionate rejection of scientific materialism; even of Dickens's satire against utilitarianism. What unites all of these disparate hostilities is the nineteenth-century writer's sense that the West has sold its heroic birthright for a mess of pottage—that material well-being is a kind of drug, to which modern man is incurably addicted.

The definitive statement of this view was offered by Nietzsche in the prologue to *Thus Spoke Zarathustra*. That is where he summons the specter of the Last Man:

> The earth has become small, and upon it hops the Last Man, who makes everything small. His race is as inexterminable as the flea; the Last Man lives longest.
>
> "We have discovered happiness," say the Last Men and blink....
>
> A little poison now and then: that produces pleasant dreams. And a lot of poison at last, for a pleasant death.
>
> They still work, for work is entertainment. But they take care the entertainment does not exhaust them.
>
> Nobody grows rich or poor any more: both are too much of a burden. Who still wants to rule? Who obey? Both are too much of a burden.

The key to understanding this vision lies in the way it is received by Zarathustra's listeners. Far from being repelled by the prospect of eternal mediocrity, the crowd clamors for it: "Give us this Last Man, O Zarathustra . . . make us into this Last Man!" The danger of the bourgeois ideal is precisely that it is so attractive to the vast majority of human beings. That is why it has to be excoriated so violently, and why those who resist it consider themselves members of a spiritual aristocracy.

The twentieth century, of course, did not turn out to be the age of the Last Man after all. The two world wars demonstrated to anyone's satisfaction that irrationality and cruelty, which Nietzsche had feared were dwindling resources, were still present in abundance just underneath the thin crust of European civilization. The masses, or at least a significant fraction of them, did not want to become Last Men, but to play at being Supermen and blond beasts, as fascism and Nazism encouraged them to do. For much of the last century, Nietzsche himself no longer seemed like the most prescient critic of European civilization, but like the evil genius urging it to commit suicide.

Then came 1989 and the end of history—or at least, *The End of History and the Last Man*, Francis Fukuyama's influential book. It is almost always referred to simply by the first part of its title; to his critics, Fukuyama is the man who declared "the end of history," triumphally and prematurely. But the second part of the book's title is actually more important, and more representative of Fukuyama's argument. No sooner had humanity emerged from a century of hot and cold wars than Fukuyama was resurrecting Nietzsche's old warning that a world of peace and prosperity would mean a world of Last Men. "The life of the last men is one of physical security and material plenty, precisely what Western politicians are fond of promising their electorates," he pointed out. "Should we fear that we will be both happy *and* satisfied with our situation, no longer human beings but animals of the species *homo sapiens*?"

Yet while Fukuyama appreciates the seriousness of the Nietzschean warning, he hears it from the perspective of a defender, not a foe, of liberalism. "We can readily accept many of Nietzsche's acute psychological observations, even as we reject his morality," he writes. The danger he foresees is not simply that bourgeois democracy will cause human beings to degenerate, but that degenerate human beings will be unable to preserve democracy. Without the sense of pride and the love of struggle that Fukuyama, following Plato, calls *thymos*, men—and there is always an implication that *thymos* is a specifically masculine virtue—cannot establish freedom or protect it. The then-recent revolutions in Eastern Europe and the Tiananmen Square demonstrations in China gave Fukuyama clear examples of the way freedom depends on extraordinary courage:

> It is only thymotic man, the man of anger who is jealous of his own dignity and the dignity of his fellow citizens, the man who feels that his worth is constituted by something more than the complex set of desires that make up his physical existence—it is this man alone who is willing to walk in front of a tank or confront a line of soldiers. And it is frequently the case that without such small acts of bravery in response to small acts of injustice, the larger train of events leading to fundamental changes in political and economic structures would never occur.

When Fukuyama published his book, in 1992, he was specifically concerned about the loss of *thymos* among Americans. It was America that had won the Cold War, thus establishing the uncontestable superiority of liberal democracy and inaugurating the end of History. Yet it was also America that, to Fukuyama, seemed to be growing soft in its prosperity—concerned with material goods and self-esteem, indifferent to duty and sacrifice. "Those earnest young people trooping off to law and business school," he wrote, "who anxiously fill out their resumes in hopes of maintaining the lifestyles to which they believe themselves entitled, seem to be much more in danger of becoming last men, rather than reviving the passions of the first man." Fukuyama granted that "the same is true in other parts of the post-historical world," such as Western Europe. But it was America that had long been identified with all the vices of the Last Man: "Nietzsche's greatest fear was that the 'American way of life' should become victorious," Fukuyama writes. In the early

1990s, a time of culture war and economic recession in the United States, it seemed all too possible that victory in the Cold War would be followed by a more insidious spiritual defeat.

Today, Fukuyama's predictions about the debility of the posthistorical world are still common currency among neoconservatives. What has changed, dramatically so, is the consensus view about where that posthistorical world can be found. The American response to the 9/11 attacks—the war on terror, the wars in Iraq and Afghanistan—have banished any fear that America might grow passive and unwarlike. The opposite complaint is much more likely to be heard, especially from European critics of America. And partly for that reason, it is to Europe that Americans now look for examples of the rise of the Last Man. The opposition of Europeans to the Iraq War can look, from a neoconservative perspective, exactly like the inability "to walk in front of a tank or confront a line of soldiers" that Fukuyama warned about.

This was the essence of Robert Kagan's argument in *Of Paradise and Power*, published in 2003 on the eve of the Iraq War. Europe, Kagan wrote, "is turning away from power" and "entering a post-historical paradise of peace and relative prosperity," while the United States "remains mired in history." Kagan granted that the European preference for cooperation over conflict, for international institutions over unilateral action, was both a natural product of its war-torn past and an inevitable reflection of its military inferiority.

But he also dwelled, in terminology very reminiscent of Nietzsche and Fukuyama, on the psychological frailty, the thymotic decay, of contemporary European society. "The real question," he writes, "is one of intangibles—of fears, passions, and beliefs." Kagan's much-quoted formula, "Americans are from Mars and Europeans are from Venus," is a more or less overt accusation of European effeminacy. The same is true of Kagan's suggestion that if America has a cowboy mentality, Europe has a saloonkeeper's—commercial, conflict-averse, and cowardly, just like the townspeople who let down Gary Cooper in *High Noon*. Or, as James Sheehan puts it, in more value-neutral terms, in *Where Have All the Soldiers Gone?*: "The eclipse of the willingness and ability to use violence that was once so central to statehood has created a new kind of European state, firmly rooted in new forms of public and private identity and power. As a result, the European Union may become a superstate—a super *civilian* state—but not a superpower."

o o o

Is it true that western Europeans, after half a century of peace and prosperity, are suffering the kind of moral malaise that Nietzsche warned about, and that Fukuyama and Kagan diagnosed? One way to answer this question is to listen, not to American pundits, but to Europeans themselves—in particular, to their novelists. In the nineteenth century, a reader of Dostoevsky and Flaubert could have gained insights into the state of Europe that a reader of newspapers would have missed. In the twenty-first, it is at least possible that the most significant European novelists can give us similar insights. Precisely because novels are not, and should not be, political documents, they offer a less guarded, more intuitive report on the inner life of a society. And when novelists from different European countries, writing in different languages and very different styles, all seem to corroborate one another's intuitions, it is at least fair to wonder whether a real cultural shift is taking place.

The three novels I want to consider are not, of course, anything like a representative sample of the fiction being written in Europe over the last two decades. But W. G. Sebald's *The Rings of Saturn*, Michel Houellebecq's *The Elementary Particles*, and Ian McEwan's *Saturday* are as distinguished a selection as might be made. All of these writers were born in the 1940s and 1950s, and emerged as major novelists in the 1990s. In other words, they are members of the post–World War II generation, and did or are doing their most important work in the post–Cold War period. They belong to, and write about, a cosmopolitan, peaceful, unified Western Europe: McEwan is English; Sebald, a German, spent most of his adult life in England; and Houellebecq, who is French, has lived in Ireland and Spain.

While all of these writers are celebrated and critically acclaimed, they in no sense form a school or movement. Houellebecq is an often crude satirist, whose misanthropic, pornographic novels have won him a scandalous reputation. He could not be more different from Sebald, who had a considerable reputation as a literary scholar before he began to publish his unclassifiable books—hybrids of fiction, memoir, and history—in the 1990s. Sebald's melancholy works were immediately acclaimed in Germany and then in the United States, and before he died, in a car accident, at the age of fifty-seven, he was often mentioned as a candidate for the Nobel Prize. McEwan has been at the center of the English literary world since the 1970s, but he has lately emerged as probably the best novelist of his generation, on the strength of books like *Amsterdam* and *Atonement*. The *New Statesman* has described him as "the closest thing we have to a 'national novelist.'"

Three more different writers could hardly be invented—which makes it all the more suggestive that their portraits of the spiritual state of contemporary Europe are so powerfully complementary. They show us a Europe that is affluent and tolerant, enjoying all the material blessings that human beings have always struggled for, and that the Europeans of seventy years ago would have thought unattainable. Yet these three books are also haunted by intimations of belatedness and decline, by the fear that Europe has too much history behind it to thrive. They suggest that currents of rage and despair are still coursing beneath the calm surface of society, occasionally erupting into violence. And they worry about what will happen when a Europe gorged on its historical good fortune has to defend itself against an envious and resentful world.

◦ ◦ ◦

The Elementary Particles, published in 1998, is the book that comes closest to confirming Nietzsche's vision of the Last Man. Indeed, the novel opens with a portentous preface, written as though in the distant future, informing us that the character we are about to meet—Michel Djerzinski, "a first-rate biologist and a serious candidate for the Nobel Prize," who is also an emotionally autistic, sexually stunted wreck of a human being—literally brought about the end of the human race in the late twentieth century. For his discoveries in genetics allowed humanity to replace itself with a new species that is not dependent on sexual reproduction, and is therefore free from suffering and death. Houellebecq gives us a glimpse of that future felicity in a poem: "We live today under a new world order . . . / What men considered a dream, perfect but remote, / We take for granted as the simplest of things."

The novel, then, is Houellebecq's portrait of a society—contemporary European society, French division—so incurably miserable that it deserves, and desires, to be made extinct. Yet the ironic message of *The Elementary Particles* is that it is precisely the plenty and safety of French society that are making it intolerable to live in. All the qualities that European social democracy prides itself on—its sexual liberation, political tolerance, and economic equality, even the free health care and the long paid vacations—become instruments of torture to Michel and his half-brother, Bruno, the novel's unlovable heroes.

They are victims of the *Zeitgeist*—of "Western Europe, in the latter half of the twentieth century," which Houellebecq describes in the novel's very first lines as "an age that was miserable and troubled," when "the relationships between . . . contemporaries were at best indifferent and more often cruel." The most destructive agent of this indifference is Bruno and Michel's mother, Janine, described by Houellebecq as an early adopter of the hedonistic, materialistic lifestyle that would become normative after the 1960s and the sexual revolution. Concerned only with her own pleasure, Janine has no interest in mothering her children, literally abandoning the infant Michel in a pile of his own excrement. No wonder he grows up to be incapable of love or sexual connection; or that Bruno, similarly maltreated, becomes a loathsome pervert, obsessed with pornography and public masturbation, and only prevented by his own cowardice from becoming a child molester.

Bruno and Michel are the prime exhibits in Houellebecq's programmatic indictment of modern European sexual mores. Starting in the 1960s, he writes, "a 'youth culture' based principally on sex and violence" began to drive out the ancient Judeo-Christian culture that valued monogamy, mutual devotion, and self-restraint. The innovative element in Houellebecq's argument is to link this new hedonism with the triumph of the European welfare state. Freed from all concern about politics and economics, men and women had nothing to occupy themselves with but the pursuit of sensual gratification. But this pursuit quickly developed into a Hobbesian war of all against all, in which the young and attractive are worshiped while the ugly and shy, like Bruno, are utterly despised. "Of all worldly goods," Bruno rages, "youth is clearly the most precious, and today we don't believe in anything but worldly goods."

"It is interesting to note," Houellebecq writes in one of many passages of armchair sociology, "that the 'sexual revolution' was sometimes portrayed as a communal utopia, whereas in fact it was simply another stage in the historical rise of individualism. As the lovely word 'household' suggests, the couple and the family would be the last bastion of primitive communism in liberal society. The sexual revolution was to destroy these intermediary communities, the last to separate the individual from the market. The destruction continues to this day." No wonder that "in the last years of Western civilization," the "general mood [was] depression bordering on masochism."

Houellebecq's powerful nostalgia for the "household"

naturally leads him to an extremely sentimental view of women. Michel and Bruno each encounter a saintly, self-sacrificing woman who longs to heal their psychological trauma. But each of them is unable to return the love they are offered, so profoundly have they been ruined by their mother and the society she represents. By the novel's end, Bruno has gone into an insane asylum and Michel has withdrawn to a hermit-like existence in Galway, where he works out the scientific discoveries that will lead to the abolition of mankind. It is not a coincidence that Galway is the westernmost city in Europe, the point where the West culminates and disappears. Nor is Houellebecq's reader surprised to learn that, in the future, humans greet their own extinction with "meekness, resignation, perhaps even secret relief." The leisure-world that is contemporary Europe, Houellebecq argues, is a trial that human beings cannot bear.

◦ ◦ ◦

To turn from *The Elementary Particles* to *The Rings of Saturn* is like exchanging the passionate complaints of an outraged teenager for the quiet, hypnotic monologue of an old man. For while Sebald was only fifty-one when the book appeared in 1995, his writerly persona seems as old as the Ancient Mariner. The narrator we meet in the book's first pages—he shares a name and a history with the author, though the identification is never totally secure—has just suffered a complete nervous breakdown: "I was taken into hospital in Norwich in a state of almost total immobility," he confides affectlessly. Unlike Houellebecq's avatars, however, Sebald is not suffering from any calamity in his personal life, about which we never hear a word. This is a strictly philosophical crisis, brought on by "the paralyzing horror that had come over me at various times when confronted with the traces of destruction, reaching far back into the past," which Sebald sees everywhere he goes.

The book can be described, in fact, as a catalogue of the

various kinds of destruction, natural and man-made, that confront the writer as he takes a walking tour along the east coast of England. *The Rings of Saturn* is not really a novel, as there is no plot and no character development. It is, rather, a branching series of stories and memories, one giving rise to the next by no logic except that of free association. In the second chapter, for instance, Sebald starts out remembering a train ride from Norwich to Lowestoft. Along the way, he observes that the countryside was once covered with windmills, which have now all disappeared; visits a country house that was an architectural marvel of Victorian England, and is now a crumbling, unvisited museum; walks down a boardwalk that was once a popular holiday destination and is now seedy and abandoned; and remembers a story he once heard about two American pilots who crashed nearby at the end of the Second World War.

Clearly, Sebald is drawn to stories of abandonment and loss, to sites where Western civilization seems to have died out, to obsolete technologies and unrecapturable pasts. As the book goes on, he assembles so many of these tales as to become a Scheherazade of destruction. And because Sebald the wanderer almost never encounters another person, he manages to produce the eerie sense that England itself has been abandoned, that he may be the last man left to catalogue its ruins. The mood of the book is beautifully captured in one of Sebald's many quotations from Sir Thomas Browne, the Renaissance polymath whose meandering, encyclopedic works are models for his own: "The shadow of night is drawn like a black veil across the earth, and since almost all creatures, from one meridian to the next, lie down after the sun has set, so . . . one might, in following the setting sun, see on our globe nothing but prone bodies, row upon row, as if leveled by the scythe of Saturn—an endless graveyard for a humanity struck by falling sickness."

This vision of a world turned into a graveyard is Sebald's metaphor for the Europe he knows. Born in Germany in the last months of World War II, he is naturally obsessed with the war and its casualties; in other books, like *The Emigrants* and *On the Natural History of Destruction*, he deals explicitly with the Holocaust and the Allied bombing of Germany. But what makes *The Rings of Saturn* uniquely powerful among his works is the way that even the war comes to seem like just another manifestation of the entropy that is constantly at work in human affairs. The book evokes a Europe where too much history has taken place, too many lives have been lived and lost, so that it is no longer possible to make sense of them all or even remember them properly. Sebald quotes Michael Hamburger, another German émigré, on the difficulty of remembering his childhood: "Too many buildings have fallen down, too much rubble has been heaped up, the moraines and deposits are insuperable." The same feeling is voiced by a random Englishman, a "Mr. Squirrel from Middletown," who "had no memory at all and was quite unable to recall what had happened in his childhood, last year, last month or even last week. How he could therefore grieve for the dead," Sebald pointedly adds, "was a puzzle to which no one knew the answer."

The answer proposed in *The Rings of Saturn* is that grieving for the dead has become so overwhelming a task, for the European inheritor of twenty centuries, that it leaves room for nothing else. In typically elliptical fashion, when Sebald describes an eccentric Irish family living in the ruins of their stately home, he is offering a metaphor for Europe on the cusp of the twenty-first century:

> The floor-boards began to give, the beams of the ceilings sagged, and the paneling and staircases, long since rotten within, crumbled to sulphurous yellow dust, at times overnight. Every so often, usually after a long period of rain or extended drought or indeed after any change in the weather, a sudden, disastrous collapse would occur in the midst of the encroaching decay that went almost unnoticed, and had assumed the

character of normality. Just as people supposed they could hold a particular line, some dramatic and unanticipated deterioration would compel them to evacuate further areas, till they really had no way out and found themselves forced to the last post, prisoners in their own homes.

o o o

The Elementary Particles and *The Rings of Saturn* both depict a civilization collapsing from within, unable to stand what it has become. It makes perfect sense that both were published in the 1990s, during the West's brief holiday from history, with no external enemy on the horizon. *Saturday*, on the other hand, appeared in 2004, at the height of the "war on terror," when the West once more felt itself under threat, this time from Islamic fundamentalism. Ian McEwan plunges his novel into this particular historical moment by dramatizing the conflict between a privileged, guilt-ridden, indecisive civilization and an angry, jealous barbarism. He asks in the form of a parable the same question Kagan asked in *Of Paradise and Power*: can Europe defend its values from its enemies, when those values include a principled aversion to violence?

The whole action of the novel takes place on one particular Saturday: February 15, 2003, the day of the worldwide protests against the impending Iraq War. Henry Perowne, the middle-aged neurosurgeon and paterfamilias who is McEwan's protagonist, finds his day of errands—a squash game, a visit to his Alzheimer's-stricken mother, grocery shopping for a dinner party—disrupted by the protest: "It's a surprise, the number of children there are, and babies in pushchairs. Despite his skepticism, Perowne in white-soled trainers, gripping his racket tighter, feels the seduction and excitement peculiar to such events; a crowd possessing the streets, tens of thousands of strangers converging with a single purpose conveying an intimation of revolutionary joy."

Yet as this passage makes clear, Perowne is divided against himself on the morality of the Iraq War. He knows too much about the evil of Saddam Hussein's regime to join the protestors in their self-righteous certainty: "by definition, none of the people now milling around Warren Street tube station happens to have been tortured by the regime, or knows and loves people who have, or even knows much about the place at all." At the same time, when he discusses the war with his squash partner and fellow surgeon, an American named Jay Strauss—whose name codes his Jewishness and his allegiance to neoconservatism—Perowne feels repelled by Strauss's bellicosity. "He's a man of untroubled certainties, impatient of talk of diplomacy, weapons of mass destruction, inspection teams, proofs of links with al-Qaeda and so on.... Whenever he talks to Jay, Henry finds himself tending towards the anti-war camp."

Perowne is a stranger to "untroubled certainties" of any kind. His ability to see both sides of the war debate, his refusal to make snap ideological judgments, is one mark of his maturity; it is part and parcel of being civilized. For McEwan makes clear that Perowne represents the best of modern European civilization. He is healthy, handsome, reasonable, generous, a good father and devoted husband and concerned citizen. His work as a brain surgeon is described in minute technical detail, to underscore the miraculous prowess that science and skill have endowed him with: in the book's first pages, we see him save one life after another with his state-of-the-art surgical tools. And what Perowne is on the individual scale, McEwan suggests, London is on the grand scale: "Henry thinks the city is a success, a brilliant invention, a biological masterpiece—millions teeming around the accumulated and layered achievements of the centuries, as though around a coral reef, sleeping, working, entertaining themselves, harmonious for the most part, nearly everyone wanting it to work."

The problem, of course, is what to do about the people who don't want it to work. In the context of *Saturday*, this is clearly a geopolitical question; but McEwan is too canny a novelist to bring Perowne directly into conflict with a terrorist, which would be almost impossible to stage convincingly. (When John Updike tried to enter the mind of an Islamic fundamentalist, in *Terrorist*, he could do little more than recite clichés.) Instead, McEwan devises a more quotidian kind of conflict, in which the resilience of Perowne's civilization is tested.

The trouble begins when Perowne gets into a fender-bender with Baxter, a young thug who quickly grows violent. Based on his behavior and certain subtle symptoms, Perowne is able to deduce that the impetuous Baxter is suffering from an incipient neurological disease: "This is how the brilliant machinery of being is undone by the tiniest of faulty cogs, the insidious whisper of ruin, a single bad idea lodged in every cell." When Perowne shows Baxter that he knows about his condition—it is inherited, and Baxter knows full well what's in store for him—the thug loses his nerve, much like the Arthurian knights overawed by the Connecticut Yankee who can predict an eclipse.

But later that day, as Perowne's family gathers for dinner, Baxter barges into his expensive home and holds the whole group hostage. With the exquisite narrative cruelty of which he is a master, McEwan makes us watch as Baxter forces Perowne's grown daughter, Daisy, to strip naked, by holding a knife at her mother's neck. That Daisy is a poet, who has come home bearing the galleys of her first book, only makes the symbolic dimension of the standoff more unmistakable: here is passive, feminine culture victimized by blind masculine violence.

Perowne, despite all his surgical skills, is unable to overcome the intruder, thanks to a fatal deficit of *thymos*: "Never in his life has he hit someone in the face, even as a child. He's only ever taken a knife to anesthetised skin in a controlled and sterile environment. He simply doesn't know how to be reckless." Perowne can understand the evil he is facing, but his understanding of evil's causes does not help him to defeat it. Indeed, McEwan suggests, the opposite may be true: he may understand Baxter so well that he is too ambivalent to fight him, just as he has been ambivalent about the justice of the Iraq War. Perowne has been plagued all day by second thoughts about his initial conflict with the criminal: "His attitude was wrong from the start, insufficiently defensive; his manner may have seemed pompous, or disdainful. Provocative perhaps." If he could only have appeased Baxter's crazy, touchy pride, he might have been left alone in the cocoon of his culture and wealth: just the same calculation that, Kagan suggests, Europe as a whole made after September 11.

It is the way McEwan resolves this deadly standoff that makes *Saturday* such an ambiguous and troubling book. At the last moment, just before Baxter is about to rape Daisy, he notices her book of poems and commands her to read one out loud. Instead, she recites "Dover Beach," Matthew Arnold's great meditation on the uncertainty and loss of confidence of modern European man: "And we are here as on a darkling plain / Swept with confused alarms of struggle and flight, / Where ignorant armies clash by night." Baxter is so overwhelmed by the beauty of the verse, by the high culture he has never known, that he lets Daisy go and drops his guard, allowing Perowne to tackle him.

It is a totally fantastic resolution to a horribly realistic dilemma; it has something of the willed unreality of Shakespeare's late romances, where the dead magically come back to life. Civilization does not have to fight barbarism, McEwan's parable suggests. It only has to display its charms, and barbarism will disarm itself. Things only get more self-flattering in the coda to this episode, when Perowne volunteers to perform the brain surgery needed to save Baxter's life after he hits his head on the stairs during their struggle. Any stain of aggression is therefore wiped away; Perowne, and the civilization he incarnates, emerge both unharmed and innocent.

It is such a complete example of wish-fulfillment as to make the reader suspect that McEwan is being deliberately, teasingly perverse. The civilization that Houellebecq depicts is not worth saving, and the one Sebald dwells in is beyond saving; but the one McEwan describes, more realistically and affirmatively than either, deserves to be saved. The troubling question he leaves us with is whether Europe is enjoying its Saturday—the last day of the week, the day of rest—too much to face the tasks the new week is sure to bring.

Under the Volcano:
Giacomo Leopardi

o o o

When Matthew Arnold published the first collection of his poems, in 1853, he made a decision that can have few parallels in literary history: he deliberately refused to include one of the best things he had ever written, on the grounds that it was too depressing. "Empedocles on Etna," which had appeared anonymously the year before, used the voice of the ancient Greek philosopher—who, according to tradition, committed suicide by leaping into the Sicilian volcano—to express Arnold's own, very modern feelings of alienation and despair. "For something has impair'd thy spirit's strength, / And dried its self-sufficing fount of joy. / Thou canst not live with men nor with thyself," Empedocles tells himself, before begging the flames, "Receive me, hide me, quench me, take me home!" But Arnold decided that he did not have the right to inflict such images of hopelessness on his fellow men. "What then are the situations, from the representation of which, though accurate, no poetical enjoyment can be derived?" he asked in a celebrated preface. "They are those in which the suffering finds no vent in action; in which a continuous state of mental distress is prolonged, unrelieved by incident, hope, or resistance; in which there is everything to be endured, nothing to be done."

What Arnold did not want, in short, was to write like Giacomo Leopardi. Leopardi, who died in 1837, was already being acclaimed as the greatest of modern Italian poets. On his gravestone outside of Naples, where he spent the last years of his life, the inscription proclaimed him a "writer of the most elevated philosophy and poetry, whose only peers are the Greeks." In Arnold's own view, "this Italian, with his pure and sure touch, with his fineness of perception, is far more of the artist" than his contemporaries, the English Romantics: Leopardi had "wider culture" and "more freedom from illusions" than Wordsworth, a greater "power of seizing the real point" than Byron.

Yet if Leopardi's book of songs, the *Canti*, was "one of the most influential works of the nineteenth century," as Jonathan Galassi writes in the introduction to his translation, its influence was owed in part to the amount of resistance it generated. For Leopardi is the supreme poet of passive, helpless suffering—a writer who constantly reiterated in verse and prose that in human life "there is everything to be endured, nothing to be done." The most concise statement of his worldview can be found in an entry he made in his vast notebook, known as the *Zibaldone*, in 1826, when he was twenty-seven years old:

> Everything is evil. I mean, everything that is, is wicked; every existing thing is an evil; everything exists for a wicked end. Existence is a wickedness and is ordained for wickedness. Evil is the end, the final purpose, of the universe. . . . The only good is nonbeing; the only really good thing is the thing that is *not*, things that are *not* things; all things are bad.

Even in these few sentences, it is possible to hear the unremitting quality of Leopardi's pessimism, the crushing insistence,

which distinguishes it from the seductive melancholy of other
Romantic poets. In several ways, Leopardi's life can be compared
to Keats's: the Italian poet was born in 1798, the English poet in
1795; the former suffered from scoliosis, which probably killed
him at the age of thirty-nine, the latter from tuberculosis, which
killed him at twenty-five; both were constantly worried about
money and moved restlessly from place to place. Yet when Keats
writes, "Now more than ever seems it rich to die, / To cease upon
the midnight with no pain," his language, like the nightingale's
song, enchants death and turns it into "an ecstasy." In Leopardi's
"Night Song of a Wandering Shepherd in Asia," on the other
hand, death is simply the last act in the pageant of pointless misery that is our existence:

> *Little old white-haired man,*
> *weak, half naked, barefoot,*
> *with an enormous burden on his back,*
> *up mountain and down valley,*
> *over sharp rocks, across deep sands and bracken,*
> *. . . till at last he comes*
> *to where his way*
> *and all his effort led him:*
> *terrible, immense abyss*
> *into which he falls, forgetting everything.*
> *This, O virgin moon,*
> *is human life.*

To find Leopardi's equal in nihilism, one would have to
turn to philosophers like Schopenhauer and Nietzsche, both of
whom admired his work. No wonder that Arnold, while prais-
ing Leopardi's artistry, finally decided that Wordsworth was the
greater poet, because his vision of life is "healthful and true,
whereas Leopardi's pessimism is not." Other critics were even
harsher: to one Italian contemporary, Leopardi was "gratuitous,
nauseatingly cold, and desolatingly bitter."

Yet next to Leopardi's frank soul-sickness—"I feel my heart break, and I'm totally / inconsolable about my destiny," he writes—Arnold's praise of the "healthful" begins to sound specious and self-deluding. "As to myself, my judgment is that I'm unhappy; in this I know I'm not wrong," says a character in the *Operette morali*, Leopardi's book of philosophical dialogues and fables. "If the others are not unhappy, I congratulate them with all my heart." And while reading Leopardi, it is hard to feel that you are really happy—that you have not simply been ignoring the hard truths he faces, about mortality, oblivion, and the futility of human endeavor. To the English critic Cyril Connolly, Leopardi was a "Grand Inquisitor" who "break[s] down our alibis of health and happiness."

One of the most common defenses against this inquisition, in the poet's lifetime and since, is to wonder whether Leopardi denied the existence of health and happiness simply because he himself never possessed them. To Alessandro Manzoni, the author of *The Betrothed*, Leopardi's philosophy could be summed up as "I am hunchbacked and ill, therefore there is no God." Naturally, Leopardi objected strongly to this kind of *ad hominem* criticism. When a German magazine published a review of his work that made a similar suggestion, he wrote, "I wish to protest against this invention of weakness and vulgarity, and beg my readers to try to controvert my remarks and my arguments, rather than to accuse my ill-health."

Yet Leopardi's deformity and physical pain are an unavoidable presence in his work. The hump came from a curvature of the spine, which began in adolescence and gradually pressed against his lungs and heart, likely accounting for his early death. In addition, he suffered from bad eyesight and mysterious nervous maladies. A friend who saw him in the late 1820s remarked, "Everything harms him: wind, air, light, every sort of food, rest or movement, work or idleness." His deformity effectively barred him from having any sort of romantic life, except for the few unrequited loves recorded in his poems, and he probably died a virgin. In "Sappho's Last Song," he invokes the ancient tradition of the poet's ugliness in order to channel his own feelings of exclusion: "Alas, the gods and pitiless fate / saved none of this endless beauty for poor Sappho. / In your proud kingdoms I am worthless, Nature, / an uninvited guest, an unloved lover."

But his own body was only one source of his misery. Leopardi hated the small town he was born in, Recanati, which he called "the deadest and most ignorant city of the Marches, which is the most ignorant and uncultivated province of Italy." His father, Count Monaldo, who had a nobleman's pride without the money to pay for it, was authoritarian and overprotective to a degree that seems almost unbelievable. Until the poet was twenty years old, he was not allowed to leave the house without a tutor, and his father continued to cut his meat for him until he was even older. In a letter Leopardi wrote to Monaldo but never sent, he complained: "In the interest of something that I have never known, but you call home and family, you have required from your children the sacrifice not only of their physical welfare, but of their natural desires, their youth, their whole life." His mother, Adelaide, was still more dreadful, thanks to her religious fanaticism. "Not only did she refuse pity to those parents who lost infant children, but she deeply and sincerely envied them, because the children had soared to a safe paradise," Leopardi wrote. "She was most solicitous in the care she gave those poor sick children, but deep in her heart she hoped it would be useless, and even confessed that the only fear she had in consulting with doctors was to hear of some improvement." It is impossible not to see the son as following in his mother's footsteps, with his hatred of this world and his longing for death's release—though the atheist Leopardi could not look forward to a reward in heaven. Certainly, when maternal images appear in his poetry, they are always terrible. In the late poem "On an Ancient Funeral Relief," he addresses nature as "mother feared and wept for / since the human family was born, / marvel that cannot be praised, / that bears and nurtures only to destroy."

Given so many sources of trauma and suffering, perhaps the most remarkable thing about Leopardi is that he was ever happy. Certainly by 1817, when he wrote his first letters to Pietro Giordani—a free-thinking ex-monk who was his earliest friend and patron—Leopardi was already complaining of "the stubborn, black, horrendous, barbarous melancholy that wears away and devours me." Yet in his poetry, what makes the torment of adult life complete is the contrast it offers to the happiness of childhood, which for Leopardi is the one enviable time of life. In "To Silvia," an elegy for a dead child, he recalls his own youth:

> *What light thoughts,*
> *what hopes, what hearts, my Silvia!*
> *What human life and fate*
> *were to us then!*
> *When I remember so much hope*
> *I'm overcome,*
> *bitter, inconsolable,*
> *and rage against my own ill luck.*
> *O Nature, Nature,*
> *why don't you deliver later*
> *what you promised then? Why do you lead on*
> *your children so?*

Yet he would come to believe that it was not just his "own ill luck" that made adulthood such a miserable sequel to childhood. His work in verse and prose—comprising the *Canti*, the *Operette morali* and the *Pensieri*, a collection of aphorisms—rests on a vision of human life and history that gives this decline a syllogistic inevitability. Reason, Leopardi argues, is always a faculty of diminution and disillusion, so that whatever we understand rationally ceases to seem valuable or significant to us. "Reason is the enemy of everything great; reason is the enemy of nature; nature is great and reason is small," he writes.

It follows that we are best off when we understand things least, because "a tiny *confused idea* is always greater than a vast one which is *clear*." In an individual life, the time of happy illusion is childhood; in historical terms, the happiest people were Leopardi's beloved Greeks, who still believed in the gods and eternal glory. On the other hand, a modern, educated European, who sees the world through the cold lens of reason, is the unhappiest person imaginable. "This is the terrible human condition and the barbarous teaching of reason," he wrote when he was just twenty-two years old: "since human pleasure and pains are mere illusions, the anguish deriving from the certainty of the nothingness of things is always the only true reality."

In this way, Leopardi constructs a metaphysical prison, from which escape is impossible; and reading him sometimes feels like being locked in a cell with him. It is not an experience for the fainthearted. Anyone with experience of depression will find Leopardi dreadfully plausible: another name for his "reason" could be depressive lucidity, and his works communicate an apathy and anhedonia that are almost contagious. He himself was certainly prey to what would now be called acute depression, as is clear from his letters to Giordani: "If in this moment I were to go mad, my madness would consist of sitting always with my eyes staring, my mouth open, and my hands between my knees, without laughing or crying, or even moving except for sheer necessity. . . . I no longer see any difference between death and this my life."

If his poetry was merely the expression in verse of this state of mind, however, it could hardly have become so beloved. Leopardi was not often moved to write verse—the *Canti* includes just thirty-six finished poems—and there were periods of years when he wrote no poetry at all. But when he did write, it was usually because something had temporarily broken up his misery—not to the extent of producing actual happiness, but enough to allow him to contemplate the dreadful facts of existence in a different, more creative light. In his very earliest poems, this factor is patriotism, which allows him to imagine that the fallenness of mankind is merely the fallenness of an Italy subjugated by French and Austrian occupiers. "O my country," Leopardi begins "To Italy," "I can see the walls / and arches and the columns and the statues / and lonely towers of our ancestors, / but I don't see the glory." He is still young enough to believe that the glory can be restored, by acts of heroism like those of the Greeks at Thermopylae.

These first poems brought Leopardi the fame of a patriotic poet, a muse for the Risorgimento. This was ironic, since he quickly lost faith in politics. Seeing human nature as he did, he could hardly help disdaining the progressive, activist faith of so many Italian literary men as a shallow delusion. One of his last poems, "Recantation," is a mock apology for his quietism, which turns immediately into a blunt satire on the nineteenth-century faith in progress, the age of "universal love, / railroads, expanded commerce, steam, / typography and cholera." The reasons for human suffering were innate and individual, not accidental and social, and it was absurd to hope to make "a joyful, happy race" from "many wretched and unhappy persons."

In his great "idylls," a series of six poems written in 1819–21 (around the time Keats was producing his Odes), Leopardi finds a source of pleasure, instead, in the very voluptuousness of his suffering. This is the period of "Infinity," perhaps the archetypal Romantic poem in any language, with its closing embrace of death: "So my mind sinks in this immensity: / and foundering is sweet in such a sea." In "To the Moon," again, Leopardi achieves an apotheosis of the vague, bittersweet longing of adolescence:

> Yet thinking back, reliving
> the time of my unhappiness, brings joy.
> Oh in youth, when hope has a long road ahead
> and memory's way is short,
> how sweet it is remembering what happened,
> though it was sad, and though the pain endures!

This is a Romantic's revision of Dante, who wrote that the worst suffering is to recall happy times when you are miserable. To Leopardi, remembering the miserable times is its own kind of happiness. It is lines like these that George Santayana must have been thinking of when he wrote that "long passages" of the *Canti* "are fit to repeat in lieu of prayers through all the watches of the night."

Between 1823 and 1828, as Leopardi moved from Milan to Bologna to Florence to Pisa in search of an affordable city with a tolerable climate, he wrote almost no verse. It says something about the nature of his genius that it was only when he returned to his loathed Recanati, and to the family home that suffocated him, that he was inspired to return to poetry. Once again, his theme was the way "youth's sweet moment flies, more dear / than fame and laurel, dearer than the simple / light of day and breath." But now youth was receding into memory, and his reflections become more impersonal and elegiac. Nothing could be more characteristic than the way Leopardi compares the period of youth not, as we might expect, to the rising sun, but to "The Setting of the Moon," the title of one of his last poems. Even at the age Leopardi believes to be the prime of life, there is no real sunlight, only the "thousand lovely / insubstantial images and phantoms" cast by the moonlight. When this moon sets, all that is left is the pitch-blackness of adulthood, when "life is forlorn, lightless."

There is, of course, a certain perversity in this metaphor, which refuses to allow any part of human life to transpire in the daytime. It is on the level of metaphor, in fact, that Leopardi's pessimism shows itself to be most oppressively partial. Take the comparison of human life, in the "Wandering Shepherd," to the journey of a weak old man over rocky terrain. The only reason that mountains and deserts can function as images of difficulty is that the earth also offers us experience of pleasant paths, just as the moon only seems poetically pale because we can compare it to the bright sun.

But Leopardi never allows his despair to be surprised by the logic of his own metaphors. In his last poem, "Broom," Leopardi offers his largest statement on human fate, comparing mankind to the tenacious shrub, *la ginestra*, which springs up in the volcanic ash around Mount Vesuvius. This inevitably leads to a reflection on Pompeii, whose immolated inhabitants the poet compares to a colony of ants crushed by a falling apple: "Nature has no more esteem / or care for the seed of man / than for the ant." That the fall of the apple is part of the reproduction of the tree, that ants feed on fallen fruit—in short, that his own metaphor offers images of growth and regeneration, as well as destruction—of all this Leopardi refuses to take account. For him, death does not just end life, it nullifies life, and the fact that we are going to die is the only fact that matters. The key to his work's terrible power is that we can never totally banish the suspicion that he might be right.

Up from Cynicism:
Peter Sloterdijk

o o o

Peter Sloterdijk has been one of Germany's best-known philosophers since the publication of his *Critique of Cynical Reason*, in 1983—a thousand-page treatise that became a bestseller. Since then, Sloterdijk has been at the forefront of European intellectual life, contributing to public debates over genetic engineering and economics and hosting a long-running discussion program on television, all while publishing a steady stream of ambitious philosophical texts—his complete bibliography includes some forty-five titles.

But while the *Critique* was published in English in the 1980s, it is only recently that Sloterdijk has begun to emerge on the American horizon. *Bubbles*, the first volume in his magnum opus, the *Spheres* trilogy, appeared here in 2011, followed by *You Must Change Your Life*, another wide-ranging and ambitious book. Along with *Rage and Time*, which appeared in English in 2010, these publications make it possible to begin to come to grips with Sloterdijk as a stirring and eclectic thinker, who addresses himself boldly to the most important problems of our time. Above all, he is concerned with metaphysics—or, rather, what to do with the empty space that is left over when metaphysics disappears, along with religion, faith in revolution, and the other grand sources of meaning that long gave shape and direction to human lives.

Sloterdijk was born in 1947, making him just the right age to participate in the student movement of the 1960s. By the early 1980s, when he wrote *Critique of Cynical Reason*, the idealism and world-changing energy of that movement had long since dwindled into splinter-group violence, on the one hand, and accommodation to the realities of capitalism and the Cold War, on the other. In this cultural moment, Sloterdijk's diagnosis of "cynicism" was very timely. "The dissolution of the student movement," he wrote, "must interest us because it represents a complex metamorphosis of hope into realism, of revolt into a clever melancholy."

Despite its parodic Kantian title, the *Critique* is no treatise in abstract logic; it is a highly personal confession of this generational world-weariness. As a philosopher, Sloterdijk is especially struck by the way he and his peers are able to master the most liberatory and radical philosophical language, but utterly unable to apply its insights to their own lives and political situation. "Because everything has become problematic, everything is also somehow a matter of indifference," he observes. The result is cynicism, which Sloterdijk defines in a neat paradox as "enlightened false consciousness": "It has learned its lessons in enlightenment, but it has not, and probably was not able to, put them into practice."

If we are to break out of this learned helplessness, Sloterdijk argues, we must ransack the Western tradition for new philosophical resources. Such ransacking is exactly the method of Sloterdijk's thought, first in the *Critique* and then, on an even grander scale, in later works like *Bubbles* and *You Must Change Your Life*. Drawing on his very wide reading, Sloterdijk excavates the prehistory of contemporary problems, and some of their possible solutions. In the *Critique*, he offers an extended analysis of the culture of Weimar Germany, in which he locates the origin of twentieth-century cynicism—as well as describing the many subvarieties of cynicism (military, sexual, religious), doing a close reading of Dostoevsky, and cataloguing the meaning of different facial expressions. The effect on the reader is of being shown around a *Wunderkammer*, where what matters is not the advancing of a consecutive argument, but the display of various intellectual treasures.

If the "cynicism" Sloterdijk describes is a post-sixties syndrome, the prescription he offers is a return to 1960s values of spontaneity, passivity, and the wisdom of the body. But he does not describe these in the language of hippiedom; instead, and characteristically, he finds a grounding for them in the oldest regions of the Western philosophical tradition. The hero of the book is Diogenes, who was himself derided as cynical—literally, "dog-like"—by the people of Athens. But there is a vast difference, Sloterdijk argues, between the exhausted cynicism of the late twentieth century and what he calls, using Greek spelling, the "kynicism" of Diogenes. When Diogenes defecated or masturbated in the street, when he slept in a bathtub or told Alexander the Great to get out of his sunlight, he was employing a joyful language of radical bodily gestures to defeat the philosophers' imprisoning language of intellectual concepts. "Neither Socrates nor Plato," Sloterdijk writes, "can deal with Diogenes—for he talks with them . . . in a dialogue of flesh and blood."

Clearly, Sloterdijk finds in Diogenes what so many of his contemporaries found in Norman O. Brown, or Zen, or for that matter in drugs and music: permission to turn off subjectivity, logocentric reason, the head. After all, wasn't it enlightened Western reason that gave us the nuclear bomb? "The bomb is not one bit more evil than reality and not one bit more destructive than we are," he writes in one of the book's prose-poetic passages. "It is merely our unfolding, a material representation of our essence. . . . In it, the Western 'subject' is consummated." Behind Sloterdijk's dark paean to the bomb, it is possible to hear, of course, those other Western abominations, Nazism and the

Holocaust, which would have shadowed his upbringing in post-war Germany. The choice, he concludes, is between the bomb or the body, cynicism or kynicism. "In our best moments, when ... even the most energetic activity gives way to passivity and the rhythmics of the living carry us spontaneously, courage can suddenly make itself felt as a euphoric clarity. ... It awakens the present within us," he writes almost mystically.

In *Critique of Cynical Reason*, Sloterdijk charts a wholly individual path to a familiar spiritual position, a Romanticism of what Wordsworth called "wise passiveness." This pattern, too, is repeated in Sloterdijk's later books: he is better at the forceful restatement of old problems than at inventing new solutions. This might be an objection to certain kinds of philosophers, who see themselves as contributors to a technical process that produces concrete results. For Sloterdijk, whose greatest influences are Nietzsche and Heidegger, it is not disqualifying, for his goal is, as he writes in *You Must Change Your Life*, "a provocative redescription of the objects of analysis." Like a literary writer—and he once told an interviewer that he thought of writing the *Spheres* trilogy as a novel—Sloterdijk's goal is to restate our basic quandaries in revelatory new language, to bring them home to us as living experiences instead of stale formulas. The prison of reason, the need for transcendence, the yearning for an absent meaning: these have been the stuff of literature and philosophy and theology for centuries. In Sloterdijk, these old subjects find a timely new interpreter.

If Sloterdijk had remained the thinker who wrote the *Critique*, he might not be terribly interesting to us today. There is already something "period" about the book's (highly intellectual) misology, its romanticizing of "kynicism," and the way it genuflects before the bomb. To compare it to his later work, however, is to see how significantly Sloterdijk evolved—both in his responses to the times and in the scope of his vision. What he saw in the *Critique* as the malaise of a disappointed generation becomes, in books like *Bubbles* and *You Must Change Your*

Life, something much bigger and more profound. It is the plight of humanity after the death of God, which Sloterdijk follows Nietzsche in seeing as a catastrophe whose true dimensions we still don't fully appreciate. At the same time, the impatience with Marxism that is already visible in the *Critique* evolves into a full-throated defense of liberal capitalism, especially in *Rage and Time*, which is largely an account of communism, and also Christianity, as ideologies driven by resentment and fantasies of revenge. (Here, too, the influence of Nietzsche is clear.)

Another way of putting this is that Sloterdijk is a thinker of, and for, the post–Cold War world. If you were to sketch Sloterdijk's understanding of history, as it emerges in his recent work, it would go something like this. From earliest times until the rise of the modern world, mankind endowed the world with purpose by means of religion, belief in the gods and God. As that belief waned, the Enlightenment faith in progress, and the more radical communist faith in revolution, replaced transcendent purposes with immanent ones. But after 1989, neither of these sets of coordinates any longer mapped our world. What Sloterdijk initially diagnosed as mere "cynicism" becomes, in his mature work, a full-fledged crisis of meaning, which can be figured as a crisis of directionality. Again and again, he refers explicitly and implicitly to Nietzsche's madman, who demanded, "Are we not plunging continually? Backward, sideward, forward, in all directions? Is there still any up or down?"

So far, this is a familiar, indeed a venerable, way of thinking about the problem of nihilism in liberal civilization. Sloterdijk's originality lies, first, in the way these old problems still strike him with undiminished force; and second, in his refusal to remain passive in the face of them. The whole thrust of Sloterdijk's thought is a rebuke to the Heidegger who mused, late in life, that "only a God can save us." On the contrary, he insists, we must save ourselves—and, what is more, we can. Salvation lies just where Heidegger believed perdition lay: that is, in the realm of technology.

Technology, for Sloterdijk, seldom has to do with machines. It is, rather, mental and spiritual technology that interests him: the techniques with which human beings have historically made themselves secure on the Earth. Sloterdijk does not talk about these strategies in terms of religion, which he sees as a vocabulary unavailable to us today. Rather, he reconfigures them with metaphors from the realms of immunology and climatology, using language that sounds respectably scientific even when its actual bearing is deeply spiritual. He is especially fond of repurposing contemporary buzzwords to give them new dimensions of philosophical meaning, as with the term "greenhouse effect." Considered spiritually, the greenhouse effect is not something to be deplored, but a necessity for human existence:

> To oppose the cosmic frost infiltrating the human
> sphere through the open windows of the Enlight-
> enment, modern humanity makes use of a delib-
> erate greenhouse effect: it attempts to balance out
> its shellessness in space, following the shattering
> of celestial domes, through an artificial civili-
> zatory world. This is the final horizon of Euro-
> American technological titanism.

Here Sloterdijk's old critique of the Enlightenment is turned inside out. Human beings need to breathe an atmosphere, not just of oxygen, but of meanings and symbols and practices. The decline of religion meant the fouling of humanity's old mental atmosphere, so that it is no longer breathable. But where the Sloterdijk of the *Critique* wanted to go backward to Diogenes—in this resembling his antagonist Heidegger, who sought salvation in the pre-Socratics—the Sloterdijk of *Bubbles*, from which this passage comes, believes that the only way out is forward. By using technological reason, we have found ways to air condition our bodies; we must also find a way to use our reason to build air-conditioning systems for our souls. Only our minds can save us.

This leads to the central metaphor of Sloterdijk's *Spheres* trilogy, which appeared in German between 1998 and 2004. "Spheres," he writes, "are air conditioning systems in whose construction and calibration . . . it is out of the question not to participate. The symbolic air conditioning of the shared space is the primal production of every society." Law, custom, ritual and art are ways we create such nurturing spheres, which for Sloterdijk are not so much topological figures as emotional and spiritual microclimates: "The sphere is the interior, disclosed, shared realm inhabited by humans—insofar as they succeed in becoming humans."

In *Bubbles*, the only part of the trilogy yet translated into English, Sloterdijk writes primarily as a historian of art and ideas, using his eccentric erudition to come up with numerous depictions of such nurturing "spheres" in human culture. A painting by Giotto depicts two faces turned sideways, joining to create a new face—an emblem of intimacy; St. Catherine of Siena imagines the eating of her heart by Christ; Marsilio Ficino theorizes that love involves a mutual transfusion of the blood, carried in superfine particles in the lovers' gaze.

It is no coincidence that many of these examples come from the iconography of Christianity, since religion has been mankind's best generator of spheres. What Sloterdijk hopes to do is to retrieve religion's power to create intimacy while shearing it of its untenable dogmas. "It will be advantageous for the free spirit to emancipate itself from the anti-Christian affect of recent centuries as a tenseness that is no longer necessary. Anyone seeking to reconstruct basic communional and communitary experiences needs to be free of anti-religious reflexes," he insists. In pointed contrast to Alain Badiou—who, on the basis of scattered statements in his books, seems to be a *bête noire* of Sloterdijk's—there is no attempt here to harness the messianism and apocalypticism of Christianity for political ends. Sloterdijk's ideal is not Pauline conversion but Trinitarian "perichoresis," a technical word he seizes on: "Perichoresis means that the milieu of the persons is entirely the relationship itself."

But if Sloterdijk is not a believer, then where does he believe we can actually experience this kind of perfectly trusting togetherness? Where do we find a sphere that is wholly earthly, yet so primal as to retain its power even now? The answer is surprising, even bizarre. In a long section of *Bubbles*, Sloterdijk argues that the original sphere, the one we all experience and yearn to recapture, is the mother's womb. This is not, for him, a place of blissful isolation, where the subject can enjoy illusions of omnipotence; if it were, the womb would be only a training ground for selfishness and disillusion. Rather, Sloterdijk emphasizes that we are all in our mother's wombs along with a placenta. The placenta is what he calls "the With"—our first experience of otherness, but a friendly and nurturing otherness, and thus a model for all future "spheres" of intimacy.

This leads Sloterdijk to what he calls, not without a sense of humor, an "ovular Platonism." There is a preexisting realm to which we long to return, but it is not in heaven. It is in the uterus, and since the uterus will always be with us (barring some remote but imaginable *Brave New World* scenario), so too will the possibility of genuine spheres. We need to recover and give to one another the trust we once gave our placentas. Indeed, Sloterdijk argues that our culture's disregard for the postpartum placenta—we simply incinerate it, instead of reverently eating it or burying it—is both a cause and symptom of our loneliness: "In terms of its psychodynamic sources, the individualism of the Modern Age is a placental nihilism."

The reader who has no patience for this kind of thing—who finds the whole "With" concept New Agey, unfalsifiable, or just wildly eccentric—will probably not get very far with Sloterdijk. This is not because placentaism is central to his thought. On the contrary, it is just one of the many provocative ideas he develops and lets fall in the course of the book, which reads less like a structured argument than a long prose poem.

But Sloterdijk's strength and appeal come from the intuitive and metaphorical quality of his thought, his unconventional approaches to familiar problems, his willingness to scandalize. As a theorem, the "With" is easy to refute; as a metaphor, it is weirdly convincing. It is another way of describing, and accounting for, the central experience of homelessness that drives all of Sloterdijk's thought. Deprived of our "With," he writes, "the officially licensed thesis 'God is dead'" must be supplemented "with the private addendum 'and my own ally is also dead.'"

There is something hopeful about this supplement, for if we cannot regain God, Sloterdijk reasons, we can still regain the sense of having an ally. Indeed, the "sphere" concept is powerful because of the way it rewrites the history of religion in respectful but fundamentally secular terms. The need for spheres—for meanings, symbols, contexts—is what is primary for human beings; that our most successful spheres have been religious ones is, for Sloterdijk, a contingent fact, not a necessary one.

An identical logic informs *You Must Change Your Life*, in which Sloterdijk reformulates his understanding of religion using a new spatial metaphor: not the nurturing sphere, this time, but the aspiring vertical line. (Indeed, he barely mentions spheres at all in the book, adding to the sense that his thoughts do not form a system but a series of improvisations.) If *Bubbles* mined religion—and science and art—for images of intimacy, *You Must Change Your Life* emphasizes instead the human proclivity for self-transcendence, for constantly remaking and exceeding ourselves, for going "higher" in every sense. Just as he half-jokingly adopted the term "greenhouse effect," now Sloterdijk seizes on the p.c. euphemism "vertically challenged": "The phrase cannot be admired enough," he writes. "The formula has been valid since we began to practice learning to live."

The word "practice" is central to Sloterdijk's argument here, and to his understanding of religion. We are living, he observes, at a time when religion is supposedly making a comeback around the world. The old assurance that all societies must inevitably converge on secularism is failing. To Sloterdijk, however, it is a mistake to think that what people are turning to is faith in the divine. Rather, the part of religion that still matters to us, for which we have a recurring need, is its practices: the technology, primarily mental and inner-directed, which allows us to reshape our ways of thinking and feeling. With typical bravado, he argues that "no 'religion' or 'religions' exist, only misunderstood spiritual regimens."

In fact, Sloterdijk argues, our time is characterized by a widespread embrace of training techniques, both physical and metaphysical. In one chapter of *You Must Change Your Life*, in a counterintuitive stroke, he pairs the rise of the modern Olympic Games with the spread of Scientology as examples of the invention of new types of spiritual-cum-athletic regimens. The sheer idiocy of the theology behind Scientology shows, for him, how irrelevant doctrines are to the contemporary appetite for religion. L. Ron Hubbard's Dianetics was a spiritual technology before it was a church, and this kind of technology can be found at the heart of all religious traditions. "If one looks to the heart of the fetish of religions," Sloterdijk writes apropos of Scientology, "one exclusively finds anthropotechnic procedures."

"Anthropotechnics" is another favorite term of Sloterdijk's, because of the way it combines a technological and a spiritual meaning. Genetic engineering and bionics are one kind of anthropotechnics, a way of working on human beings to improve them. But so too, he insists, are the exercises of Ignatius de Loyola, or the harsh training procedures of Buddhist monks. Fasting, memorization of sacred texts, hermitism, self-flagellation—such practices actually transform the human being, building a new and "higher" inner life on the foundations of the old one.

Much of *You Must Change Your Life* is devoted to a cultural history and typology of these kinds of training practices, passing freely between Eastern and Western traditions. When Jesus on the Cross declares "*Consummatum est*," for instance, Sloterdijk says that we ought to see this as a victor's cry, equivalent to that of a Greek athlete winning a race or a wrestling match. The phrase should be translated not as a passive "It is finished," he argues, but as "Made it!" or "Mission acomplished!" For the conquest of death is the ultimate goal of all spiritual training, and the great founders—Jesus, Buddha, Socrates—are those who won the championship by dying on their own terms. This phenomenon is what Sloterdijk refers to as "the outdoing of the gladiators by the martyrs."

To identify religion as a form of competitive training is to reimagine history, and in *You Must Change Your Life*, Sloterdijk offers a mock-Hegelian account of the evolution of the human subject. In the beginning, he writes, all human beings lived in a swamp of habit and mass-mindedness. A few rare and gifted individuals lifted themselves up to the dry ground, where they could look back on their old lives in a self-conscious and critical spirit. This constitutes the true birth of the subject: "anyone who takes part in a program for depassivizing themselves, and crosses from the side of the merely formed to that of the forming, becomes a subject."

These pioneers in turn draw imitators after them, people eager to remake themselves in the image of the miraculous founders: Jesus has his Paul, Socrates his Plato. In the modern age, society attempts to universalize this experience of enlightenment, to awaken all the sleepers, but with uneven and sometimes disastrous effects. For humans live on a vertical, and the definition of a vertical is that there will always be a top and a bottom: "the upper class comprises those who hear the imperative that catapults them out of their old life, and the other classes all those who have never heard or seen any trace of it."

If this is elitism—and it is, with a vengeance—then Sloterdijk says, so be it. "Egotism," he writes, "is often merely the despicable pseudonym of the best human possibilities." Indeed, it is not hard to see that what Sloterdijk has written is a reformulation and defense of the idea of the *Übermensch*. The whole book could be thought of as a commentary on a single line of Nietzsche's from *Thus Spoke Zarathustra*, which Sloterdijk repeatedly quotes: "Man is a rope, stretched between beast and Übermensch." Here is the original vertical—or, as Sloterdijk also has it, a kind of Jacob's ladder, on which men ascend toward the heavens and descend toward the earth.

For a German thinker of Sloterdijk's generation to rehabilitate the idea of the *Übermensch* might seem like a dangerous proposition. But in his hands, the concept is totally disinfected of any taints of blond beastliness or will-to-power. Indeed, the figures Sloterdijk cites as the supreme self-trainers, at the top of the human vertical, are Jesus and Socrates—the very ones Nietzsche despised as teachers of herd morality. It is central to Sloterdijk's vision that, for him, supremacy is totally divorced from domination. He imagines that only self-mastery is what matters to human beings, that the training of the self is more noble and satisfying than control over others. If this is a blind spot, it is one that allows him to take his Nietzsche guilt-free.

The image of the stretched rope appeals to Sloterdijk because it manages to sustain the idea of verticality—which also means, of hierarchy and value—in the absence of the divine. Like a snake charmer, Sloterdijk needs to make the rope of human existence stand up straight without attaching it to anything on high; this is what he calls "the problematic motif of the transcendence device that cannot be fastened at the opposite pole." The main intuition, and gamble, of *You Must Change Your Life* is that the human instinct for verticality can survive the relativizing of space in a Godless world. What remains is a sort of highly intellectualized and sublimated vitalism: "Vitality, understood both somatically and mentally, is itself the medium that contains a gradient between more and less," he writes. "It therefore contains the vertical component that guides ascents within itself, and has no need of additional external or metaphysical attractors. That God is supposedly dead is irrelevant in this context."

The line, then, like the sphere, becomes for Sloterdijk a substitute for metaphysics. Metaphysics, he says in an aside that captures his whole argument, really ought to be called metabiotics: it is life itself that aspires upward, even if space has no up or down to speak of. "Even without God, or the Übermensch, it is sufficient to note that every individual, even the most successful, the most creative and the most generous, must, if they examine themselves in earnest, admit that they have become less than their potentialities of being would have required," he writes near the end of the book, revealing the deep Protestant roots of this conception of the conscience.

One of the most appealing things about Sloterdijk's philosophy is that, like literature, it leaves itself vulnerable, instead of trying to anticipate and refute all possible objections. And the objections to *You Must Change Your Life*, as with *Bubbles*, are not far to seek. For one thing, by conceiving of religion as an elite training regimen, Sloterdijk implies that a religion is justified by its saints. Anyone who is not a saint doesn't count, and so the average person's experience of religious meanings—whether metaphysical doctrine or spiritual consolation or tradition or identity or communion—is dismissed out of hand. This is false to the lived reality of religion for most people, and shows how tendentious Sloterdijk's equation of religion with "practice" really is.

Then there is the question-begging insistence that metabiotics will do in the absence of metaphysics. It is certainly true that even nonbelievers continue to act as if there is such a thing as excellence, self-improvement, self-overcoming. But it is not certain that these "salutogenic energies," as Sloterdijk calls them, are capable of sustaining themselves indefinitely in the absence of some metaphysical validation. Much of modern literature, from Leopardi to Beckett, suggests that they cannot. What is missing from *You Must Change Your Life* is an investigation of what happens when the vertical collapses, as it does sometimes for everyone, even believers; Sloterdijk needs to offer a psychology of depression to complement his psychology of aspiration. This is as much as to say that Sloterdijk has not solved the immense problems he raises, even though he claims to know the way toward the solution. But it is not necessary for a philosopher to solve problems, only to make them come alive; and this Sloterdijk does as well as any thinker at work today.

The Deadly Jester:
Slavoj Žižek

o o o

In 2007, the Slovenian philosopher Slavoj Žižek published an editorial in the *New York Times* deploring America's use of torture to extract a confession from Khalid Shaikh Mohammed, the Al Qaeda leader who is thought to have masterminded the attacks of September 11. The arguments that Žižek employed could have been endorsed without hesitation by any liberal-minded reader. Yes, he acknowledged, Mohammed's crimes were "clear and horrifying"; but by torturing him the United States was turning back the clock on centuries of legal and moral progress, reverting to the barbarism of the Middle Ages. We owe it to ourselves, Žižek argued, not to throw away "our civilization's greatest achievement, the growth of our spontaneous moral sensitivity."

For anyone who is familiar with Žižek's many books, what was striking about the piece was how un-Žižekian it was. Yes, there were the telltale marks—quotations from Hegel and Agamben kept company with a reference to the television show *24*, creating the kind of high-low frisson for which he is celebrated. But for the benefit of *Times* readers, Žižek was writing, rather surprisingly, as if the United States was basically a decent country that had strayed into sin.

What Žižek really believes about America and torture can be seen in his book *Violence*, where he discusses the notorious torture photos from Abu Ghraib: "Abu Ghraib was not simply a case of American arrogance towards a Third World people; in being submitted to humiliating tortures, the Iraqi prisoners were effectively initiated into American culture." Torture, far from being a betrayal of American values, actually offers "a direct insight into American values, into the very core of the obscene enjoyment that sustains the U.S. way of life." This, to Žižek's many admirers, is more like it. It provides a fine illustration of the sort of dialectical reversal that is Žižek's favorite intellectual stratagem, and which gives his writing its disorienting, counterintuitive dazzle.

Nor does Žižek simply condemn Al Qaeda's violence as "horrifying." Fundamentalist Islam may seem reactionary, but "in a curious inversion," he characteristically observes, "religion is one of the possible places from which one can deploy critical doubts about today's society. It has become one of the sites of resistance." And the whole premise of *Violence*, as of Žižek's work in general, is that resistance to the liberal-democratic order is so urgent that it justifies any degree of violence. "Everything is to be endorsed here," he writes in *Iraq: The Borrowed Kettle*, "up to and including religious 'fanaticism.'"

The curious thing about the Žižek phenomenon is that the louder he applauds violence and terror—especially the terror of Lenin, Stalin, and Mao, whose "lost causes" he takes up in *In Defense of Lost Causes*—the more indulgently he is received by the academic left, which has elevated him into a celebrity and the center of a cult. A glance at the blurbs on his books provides a vivid illustration of the power of repressive tolerance. In *Iraq: The Borrowed Kettle*, Žižek claims, "Better the worst Stalinist terror than the most liberal capitalist democracy"; but on the back cover of the book we are told that Žižek is "a stimulating writer" who "will entertain and offend, but never bore." In *The Fragile Absolute*, he writes that "the way to fight ethnic hatred effectively is not through its immediate counterpart, ethnic tolerance; on the contrary, what we need is even more hatred, but proper political hatred"; but this is an example of his "typical brio and boldness." And in *In Defense of Lost Causes*, Žižek remarks that "Heidegger is 'great' not in spite of, but because of his Nazi engagement," and that "crazy, tasteless even, as it may sound, the problem with Hitler was that he was not violent enough, that his violence was not 'essential' enough"; but this book, its publisher informs us, is "a witty, adrenalin-fueled manifesto for universal values."

In the same witty book Žižek laments that "this is how the establishment likes its 'subversive' theorists: harmless gadflies who sting us and thus awaken us to the inconsistencies and imperfections of our democratic enterprise—God forbid that they might take the project seriously and try to live it." How is it, then, that Slavoj Žižek, who wants not to correct democracy but to destroy it, has been turned into one of the establishment's pet subversives, who "tries to live" the revolution as a professor at the European Graduate School, a senior researcher at the University of Ljubljana's Institute of Sociology, and the international director of the Birkbeck Institute for the Humanities?

A part of the answer has to do with Žižek's enthusiasm for American popular culture. Despite the best attempts of critical theory to demystify American mass entertainment, to lay bare the political subtext of our movies and pulp fiction and television shows, pop culture remains for most Americans apolitical and antipolitical—a frivolous zone of entertainment and distraction. So when the theory-drenched Žižek illustrates his arcane notions with examples from *Nip/Tuck* and *Titanic*, he seems to be signaling a suspension of earnestness. The effect is quite deliberate. In *The Metastases of Enjoyment*, for instance, he writes that "*Jurassic Park* is a chamber drama about the trauma of fatherhood in the style of the early Antonioni or Bergman." Elsewhere he asks, "Is Parsifal not a model for Keanu Reeves in *The Matrix*, with

Laurence Fishburne in the role of Gurnemanz?" These are laugh lines, and they cunningly disarm the anxious or baffled reader with their playfulness. They relieve the reader with an expectation of comic hyperbole, and this expectation is then carried over to Žižek's political proclamations, which are certainly hyperbolic but not at all comic.

When, in 1994, during the siege of Sarajevo, Žižek wrote that "there is no difference" between life in that city and life in any American or Western European city, that "it is no longer possible to draw a clear and unambiguous line of separation between us who live in a 'true' peace and the residents of Sarajevo"—well, it was only natural for readers to think that he did not really mean it, just as he did not really mean that *Jurassic Park* is like a Bergman movie. This intellectual promiscuity is the privilege of the licensed jester, of the man whom the *Chronicle of Higher Education* dubbed "the Elvis of cultural theory."

In person, too, Žižek plays the jester with practiced skill. Every journalist who sits down to interview him comes away with a smile on his face. Robert Boynton, writing in *Lingua Franca* in 1998, found Žižek "bearded, disheveled, and loud . . . like central casting's pick for the role of Eastern European Intellectual." Boynton was amused to see the manic, ranting philosopher order mint tea and sugar cookies: "'Oh, I can't drink anything stronger than herbal tea in the afternoon,' he says meekly. 'Caffeine makes me too nervous.'" The intellectual parallel is quite clear: in life, as in his writing, Žižek is all bark and no bite. Like a naughty child who flashes an irresistible grin, it is impossible to stay angry at him for long.

The same act was on display when Žižek appeared with Bernard-Henri Lévy at the New York Public Library in 2008. The two philosopher-celebrities came on stage to the theme music from *Superman*, and their personae were so perfectly opposed that they did indeed nudge each other into cartoonishness: Lévy was all the more Gallic and debonair next to Žižek, who seemed all the more wild-eyed and Slavic next to Lévy.

Thus it was perfectly natural for the audience to erupt in laughter when Žižek, at one point in the generally unacrimonious evening, told Lévy: "Don't be afraid—when we take over you will not go to the Gulag, just two years of reeducation camp." Solzhenitsyn had died only a few weeks earlier, but it would have been a kind of *bêtise* to identify Žižek's Gulag with Solzhenitsyn's Gulag. When the audience laughed, it was playing into his hands, and hewing to the standard line on Žižek, which Rebecca Mead laid down in a profile of him in the *New Yorker*: "Always to take Slavoj Žižek seriously would be to make a category mistake."

⁰ ⁰ ⁰

Whether or not it would always be a mistake to take Slavoj Žižek seriously, surely it would not be a mistake to take him seriously just once. He is, after all, a famous and influential thinker. So it might be worthwhile to consider Žižek's work as if he means it—to ask what his ideas really are, and what sort of effects they are likely to have.

Žižek is a believer in the Revolution at a time when almost nobody, not even on the left, thinks that such a cataclysm is any longer possible or even desirable. This is his big problem, and also his big opportunity. While "socialism" remains a favorite hate-word for the Republican right, the prospect of communism overthrowing capitalism is now so remote, so fantastic, that nobody feels strongly moved to oppose it, as conservatives and liberal anti-Communists opposed it in the 1930s, the 1950s, and even the 1980s. When Žižek turns up speaking the classical language of Marxism-Leninism, he profits from the assumption that the return of ideas that were once the cause of tragedy can now occur only in the form of farce. In the visual arts, the denaturing of what were once passionate and dangerous icons has become commonplace, so that emblems of evil are transformed into perverse fun, harmless but very profitable statements of postideological camp; and there is a kind of intellectual equivalent of this development in Žižek's work. The cover of his book *The Parallax View* reproduces a Socialist Realist portrait of *Lenin at the Smolny Institute* in the ironically unironic fashion made familiar by the pseudoiconoclastic work of Komar and Melamid, Cai Guo-Qiang, and other post-Soviet, post-Mao artists. But there is a difference between Žižek and the other jokesters. It is that he is not really joking.

Like them, Žižek, who was born in Ljubljana, the capital of Slovenia, in 1949, spent his formative years under communism. As an undergraduate, he acquired what would become a lifelong fascination with the work of Jacques Lacan; later he went to Paris to be analyzed by Lacan's son-in-law and heir, Jacques-Alain Miller, and to this day Lacanian ideas form one of the foundations of Žižek's thought. His academic career was evidently sidetracked by communist bureaucrats who believed, no doubt correctly, that his eccentric brilliance would make him politically unreliable. In the 1980s, he was involved in establishing Slovenia's opposition Liberal Democratic Party, and he even ran for office, unsuccessfully, in the newly independent country's elections in 1990. It would be interesting to know more about Žižek's activities in this period, so as to understand how this erstwhile liberal democrat emerged as an idolator of Lenin and a contemptuous foe of liberal democracy.

For if Žižek benefits, practically speaking, from the repudiation of the communist dream, it is also his central grievance. Since he mixes high theory and low culture—one of his books, *Enjoy Your Symptom!*, is a primer on Lacan that illustrates his ideas with examples from Hollywood movies—it is tempting to classify him as another postmodernist. But Žižek is quite capable of distinguishing between pop culture, which is the air we all breathe, and postmodern relativism, which he unequivocally rejects. His recent work, in fact, is strictly conservative in its hostility to the libertarian and improvisatory aspects of contemporary Western culture. His attitude toward homosexuality, for instance, is that of a mid-century Freudian: he regards it as a symptom of debilitating narcissism. In *Violence*, he suggests that homosexuality is a step on the road to onanism: "first, in homosexuality, the other sex is excluded (one does it with another person of the same sex). Then, in a kind of mockingly Hegelian negation of negation, the very dimension of otherness is canceled: one does it with oneself." Transsexuals are even more threatening: "The ultimate difference, the 'transcendental' difference that grounds human identity itself, thus turns into something open to manipulation: the ultimate plasticity of being human is asserted instead." When it comes to the brave new world of contemporary bioethics, Žižek is as hidebound as any Catholic traditionalist.

Žižek suspects all these postmodernist twenty-first-century phenomena because his political program is, as he recognizes, a throwback to the political modernism of the twentieth century, with its utopian longing for a violent, total transformation of human society. Only this kind of revolution, he believes, is real politics. More: only in the violence of revolution do we touch reality at all. "The ultimate and defining experience of the twentieth century," he declares, "was the direct experience of the Real as opposed to the everyday social reality—the Real in its extreme violence as the price to be paid for peeling off the deceptive layers of reality." Žižek, too, feels this longing for the Real, and he recognizes that this puts him in opposition to his times, in which the Virtual does quite nicely. He deplores "one of the great postmodern motifs, that of the Real Thing towards which one should maintain a proper distance." He wants to close that distance, to seize the Real Thing.

It makes sense, then, that the pop-culture artifact that speaks most deeply to Žižek, and to which he returns again and again in his work, is *The Matrix*. In this film, you will remember, the hero, played by Keanu Reeves, is initiated into a terrible secret: the world as we know it does not actually exist, but is merely a vast computer simulation projected into our brains. When the hero is unplugged from this simulation, he finds that the human race has in reality been enslaved by rebellious robots, who use the Matrix to keep us docile while literally sucking the energy from our bodies. When Laurence Fishburne, Reeves's mentor, shows him the true state of the Earth, blasted by nuclear bombs, he proclaims: "Welcome to the desert of the real!"

When Žižek employed this phrase as the title of a short book about the September 11 attacks and their aftermath, he was not making an ironic pop reference. He was drawing an edifying parallel. Why is it, the communist revolutionary must inevitably reflect, that nobody wants a communist revolution? Why do people in the West seem so content in what Žižek calls "the Francis Fukuyama dream of the 'end of history'"? For most of us, this may not seem like a hard question to answer: one need only compare the experience of communist countries with the experience of democratic ones. But Žižek is not an empiricist, or a liberal, and he has another answer. It is that capitalism is the Matrix, the illusion in which we are trapped.

This, of course, is merely a flamboyant sci-fi formulation of the old Marxist concept of false consciousness. "Our 'freedoms,'" Žižek writes in *Welcome to the Desert of the Real*, "themselves serve to mask and sustain our deeper unfreedom." This is the central instance in Žižek's work of the kind of dialectical reversal, the clever antiliberal inversion, that is the basic movement of his mind. It could hardly be otherwise, considering that his intellectual gods are Hegel and Lacan—masters of the dialectic, for whom the real never appears except in the form of the illusion or the symptom. In both their systems, the interpreter—the philosopher for Hegel, the analyst for Lacan—is endowed with privileged insight and authority. Most people are necessarily in thrall to appearances, and thereby to the deceptions of power; but the interpreter is immune to them, and can recognize and expose the hidden meanings, the true processes at work in History or in the Unconscious.

This sacerdotal notion of intellectual authority makes both thinkers essentially hostile to democracy, which holds that the truth is available in principle to everyone, and that every individual must be allowed to speak for himself. Žižek, too, sees the similarity—or, as he says, "the profound solidarity"—between his favorite philosophical traditions. "Their structure," he acknowledges, "is inherently 'authoritarian': since Marx and Freud opened up a new theoretical field which sets the very criteria of veracity, their words cannot be put to the test the same way one is allowed to question the statements of their followers." Note that the term "authoritarian" is not used here pejoratively. For Žižek, it is precisely this authoritarianism that makes these perspectives appealing. Their "engaged notion of truth" makes for "struggling theories, not only theories about struggle."

But to know what is worth struggling for, you need theories about struggle. Only if you have already accepted the terms of the struggle—in Žižek's case, the class struggle—can you move on to the struggling theory that teaches you how to fight. In this sense, Žižek the dialectician is at bottom entirely undialectical. That liberalism is evil and communism good is not his conclusion, it is his premise; and the contortions of his thought, especially in his most political books, result from the need to reconcile that premise with a reality that seems abundantly to indicate the opposite.

Hence the necessity of the Matrix, or something like it, for Žižek's worldview. And hence his approval of anything that unplugs us from the Matrix and returns us to the desert of the real—for instance, the horrors of September 11. One of the ambiguities of Žižek's recent work lies in his attitude toward the kind of Islamic fundamentalists who perpetrated the attacks. On the one hand, they are clearly reactionary in their religious dogmatism; on the other hand, they have been far more effective than the Zapatistas or the Porto Alegre movement in discomfiting American capitalism. As Žižek observes, "while they pursue what appear to us to be evil goals with evil means, the very form of their activity meets the highest standard of the good." Yes, the good: Mohammed Atta and his comrades exemplified "good as the spirit of and actual readiness for sacrifice in the name of some higher cause." Žižek's dialectic allows him to have it all: the jihadis may say they are motivated by religion, but they are actually casualties of capitalism, and thus objectively on the left. "The only way to conceive of what happened on September 11," he writes, "is to locate it in the context of the antagonisms of global capitalism."

∘ ∘ ∘

"Will America finally risk stepping through the fantasmatic screen that separates it from the Outside World, accepting its arrival in the Real world?" Žižek asked in 2002. The answer was no. Even September 11 did not succeed in robbing the West of its liberal illusions. What remains, then, for the would-be communist? The truly dialectical answer, the kind of answer that Marx would have given, is that the adaptations of capitalism must themselves prove fatally maladaptive. This is the answer that Antonio Negri and Michael Hardt gave in their popular neo-Marxist treatises *Empire* and *Multitude*: as global capitalism evolves into a kind of disembodied, centerless, virtual reality, it makes labor autonomous and renders capital itself unnecessary.

But Žižek, in *In Defense of Lost Causes*, has no use for Negri's "heroic attempt to stick to fundamental Marxist coordinates." When it comes to the heart of the matter, what Žižek wants is not dialectic, but repetition: another Robespierre, another Lenin, another Mao. His "progressivism" is not linear, it is cyclical. And if objective conditions are different from what they were in 1789 or 1917, so much the worse for objective conditions. "True ideas are eternal, they are indestructible, they always return every time they are proclaimed dead," Žižek writes in his introduction. One of the sections in the book is titled "Give the dictatorship of the proletariat a chance!"

Of course, Žižek knows as well as anyone how many chances it has been given, and what the results have been. In his recent books, therefore, he has begun to articulate a new rationale for revolution, one that acknowledges its destined failure in advance. "Although, in terms of their positive content, the Communist regimes were mostly a dismal failure, generating terror and misery," he explains, "at the same time they opened up a certain space, the space of utopian expectations." He adds elsewhere: "In spite of (or, rather, because of) all its horrors, the Cultural Revolution undoubtedly did contain elements of an enacted utopia." The crimes denoted not the failure of the utopian experiments, but their success. This utopian dimension is so precious that it is worth any number of human lives. To the tens of millions already lost in Russia, China, Cambodia, and elsewhere, Žižek is prepared to add however many more are required. He endorses the formula of Alain Badiou: "*mieux vaut un désastre qu'un désêtre*," better a disaster than a lack of being.

This ontology of revolution raises some questions. On several occasions, Žižek describes the "utopian" moment of revolution as "divine." In support of this notion he adduces Walter Benjamin on "divine violence." "The most obvious candidate for 'divine violence,'" he writes in *Violence*, "is the violent explosion of resentment which finds expression in a spectrum that ranges from mob lynchings to revolutionary terror." It is true that Benjamin did, in his worst moments, endorse revolutionary violence in these terms. But for Benjamin, who had a quasi-mystical temperament, the divine was at least a real metaphysical category: when he said divine, he meant divine. For Žižek, who sometimes employs religious tropes but certainly does not believe in religion, "divine" is just an honorific—a lofty way of justifying his call for human sacrifices.

"In the revolutionary explosion as an Event," Žižek explains in *In Defense of Lost Causes*, "another utopian dimension shines through, the dimension of universal emancipation which, precisely, is the excess betrayed by the market reality which takes over 'the day after'—as such, this excess is not simply abolished, dismissed as irrelevant, but, as it were, transposed into the virtual realm." But if utopia is destined to remain virtual—if

Robespierre is always followed by Bonaparte, and Lenin by Stalin—why should actual lives be sacrificed to it? Would it not be wiser to seek this "dimension," this "divinity," bloodlessly, outside politics, by means of the imagination?

But what if it is not the utopia that appeals to Žižek, but the blood and the sacrifice? That is certainly the impression he gives with his strange misreading of Benjamin's most famous image. In *Violence*, Žižek cites the passage in Benjamin's "Theses on the Philosophy of History" that was inspired by Paul Klee's *Angelus Novus*: "This is how one pictures the angel of history. His face is turned toward the past. Where we perceive a chain of events, he sees one single catastrophe which keeps piling wreckage and hurls it in front of his feet. The angel would like to stay, awaken the dead, and make whole what has been smashed. But a storm is blowing in from Paradise; it has got caught in his wings with such a violence that the angel can no longer close them. The storm irresistibly propels him into the future to which his back is turned, while the pile of debris before him grows skyward. This storm is what we call progress."

The moral sublimity of this image, which has made it a touchstone for so many postwar thinkers, lies in Benjamin's opposition between the violence of history and the ineffectual but tireless witness of the angel. Violence lies in the nature of things, but the angel, who is the always-imminent messiah, resists this nature absolutely: his one desire is to "make whole what has been smashed." Yet here is Žižek's response to Benjamin: "And what if divine violence is the wild intervention of this angel?" What if "from time to time he strikes back to restore the balance, to enact a revenge"? Benjamin's point could not be more completely traduced: if the angel struck back, he would no longer be the angel. He would have gone over to the side of the "progress" that kills.

That is not Benjamin's side, but it is Žižek's. And in his recent writings, as the actual—or, in his Heideggerian terminology, the "ontic"—possibility of revolution recedes, its "ontological" importance has increased. No, the revolution will not bring the millennium. As a historical science, Marxism is false. Divine violence "strikes from out of nowhere, a means without an end." And yet "one should nevertheless insist that there is no 'bad courage.'" The courage displayed in the Revolution is its own justification, it is the image of the utopia it cannot achieve. "The urge of the moment is the true utopia."

Žižek is hardly the only leftist thinker who has believed in the renovating power of violence, but it is hard to think of another one for whom the revolution itself was the *acte gratuit*. For the revolutionary, Žižek instructs, violence involves "the heroic assumption of the solitude of a sovereign decision." He becomes the "master" (Žižek's Hegelian term) because "he is not afraid to die, [he] is ready to risk everything." True, "democratic materialism furiously rejects" the "infinite universal Truth" that such a figure brings, but that is because "democracy as a rule cannot reach beyond pragmatic utilitarian inertia...a leader is necessary to trigger the enthusiasm for a Cause." In sum, "without the Hero, there is no Event"—a formula from a video game that Žižek quotes with approval. He grants that "there is definitely something terrifying about this attitude—however, this terror is nothing less than the condition of freedom."

There is a name for the politics that glorifies risk, decision, and will; that yearns for the hero, the master, and the leader; that prefers death and the infinite to democracy and the pragmatic; that finds the only true freedom in the terror of violence. Its name is not communism. Its name is fascism, and in his most recent work Žižek has inarguably revealed himself as some sort of fascist. He admits as much in *Violence*, where he quotes the German philosopher Peter Sloterdijk on the "re-emerging Left-Fascist whispering at the borders of academia"—"where, I guess, I belong." There is no need to guess.

Žižek endorses one after another of the practices and the values of fascism, but he obstinately denies the label. Is "mass choreography displaying disciplined movements of thousands of bodies," of the kind Leni Riefenstahl loved to photograph, fascist? No, Žižek insists, "it was Nazism that stole" such displays "from the workers' movement, their original creator." (He is willfully blind to the old and obvious conclusion that totalitarian form accepts content from the left and the right.) Is there something fascist about what Adorno long ago called the jargon of authenticity—"the notions of decision, repetition, assuming one's destiny . . . mass discipline, sacrifice of the individual for the collective, and so forth"? No, again: "there is nothing 'inherently fascist'" in all that. Is the cult of martyrdom that surrounds Che Guevara a holdover from the death worship of reactionary Latin American Catholicism, as Paul Berman has argued? Perhaps, Žižek grants, "but—so what?" "To be clear and brutal to the end," he sums up, "there is a lesson to be learned from Hermann Goering's reply, in the early 1940s, to a fanatical Nazi who asked him why he protected a well-known Jew from deportation: 'In this city, I decide who is a Jew!'. . . In this city, it is we who decide what is left, so we should simply ignore liberal accusations of inconsistency."

o o o

That sentence is a remarkable moment in Žižek's writing. It stands out even among the many instances in which Žižek, before delivering himself of some monstrous sentiment, warns the reader of the need to be harsh, never to flinch before liberal pieties. In order to defend himself against the charge of proto-fascism, Žižek falls back on Goering's joke about Jews! This is not just the "adrenalin-fueled" audacity of the bold writer who "dares the reader to disagree." To produce this quotation in this context is a sign, I think, of something darker. It is a dare to himself to see how far he can go in the direction of indecency, of an obsession that has nothing progressive or revolutionary about it.

It is not surprising that it is the subject of the Jews that calls forth this impulse in Žižek, because the treatment of Jews and

Judaism in his work has long been unsettling—and in a different way from his treatment of, say, the United States, which he simply denounces. Žižek's books are loosely structured and full of digressions, more like monologues than treatises, but for that very reason, his perpetual return to the subject of the Jews functions in his writing the way a similar fixation might function in an analysand's recital: as a hint of something hidden that requires critical examination.

Typically, the form that Žižek's remarks on Jews take is that of an exposition of the mentality of the anti-Semite. This is an unimpeachable and rather common forensic device, but somehow it does not quite account for the passionate detail of Žižek's explorations. Consider, for instance, the passage in *The Metastases of Enjoyment* in which Žižek, in order to explicate John McCumber's theory about "the logic of the signifier" in Hegel, writes: "In order to explain this 'reflexivity,' let us resort to the logic of anti-Semitism. First, the series of markers that designate real properties are abbreviated-immediated in the marker 'Jew': (avaricious, profiteering, plotting, dirty . . .)—Jew. We then reverse the order and 'explicate' the marker 'Jew' with the series (avaricious, profiteering, plotting, dirty . . .)—that is, this series now provides the answer to the question 'What does "Jew" mean?'" In the ensuing discussion, Žižek goes on to recite this list of "Jewish" adjectives six more times.

It is an odd way to demonstrate a point of linguistic theory. Odd, too, is the passage in *Iraq: The Borrowed Kettle* where Žižek discusses the ideological function of Nazi anti-Semitism: "one could say that even if most of the Nazi claims about the Jews had been true (that they exploited the Germans, that they seduced German girls, and so forth . . .) their anti-Semitism would still have been (and was) pathological, since it repressed the true reason why the Nazis needed anti-Semitism in order to sustain their ideological position." Why this need to keep open, as if for the sake of argument, the possibility that the Jews really were guilty of all the things of which the Nazis accused them? Why, when

Žižek returns to this same line of reasoning in *Violence*—"even if rich Jews in the Germany of the 1930s 'really' exploited German workers, seduced their daughters," and so on—are there quotation marks around "really," as though the truth or falsehood of Jewish villainy were a question to be postponed until it can be given fuller consideration?

These moments, unpleasant as they are, are not quite expressions of anti-Semitism. But in *In Defense of Lost Causes*, Žižek does make plain what he might call the "fantasmatic screen" through which he sees Jews. This occurs in his discussion of *Man Is Wolf to Man*, the Gulag memoir of a Polish Jew named Janusz Bardach. In his book, Žižek writes, Bardach relates that when he was freed from the Kolyma camp but still forced to remain in the region, he took a job in a hospital, where he worked with a doctor on "a desperate method of providing the sick and starving prisoners with some vitamins and nutritious foodstuffs. The camp hospital had too large a stock of human blood for transfusions which it was planning to discard; Bardach reprocessed it, enriched it with vitamins from local herbs, and sold it back to the hospital." Later, when the hospital objected to this technique, Bardach found a way to do the same thing with deer blood, "and soon developed a successful business." Here is Žižek's reaction to this story: "My immediate racist association was, of course: 'Typical Jews! Even in the worst gulag, the moment they are given a minimum of freedom and space for maneuver, they start trading—in human blood!'"

Now, Žižek is telling this story against himself, as an illustration of the way "racism works as a spontaneous disposition lurking beneath the surface" of all our minds. Still, there is something chilling about that "of course": his implication is that we all harbor the association of Jews with profiteering and blood-drinking, though we ought to try to suppress it. It is at such a moment that one realizes that for Žižek, Jews are a mere abstraction, objects of fantasy and speculation, that can be forced to play any number of roles in his psychic economy.

In his recent writings, as his concerns have shifted more and more toward the political, the roles reserved for Jews and Judaism have become decidedly more negative. True, Žižek is less straightforwardly hostile to Israel than many European leftists. In his chapter on the subject in *Violence*, he writes that "everybody knows the only viable solution" to the Middle East stalemate is the two-state solution, with a Jewish state and a Palestinian state side by side. Yet Žižek's sovereign disdain for fact, along with his imaginative fixation on the Jews, ensures that his portrait of Israel is a malign fantasy.

"In all honesty I have to admit that every time I travel to Israel, I experience that strange thrill of entering a forbidden territory of illegitimate violence," he declares. "Does this mean I am (not so) secretly an anti-Semite?" (Note the disarming sincerity that expects absolution, and in Žižek's case usually receives it.) One manifestation of this illegitimate violence, he writes, is that "the Jews, the exemplary victims . . . are now considering a radical 'ethnic cleansing' (the 'transfer'—a perfect Orwellian misnomer—of the Palestinians from the West Bank)." In fact, "the Jews" are not considering this at all; the only political party in Israel that did advocate such an obscenity, Meir Kahane's Kach, was banned from the Knesset for exactly that reason. But such merely empirical considerations cannot be allowed to stand in the way of Žižek's "dialectical" conclusion. As far back as World War II, he remarks, rehearsing one of the oldest and most pointless "ironies" of modern history, "the Nazis and the radical Zionists shared a common interest. . . . In both cases, the purpose was a kind of 'ethnic cleansing.'"

This method of alleviating European guilt by casting "the exemplary victims" of the Holocaust as in some sense the agents of holocaust is far from unknown on the European left. But what is less common, even there, is Žižek's resurrection of some of the oldest tropes of theological and philosophical anti-Semitism. The key text here is Žižek's book *The Fragile Absolute: Or, Why Is the Christian Legacy Worth Fighting For?* which appeared in 2000.

It addresses "the delicate question of the relationship between Judaism and Christianity."

In Žižek's telling, that relationship is sickeningly familiar. Invoking Freud's *Moses and Monotheism*, Žižek asserts that Judaism harbors a "'stubborn attachment'. . . to the unacknowledged violent founding gesture that haunts the public legal order as its spectral supplement." Thanks to this Jewish stubbornness, he continues, "the Jews did not give up the ghost; they survived all their ordeals precisely because they refused to give up the ghost." This vision of Judaism as an undead religion, surviving zombie-like long past the date of its "natural" death, is taken over from Hegel, who writes in *The Phenomenology of Spirit* about the "fatal unholy void" of this "most reprobate and abandoned" religion. This philosophical anti-Judaism, which appears in many modern thinkers, including Kant, is a descendant of the Christian anti-Judaism that created the figure of the Wandering Jew, who also "refused to give up the ghost."

It makes sense, then, that Žižek should finally cast his anti-Judaism in explicitly theological terms. Why is it that so many of the chief foes of totalitarianism in the second half of the twentieth century were Jews—Arendt, Berlin, Levinas? One might think it is because the Jews were the greatest victims of Nazi totalitarianism, and so had the greatest stake in ensuring that its evil was recognized. But Žižek has another explanation: the Jews are stubbornly rejecting the universal love that expresses itself in revolutionary terror, just as they rejected the love of Christ. "No wonder," he writes in the introduction to *In Defense of Lost Causes*, "that those who demand fidelity to the name 'Jews' are also those who warn us against the 'totalitarian' dangers of any radical emancipatory movement. Their politics consists in accepting the fundamental finitude and limitation of our situation, and the Jewish Law is the ultimate mark of this finitude, which is why, for them, all attempts to overcome Law and tend towards all-embracing Love (from Christianity through the French Jacobins to Stalinism) must end up in totalitarian terror."

Stalinism, in this reading, is the heir to Christianity, and yet another attempt to overcome law with love. Here Žižek is explicating the views of Badiou, to whom the book is dedicated, but it is safe to say that Žižek endorses those views, since precisely the same logic is at work in *The Fragile Absolute*, where he writes of "the Jewish refusal to assert love for the neighbor outside the confines of the Law," as against the Christian "endeavor to break the very vicious cycle of Law/sin." "No wonder," Žižek says, "that, for those fully identified with the Jewish 'national substance'... the appearance of Christ was a ridiculous and/or traumatic scandal."

It does not bother Žižek that this hoary dichotomy is built on a foundation of complete ignorance of both Judaism and Christianity. Nothing could be lazier than to recycle the ancient Christian myth of Judaism as a religion of "mere law." And nothing could be more insulting to Christianity than to reduce it romantically to antinomianism, which has always been a Christian heresy. "Christianity," Žižek remarks, "is... a form of anti-wisdom par excellence, a crazy wager on Truth." But surely it is no part of the Pascalian wager that murdering millions of people will help to win it.

And there is no doubt that this scale of killing is what Žižek looks forward to in the Revolution. "What makes Nazism repulsive," he writes, "is not the rhetoric of a final solution as such, but the concrete twist it gives to it." Perhaps there is supposed to be some reassurance for Jews in that sentence; but perhaps not. For in *In Defense of Lost Causes*, again paraphrasing Badiou, Žižek writes: "To put it succinctly, the only true solution to the 'Jewish question' is the 'final solution' (their annihilation), because Jews... are the ultimate obstacle to the 'final solution' of History itself, to the overcoming of divisions in all-encompassing unity and flexibility." I hasten to add that Žižek dissents from Badiou's vision to this extent: he believes that Jews "resisting identification with the State of Israel," "the Jews of the Jews themselves," the "worthy successors to Spinoza," deserve to be exempted on account of their "fidelity to the Messianic impulse."

In this way, Žižek's allegedly progressive thought leads

directly into a pit of moral and intellectual squalor. In his *New York Times* editorial against torture, Žižek worried that the normalization of torture as an instrument of state was the first step in "a process of moral corruption: those in power are literally trying to break a part of our ethical backbone." This is a good description of Žižek's own work. Under the cover of comedy and hyperbole, in between allusions to movies and video games, he is engaged in the rehabilitation of many of the most evil ideas of the last century. He is trying to undo the achievement of all the postwar thinkers who taught us to regard totalitarianism, revolutionary terror, utopian violence, and anti-Semitism as inadmissible in serious political discourse. Is Žižek's audience too busy laughing at him to hear him? I hope so, because the idea that they can hear him without recoiling from him is too dismal, and frightening, to contemplate.

Still the Good War?

∘ ∘ ∘

In February 2011, the last surviving American veteran of the First World War died. It is hard to imagine the day when we say goodbye to the last survivor of the Second World War, so large do the "good war" and the "greatest generation" continue to loom in our national imagination. But the calendar and the census do not lie. Some 16 million Americans served in the military during World War II. On the sixtieth anniversary of Pearl Harbor Day, in 2001, about 5.5 million were still living. By the seventieth anniversary, the number was closer to 1.5 million, and it drops by almost a thousand a day.

The passage of time doesn't just turn life into history; it also changes the shape of history itself. Over the last several years, historians, philosophers, and other writers have begun to think about the Second World War in challenging new ways, reflecting the growing distance between the country that fought the war and the country that remembers it. The purpose of the new World War II history is not so much to uncover new facts about the war—most of its secrets, from British codebreaking at Bletchley Park to the Soviet massacre of Poles at Katyn, were exposed long ago—as to reshape the way we think about its moral legacy.

The passing of the World War II generation itself accounts for part of this change. In the 1990s, as the veterans began to die out, Americans embraced histories that celebrated the democratic heroism of the G.I. The emblematic books of that decade were Stephen Ambrose's *Band of Brothers* and Tom Brokaw's *The Greatest Generation*, which coined a permanent catchphrase. Both books emphasized the extraordinary achievements of ordinary Americans, and their success had much to do with their tone of filial guilt—the way they expressed the younger generation's fear of being unable to live up to the veterans' achievement.

The appeal of this kind of World War II history has not disappeared, and probably never will. Laura Hillenbrand's *Unbroken*, which spent months near the top of the bestseller list, is the latest incarnation of the classic G.I. tale. She, too, focuses on an ordinary American swept up by the war and transformed into a hero; that Louis Zamperini was an Olympic track star only seems to reinforce his everyman charisma. But what makes Zamperini the perfect war hero for Americans, with our enduring ambivalence about the martial virtues, is that his heroism is largely passive, a matter of enduring suffering, not inflicting it.

Unbroken opens with a panorama of Zamperini and his fellow downed airmen on a raft, "alone on sixty-four million square miles of ocean," and goes on to describe his ordeals at sea and in a Japanese prison camp. Zamperini's greatness was, the title suggests, his refusal to break, and not his ability to break others—which is an equally important part of the soldier's job, and one that is far less comfortable to read about. Zamperini was a bombardier on a B-24, and at the very time he was being tortured by the Japanese, other B-24 crews, made up of men no better or worse than him, carried out Operation Gomorrah—the weeklong raid on Hamburg, Germany that, in July 1943, killed some 40,000 civilians and destroyed virtually the entire city.

Do we have room for that story, and others like it, in our memory of the Second World War? This is the question that a number of historians and philosophers have begun asking with renewed force. Of course, the horrors of the Allied bombing campaign have never been a secret; Kurt Vonnegut's *Slaughterhouse-Five*, with its nightmare evocation of the bombing of Dresden, is one of the most popular American war novels. But American debates on the morality of bombing have traditionally focused on the atom bomb, a unique weapon that raises unique questions.

Recently, historical debate has focused much more on the European theater, and on the conventional bombs employed by the Allied air forces. What makes this shift especially important is that it has been driven, for the first time since the war's end, by the memories of the Germans who were targeted. In a landmark essay, "Air War and Literature" (published in English in *On the Natural History of Destruction*), the German novelist W. G. Sebald wondered why the experience of Allied bombing—which killed half a million Germans and devastated most German cities—"seems to have left scarcely a trace of pain behind in the collective consciousness." He suggested that "there was a tacit agreement, equally binding upon everyone, that the true state of material and moral ruin in which the country found itself was not to be described."

A few years later, as if in response, the German historian Jörg Friedrich published *The Fire: The Bombing of Germany, 1940–1945*. This comprehensive history uses words and photographs to evoke Sebald's "material and moral ruin." Friedrich describes the kinds of scenes that took place on German streets in the aftermath of bombing raids: for instance, "a man dragging a sack with five or six bulges in it as if he were carrying heads of cabbage. It was the heads of his family, a whole family, that he had found in the cellar."

Friedrich was criticized for using language that implicitly equated Allied bombing with Nazi war crimes. For instance, he referred to RAF squadrons as *Einsatzgruppen*, the term used for the German death squads who murdered millions of Jews in Eastern Europe. But when Friedrich concluded that the lesson of the Second World War is that "civilians do not show mercy to civilians. . . . Total war consumes the people totally, and their sense of humanity is the first thing to go," he challenged the Anglo-American memory of the war in ways that were impossible to ignore. Can we still remember World War II as a good war if the Allies were just as consumed and merciless as the Axis?

Among the Dead Cities, by the English philosopher A. C. Grayling, offers one of the most earnest answers to that question. "What should we, the descendants of the Allies who won the victory in the Second World War, reply to the moral challenge of the descendants of those whose cities were targeted by Allied bombers?" Grayling asks. He begins by making clear that he, like almost everyone in England and America (and in today's Germany, too), regards World War II as "a just war against morally criminal enemies."

Still, Grayling concludes that the practice of area bombing—in which the RAF's Bomber Command, in particular, indiscriminately bombed urban areas, in the hope of inflicting damage on Germany's economy and morale—was "a moral crime." After all, "What is the moral difference between bombing women and children and shooting them with a pistol? . . . the anonymity of the act of killing from 20,000 feet?" In the end, Grayling is carried by the force of his own argument to a controversial verdict: "there comes to seem very little difference in principle between the RAF's Operation Gomorrah, or the USAAF's atom bomb attacks on Hiroshima and Nagasaki, and the destruction of the World Trade Center in New York by terrorists on September 11, 2001. . . . All these terrorist attacks are atrocities."

The Allies as Al Qaeda: is this the conclusion to which a reevaluation of the Second World War must lead us? If so, it's no wonder that some historians grow impatient with the whole project. The title of *Moral Combat: Good and Evil in World War II*, by the English historian Michael Burleigh, summarizes his response to the revisionists: yes, this really was a *moral* combat. In his introduction, Burleigh is at least willing to grant that there were moral ambiguities involved, even saying that he does not "seek to excuse Allied war crimes."

Yet when he comes to discuss Allied bombing, it is under the chapter heading "The King's Thunderbolts are Righteous"—the motto of the RAF's 44th Bomber Squadron. And while Burleigh acknowledges that Arthur Harris, the head of Bomber Command, was "obsessed with wrecking German cities," he is far more angered by those who would second-guess Harris after the fact. With an eye on Grayling, Burleigh fulminates, "Wars are not conducted according to the desiccated deliberations of a philosophy seminar full of purse-lipped old maids."

It is no coincidence that this vulgar, bad-tempered aside comes in the course of Burleigh's defense of Winston Churchill, who is the hero of *Moral Combat*. For it is the reputation of Churchill that has been the most rancorous battleground in recent writing about the war. Was Churchill the resolute war leader who saved Britain in its darkest hour, and thereby saved Western civilization from Nazism? Or was he a kind of charlatan—impetuous, irresponsible, grandiose, belligerent, imperialist, racist?

The subtext of this debate, and the reason for its vehemence, has to do with the outsized symbolic role Churchill came to play in American foreign-policy debates after the September 11 attacks. In his first address to Congress after 9/11, President Bush declared, "We will not tire, we will not falter, and we will not fail . . . I will not yield, I will not rest, I will not relent in waging this struggle for freedom and security for the American people."

Bush and his speechwriters were demonstratively borrowing the rhythms of Churchill's most famous speech, which he delivered on June 4, 1940, after the fall of France, promising: "We shall not flag or fail. We shall go on to the end." "With these words," Norman Podhoretz writes in *World War IV*, "Bush unmistakably and unambiguously placed the war against the global terrorist network in the direct succession to World War II." Famously, Bush kept a bust of Churchill in the Oval Office.

It is not surprising, then, that historians began to view Churchill, for good or ill, through the lens of Bush and the War on Terror. Admirers of Churchill dwelled on his moral certainty and his indifference to elite opinion: "Churchill's heart . . . beat in accord with that of the mass of the people of Britain, though not yet with some of the representatives of his party, or with some of the upper classes or with some intellectuals. Never mind," John Lukacs writes in his short book *Blood, Toil, Tears, and Sweat: The Dire Warning*. "What matters is what Churchill knew Britain and Western civilization were up against."

At the same time, revisionist accounts of Churchill have proliferated. The titles tell the story: *Churchill's Folly: How Winston Churchill Created Modern Iraq*; *Blood, Sweat, and Arrogance: The Myths of Churchill's War*. Nicholson Baker, who fantasized about the assassination of George W. Bush in the novel *Checkpoint*, wrote a revisionist account of World War II called *Human Smoke*, in which Churchill comes across as rather more responsible for the war than Hitler. Meanwhile, on the far right, Pat Buchanan produced *Churchill, Hitler, and "The Unnecessary War,"* blaming Churchill for getting involved in World War II in the first place. This isolationist lesson was directed, Buchanan explicitly said, at "the Churchill cult" that convinced Bush, "an untutored president," to invade Iraq. "The Churchill cult gave us our present calamity. If not exposed, it will produce more wars and more disasters, and, one day, a war of the magnitude of Churchill's wars that brought Britain and his beloved empire to ruin," Buchanan warned.

The word "empire" lies at the heart of these debates. In a period that saw historians like Niall Ferguson try to redeem the reputation of the British Empire, and urge America to follow its world-policing example, the connection between Churchill's wartime leadership and his lifelong imperialism and racial prejudice became a major problem. How could the savior of the free world also have been the man who—as Richard Toye documents in *Churchill's Empire*—said "I hate people with slit-eyes and pig tails," and "did not really think that black people were as capable or as efficient as white people," and reminisced about Britain's "jolly little wars against barbarous peoples"?

Still more serious than this casual racism is the charge leveled at Churchill by Madhusree Mukerjee in *Churchill's Secret War: The British Empire and the Ravaging of India During World War II.* Mukerjee lays responsibility for the 1943 Bengal famine, which killed some 3 million people, right at Churchill's doorstep: "One primary cause of the famine was the extent to which Churchill and his advisers chose to use the resources of India to wage war against Germany and Japan, causing inflation and scarcity within the colony." Like Friedrich, Mukerjee sharpens her point by drawing provocative analogies between the English and the Nazis. At the height of the famine, she writes, relief kitchens in Bengal were offering the dying just 400 calories worth of rice a day, "at the low end of the scale on which, at much the same time, inmates at Buchenwald were being fed."

The comparison is unjust, and reviewers have challenged Mukerjee's conclusions about the relative share of responsibility for the famine borne by the British, the invading Japanese, bad weather in Bengal, and hoarding. But *Churchill's Secret War* does make one fundamental point quite convincingly. The famine in Bengal was allowed to continue because the Empire's rulers, including Churchill, prioritized the welfare of Britons over the welfare of Indians.

Does this mean that 3 million deaths must be placed against the moral account of Britain in World War II? And if so, does that affect the way we as Americans remember the war we fought alongside Britain? But then again, other historians are now reminding us, Americans have long been used to protecting our memories of a good war from the fact of our alliance with an undeniably evil power—Stalin's USSR. In fact, of all the recent challenges to our traditional understanding of World War II, the most powerful comes from historians who emphasize how much of the work of defeating Hitler was done by Stalinist Russia, and how little by democratic America.

In the Pacific theater, World War II was largely an American war. But the moral legacy of the war, the reason we remember it as a war of good against evil, has more to do with what happened in Europe: the crusade against Nazism, the liberation of France, the discovery of the concentration camps, the Nuremberg Trials. Yet in *No Simple Victory: The World War in Europe, 1939–1945*, Norman Davies starts from the premise that "the war effort of the Western powers was something of a side-show." America lost 143,000 soldiers in the fight against Germany, he points out, while the USSR lost 11 million.

And if the main show was a war between Hitler and Stalin, Davies asks, wasn't World War II a clash of nearly equivalent evils? "Anyone genuinely committed to freedom, justice and democracy is duty-bound to condemn both of the great totalitarian systems without fear or favor," he concludes. "If one finds two gangsters fighting each other, it is no valid approach at all to round on one and to lay off the other. The only valid test is whether or not they deserve the name of gangsters."

But the recent book that may do most to change the way we think about World War II is one that hardly mentions America at all. *Bloodlands: Europe Between Hitler and Stalin*, by Timothy Snyder, does not need to take account of the United States' role, because it focuses on a region—East-Central Europe from the Baltics to Belarus to Ukraine—where no American soldiers fought. Yet this area, which Snyder calls "the bloodlands," was the greatest killing field of the Second World War. Not only was it the scene of the titanic battles between the Wehrmacht and the Red Army: it was the site of 14 million *noncombatant* deaths between 1933 and 1945. This includes 10 million civilians and prisoners of war killed by the Nazis—including 6 million Jews murdered in the Holocaust—and 4 million civilians and POWs killed by the Soviets.

In grouping German and Soviet casualties together like this, Snyder is making a polemical point. But because he writes with exemplary gravity and care—far removed from the polemical bluntness of Burleigh or Davies—he builds a case that is hard to argue with. Weren't the 3 million Ukrainians starved by Stalin in 1932–33 deliberate victims of state aggression and ideological terror, no less than the 3 million Soviet POWs starved by Hitler in 1941–42? "Only an unabashed acceptance of the similarities between the Nazi and Soviet systems permits an understanding of their differences," Snyder concludes.

If the Second World War is the story of America fighting alongside one of these mass-murdering tyrannies to defeat the other, it becomes a very different kind of war. As Anne Applebaum wrote, reviewing *Bloodlands* in the *New York Review of Books*: "we liberated one half of Europe at the cost of enslaving the other half for fifty years. . . . There was a happy end for us, but not for everybody. This does not make us bad—there were limitations, reasons, legitimate explanations for what happened. But it does make us less exceptional. And it does make World War II less exceptional, more morally ambiguous, and thus more similar to the wars that followed."

Unexceptional and ambiguous: these are not the kind of words we can expect to hear from speechmakers on Pearl Harbor Day. Nor should they be. Even if we accept the most reasonable and best-documented attempts to change the way we think about the Second World War, we should not lose our ability to be inspired by what America, and Americans, accomplished from 1941 to 1945. The patriotism, sacrifice, and bravery that we read about in *Band of Brothers* cannot be nullified by knowing more about the war in which they flourished.

On the contrary, the best of the new World War II histories can be seen as attempts to give us, in the twenty-first century, a more vital sense of what the war was actually like to those fighting it. That the Allies were firebombing German cities, that Churchill was an unapologetic imperialist, that the vast bulk of the fighting and dying was being done by the Red Army—these are all things that would have been clear to knowledgeable Americans during the war itself. Knowing these truths did not make them see the war as ignoble, or lead them to embrace pacifism and isolationism, as Baker or Buchanan suggest we should today. On the contrary, the history of World War II plainly shows that it was the irresolution and military weakness of the democracies that allowed Nazi Germany to provoke a world war, with all its horrors and moral ambiguities.

But then, the present is always lived ambiguously. It is only in retrospect that we begin to simplify experience into myth—because we need stories to live by, because we want to honor our ancestors and our country instead of doubting them. Events give way to books and movies and television shows, gray becomes black and white, and in time the seeming clarity and monumentality of the past makes us feel shy, guilty, or resentful before it.

The best history writing reverses this process, restoring complexity to our sense of the past, helping us to understand that the people who fought the war were as imperfect as ourselves. This requires objectivity, but it should not breed detachment. On the contrary, if we feel proud of our forefathers' virtues and pained by their sufferings and sins, that is because World War II is still *our* history—as the Civil War is still our history, long after the last veteran has been laid to rest.

Beware of Pity:
Hannah Arendt

o o o

In 1999, the Croatian novelist Slavenka Drakulić went to the Hague to observe the trials for war crimes in the former Yugoslavia. Among the defendants was Goran Jelisić, a thirty-year-old Serb from Bosnia, who struck her as "a man you can trust." With his "clear, serene face, lively eyes, and big reassuring grin," he reminded Drakulić of one of her daughter's friends. Many of the witnesses at the Hague shared this view of the defendant—even many Muslims, who told the court how Jelisić helped an old Muslim neighbor to repair her windows after they were shattered by a bomb, or how he helped another Muslim friend escape Bosnia with his family. But the Bosnian Muslims who had known Jelisić seven years earlier, when he was a guard at the Luka prison camp, had different stories to tell. Over a period of eighteen days in 1992, they testified, Jelisić personally killed more than a hundred prisoners. As Drakulić writes, he would choose his victims at random, by asking "a man to kneel down and place his head over a metal drainage grating. Then he would execute him with two bullets in the back of the head from his pistol, which was equipped with a silencer." He liked to introduce himself with the words, "Hitler was the first Adolf, I am the second." He was sentenced to forty years in prison.

None of Drakulić's experience creating fictional characters could help her understand such a mind, which remained all the more unfathomable because of Jelisić's apparent normality, even gentleness. "The more you realize that war criminals might be ordinary people, the more afraid you become," she wrote. What Drakulić discovered, in other words, is what Hannah Arendt, at the trial of Adolf Eichmann forty years earlier, famously called "the fearsome, word-and-thought-defying *banality of evil*." Arendt's phrase has been so influential that it is hard to remember how bitterly controversial it was when she first used it. Many readers resisted what looked like an attempt to trivialize the Nazis: "No banality of a man could have done so hugely evil a job so well," one critic wrote. Yet even those who dispute Arendt's judgment acknowledge her influence on the way we think about political evil. As long as ordinary people can be transformed overnight into mass murderers, we are still living in Hannah Arendt's world.

It is an ambiguous tribute to Arendt, then, that her scholarly and popular profile is as high today as at any time since she died in 1975, at the age of sixty-nine. In the 2000s, a number of Arendt's works were reissued in new editions by Schocken Books, where she worked as an editor in the 1940s—most notably *The Jewish Writings*, which includes Arendt's wartime journalism, never before translated. Scholars around the world have kept pace with a torrent of studies—on Arendt and international relations, Arendt and human rights, Arendt and the Jewish question. Few thinkers of the twentieth century are more sought after as guides to the dilemmas of the twenty-first.

Yet it is not only political theorists who find Arendt a source of fascination. The most intense curiosity about Arendt in recent years has had less to do with her work than with her life. Above all, the publication in 2004 of Arendt's correspondence with Martin Heidegger, after decades of speculation about their relationship, brought renewed scrutiny to her intimate life. To a thinker who believed that the personal was emphatically not political, this kind of attention would be very unwelcome. Arendt derided the "pseudoscientific apparatuses of depth-psychology, psychoanalysis, graphology, etc." as nothing more than "curiosity-seeking." Yet her deeply ambivalent relationship with Heidegger, her lover, teacher, and friend, has a more than personal significance, since it casts light on the most vexed issue in her work: her tangled relationship with Jewishness and Germanness.

Arendt's image has become as important to posterity as her theories. In part, of course, this is because she is one of the few women in the traditionally male pantheon of political philosophy. It makes sense that it is feminist readers who find the most food for thought in Arendt's image—even though she denied that she was a feminist. Julia Kristeva even devotes a section of her book *Hannah Arendt: Life Is a Narrative* to Arendt's changing appearance, as documented in photographs: from the girlish "seductress" of the nineteen-twenties, gazing poetically at the camera, to the confident intellectual of the fifties, whose "femininity . . . beats a retreat" as her face becomes "a caricature of the . . . battle scars" earned during her public career.

Kristeva's reverie on Arendt's "psychic bisexuality" is not the kind of attention that gets paid to Kant, or Heidegger. Yet it is a tribute to the way Arendt has emerged as something more and less than a political theorist. The most rewarding way to read Arendt, and the best way to make sense of her work's strengths and limitations, is to approach her as Michelle-Irène Brudny does in *Hannah Arendt: Essai de biographie intellectuelle*: "I definitely take Hannah Arendt to be less a political philosopher or a political theorist . . . than an author in the strong sense of the word." More emphatically still, Kristeva considers Arendt's writings "to be less a body of work than an action." Like so many Jewish writers of her generation, Arendt's work was an attempt to shine the light of intellect on the extreme darkness she lived through. That she chose to do this in the most impersonal of genres—philosophy and history—rather than through memoir, or even poetry (which she loved to read, and wrote from time to time), is itself a clue to the immense psychological pressures that shaped her work, and in the end partly disfigured it.

o o o

The power of the impersonal is, in fact, the great theme of Arendt's work, and it is no coincidence that she first discovered it in the most literary, least theoretical of her books: *Rahel Varnhagen: The Life of a Jewess*. It was the first book she wrote (not counting her doctoral dissertation), but it was not published for almost two decades, and it remains, even today, a kind of orphan in Arendt's canon. Readers of *Eichmann in Jerusalem* and *The Origins of Totalitarianism* tend to ignore this impressionistic biography of a late-eighteenth-century hostess and letter-writer, whose Berlin salon was one of the breeding grounds of German Romanticism. Yet the Rahel biography, as Kristeva says, is "a veritable laboratory of Arendt's political thought."

Arendt acknowledged her deep affinity with Rahel Varnhagen, née Levin, calling her "my very closest woman friend, unfortunately dead a hundred years now." What they had in common was their predicament as highly gifted Jewish women in a culture that exacted a terrible psychic toll on both women and Jews. In Berlin during the period of the French Revolution, Rahel's friends included some of Germany's greatest minds. They were drawn to her freedom from social convention, and to the exquisite sensibility that informed her cult of Goethe, her extensive correspondence, and her love affairs. Yet during the Napoleonic Wars, as Prussian nationalism began to flourish, Rahel's German friends deserted her; her Gentile lover, whom she saw as her ticket to respectable society, refused to marry her. She was left alone with her inwardness, mourning "the thing which all of my life seemed to me the greatest shame, which was the misery and misfortune of my life—having been born a Jewess."

Not until she was dying did she decide that, all the same, Jew-ishness was the one thing "I should on no account now wish to have missed."

When Arendt first discovered Rahel in the late 1920s, she recognized her as both a tutelary spirit and a cautionary tale. Arendt was born in 1906 into a family that, like so many German Jews, ardently pursued Rahel's ideal of culture or *Bildung*. "With us from Germany," she wrote bitterly during the Second World War, "the word 'assimilation' received a 'deep' philosophical meaning. You can hardly realize how serious we were about it." Again like Rahel, Arendt was conspicuous for her intelligence from an early age; as a young woman, her nickname was "Pallas Athene." When she went to the University of Marburg, in 1924, she entered into the study of theology and German philosophy as into her own inheritance, even though she recognized that they might be uncomfortable subjects for a Jew. When she signed up for a seminar on the New Testament, she warned the professor sternly that "there must be no anti-Semitic remarks."

Yet Arendt could not have suspected just how fraught her encounter with philosophy would turn out to be. In her first semester, like all the most enterprising students, she signed up for a class with Martin Heidegger. Heidegger was then at work on his magnum opus, *Being and Time*, but already he had a reputation as a thrilling teacher. As Arendt remembered a lifetime later, in her tribute on Heidegger's eightieth birthday, "Little more than a name was known, but the name made its way through all of Germany like the rumor of a secret king." She was thus more than prepared to respond when, during a visit to Heidegger's office hours, the married thirty-five-year-old professor began to fall in love with her.

The fact that Heidegger and Arendt were lovers was not a secret to her close friends—"Oh, how very exciting!" Karl Jaspers exclaimed when Arendt told him—and it has been public knowledge since Elisabeth Young-Bruehl revealed it in her 1982 biography. But the affair became a kind of highbrow scandal in

1995, when Elzbieta Ettinger, a professor at MIT, wrote about it in a short book, *Hannah Arendt/Martin Heidegger*. Ettinger, who had been granted access to the Heidegger-Arendt correspondence for the purpose of writing a new biography of Arendt, instead made it the subject of a sensational exposé. The book was loftily derided by Arendtians; yet without the curiosity Ettinger excited, it is doubtful that Arendt's and Heidegger's estates would have consented to the publication of their letters, which cast a fascinating new light on this most important chapter in Arendt's life.

The *Letters: 1925–1975* are revealing, first of all, in their very incompleteness. Arendt kept all of Heidegger's letters from the very beginning; he kept few of hers, and none from the early years. As a result, Heidegger's voice dominates the book, just as his personality and his decisions dominated their affair. Just as one would expect, Heidegger—as an older male professor, who also happened to be one of Europe's greatest philosophers—treats his teenage lover with a combination of passion and condescension. He is capable of poetic raptures: "The demonic struck me. . . . Nothing like it had ever happened to me," he writes a few weeks after they met. Yet while it was Arendt's intellect that helped draw him to her, Heidegger is deeply patronizing about her intellectual ambitions. He urges her to take a "decisive step back from the path toward the terrible solitude of academic research, which only man can endure," and to concentrate instead on becoming "a woman who can give happiness, and around whom all is happiness."

Understandably, after a year of covert meetings and emotional confrontations, Arendt left Marburg for Heidelberg, where she found a more equable teacher in Jaspers. It is just possible to glimpse in the letters the pain the affair caused Arendt—above all, by enforcing a sense of powerlessness. Early on, in an autobiographical composition she titled "Shadows," Arendt described herself to Heidegger in the third person: "her sensitivity and vulnerability, which had always given her an exclusive air, grew to almost grotesque proportions." As late as 1929, when Arendt ran into Heidegger at a train station and he failed to recognize her for a moment, she found the experience shattering: "When I was a small child, that was the way my mother once stupidly and playfully frightened me. I had read the fairy tale about Dwarf Nose, whose nose gets so long nobody recognizes him anymore. My mother pretended that had happened to me. I still vividly recall the blind terror with which I kept crying: but I am your child, I am your Hannah.—That is what it was like today."

The full significance of her experience with Heidegger did not unfold, however, until the early 1930s. As the Weimar Republic collapsed and Nazi violence grew, Arendt began to hear unsettling rumors about Heidegger's sympathy with National Socialism. Her letter to him on the subject is lost, but we can gauge her anxiety from Heidegger's response, which is tentatively dated "Winter 1932/33." "The rumors that are upsetting you are slanders," he begins, and proceeds to give an evasively technical defense of his treatment of Jewish students and colleagues. (If he refused to supervise a Jewish student's dissertation, he explains, it was only because "I am on sabbatical this winter semester"; and besides, "the man who, with my help, got a stipend to go to Rome is a Jew.") Nowhere in the letter is there any denial of Nazi sympathies. Instead, Heidegger simply assures Arendt that, whatever happens, "it cannot touch my relationship to you." After reading this letter, Arendt could not have been entirely surprised when, in 1933, Heidegger joined the Nazi Party and became the rector of Marburg, with the mission of aligning the university with the new party-state.

By that time, Arendt was already in exile from the land of her birth. In the spring of 1933, just after Hitler took power, she began to do clandestine work for a Zionist organization, documenting anti-Semitism in the new Germany. She was arrested and interrogated for eight days before being released. Immediately, she and her mother fled the country, slipping across the Czech border at night. But while she later dated her political awakening to the Reichstag Fire, it is clear that, for several years before 1933, she had been growing more and more alert to the untenable position of Jews in Germany. The private humiliation and political betrayal she suffered at the hands of Heidegger, the living embodiment of German intellect, only brought home to her the lessons she was already learning from her study of Rahel Varnhagen.

When she came to write about Rahel's life, then, Arendt brought to the task a passion and personal commitment born of her own experience. No one could have believed more seriously than Rahel in the cultivation of the spirit. Yet to Arendt she appears as the victim of a terrible illusion—"the hapless human being, the *shlemihl*, who has anticipated nothing." The lesson Arendt drew was that a beautiful soul is not enough, for "it was precisely the soul for which life showed no consideration." To live fully and securely, every human being needs what Arendt calls "specificity," the social and political status that comes with full membership in a community. Arendt had said of herself, in the "Shadows" letter, "she did not belong to anything, anywhere, ever"; so, too, Rahel was "exiled . . . all alone to a place where nothing could reach her, where she was cut off from all human things, from everything that men have a right to claim." To avoid that helpless "place" became the goal of Arendt's life and thought. The categorical imperative of her political theory might be phrased: thou shalt not be a *shlemihl*.

o o o

By the time she finished writing *Rahel Varnhagen*, in 1938—thanks in part to the prodding of Walter Benjamin, her friend and fellow exile—Arendt had come to see Rahel's predicament as an early example of the political naïveté that left European Jewry so vulnerable to Nazi persecution. The biography was written, she later said, "with an awareness of the doom of German Judaism (although, naturally, without any premonition of how far the physical annihilation of the Jewish people in Europe would be carried)." And just as Arendt's attitude toward Rahel was an unstable mixture of sympathy and criticism, so her reaction to the Jewish crisis would blend urgent concern and haughty contempt.

Arendt's tendency to blame the victim, which produced such an explosive effect in *Eichmann in Jerusalem* in the 1960s, is already obvious in the articles she wrote during the war for *Aufbau*, the German-language Jewish newspaper in New York. Arendt and her husband Heinrich Blücher had been able to flee Vichy France for the United States in 1941, thanks to the visas they received from the Emergency Rescue Committee, a volunteer group that used both legal and illegal means to get Jews out of the country. They set up housekeeping in two rooms on West 95th Street, joined a few weeks later by Arendt's mother, who also managed to escape France by way of Lisbon. It is a measure of Arendt's dauntlessness, and her determination to make her voice heard publicly, that before the year was out she had been hired as a columnist for *Aufbau*. It was the first step in an American journalistic career that eventually, as her facility in English improved, led her to become a contributor to *Partisan Review*, the *New Yorker*, and the *New York Review of Books*.

Arendt's wartime articles, collected in *The Jewish Writings*, offer a crucial insight into the political experiences that shaped her theoretical work. In particular, they show Arendt developing a self-contradictory brand of Zionism, which might be called a Zionism of necessity. Faced with the collapse of Jewish assimilation, Arendt turned to Zionism as an "escape route from illusion into reality, from mendacity and self-deception to an honest existence." And the major subject of her wartime writing is the need for Jews to regain their political self-respect—to refuse any longer to be *shlemihls*. As she wrote in 1941, "One truth that is unfamiliar to the Jewish people, though they are beginning to learn it, is that *you can only defend yourself as the person you are attacked as*. A person attacked as a Jew cannot defend himself as an Englishman or a Frenchman. The world would only conclude that he is simply not defending himself." That is why Arendt strongly urged the creation of a Jewish army, which would enable the Jews to hold up their heads as equals among the Allied powers.

What Arendt's Zionism lacked, however, was any positive content, any genuine interest in Judaism or Jewish history. This attitude was typical of the assimilated German Jews of Arendt's generation, the natural product of an upbringing in which, as she remembered, "I did not know from my family that I was Jewish. ... The word 'Jew' never came up when I was a small child." Arendt's Jewishness was constituted by anti-Semitism: "I first met up with it through anti-Semitic remarks ... from children on the street. After that I was, so to speak, enlightened."

It stood to reason, then, that in 1948, when the State of Israel was established and the existential threat to the Jewish people receded, Arendt rapidly disembarrassed herself of her Zionism. While she retained a lifelong interest in the fate of the Jewish state—"any real catastrophe in Israel would affect me more deeply than almost anything else," she told Mary McCarthy— she had an equally strong distaste for its politics and most of its citizens. Among the posthumous revelations that have damaged Arendt's reputation are the letters she wrote from Jerusalem in 1961, when she was attending the Eichmann trial. Her description of the crowd at the courthouse, in a letter to Jaspers, passes beyond condescension to outright racism: "On top, the best of German Jewry. Below them, the prosecuting attorney, Galicians, but still Europeans. Everything is organized by a police force that gives me the creeps, speaks only Hebrew, and looks Arabic. Some downright brutal types among them. They would obey any order. And outside the doors, the oriental mob, as if one were in Istanbul or some other half-Asiatic country."

The venom of this description, like the undisguised pleasure Arendt took in leaving Israel—"I have never before grasped the *concrete* meaning of 'relief' so clearly," she wrote at the end of a 1955 trip—suggests the great emotional forces at play. As she put down roots in New York City—she lived on the West Side of Manhattan from 1941 until her death—and became a sought-after writer and lecturer, Arendt's ideas about self-respect, that Rahelian imperative, began to change. Now the solidarity she had once sought in Zionism began to appear as not a source of strength, but another evidence of weakness—a way of clinging to one's people because one was too weak to stand alone.

She described this phenomenon in a 1959 speech in Hamburg, which had awarded her the Lessing Prize: "it is as if under the pressure of persecution the persecuted have moved so closely together that the interspace which we have called world . . . has simply disappeared. This produces a warmth of human relationships which may strike those who have had some experience with such groups as an almost physical phenomenon." But the price of that warmth was too high to pay: "in extreme cases, in which pariahdom has persisted for centuries, we can speak of real worldlessness. And worldlessness, alas, is always a form of barbarism." For a Jew to tell a German audience, less than fifteen years after the Holocaust, that Jews were barbarians was a shockingly effective means of reclaiming the isolation, the "interspace," Arendt so urgently needed.

It was this refusal of solidarity, as much as any specific assertion, that led so many Jewish readers to react with fury to *Eichmann in Jerusalem* when it appeared in the *New Yorker*, in five installments in 1963. Arendt's report from the trial of Adolf Eichmann, the chief bureaucratic organizer of the Jewish genocide, remains one of the touchstones of American thinking about the Holocaust. But the anger her work provoked among many Jews—according to the historian Peter Novick, she "became, for a time, American Jewish Public Enemy Number One"—has proved just as durable. At the time, Arendt's critics objected to her blanket condemnation of the Jews drafted to serve on the *Judenräte*—the Jewish Councils established by the Nazis to manage the ghettos—and to her phrase about "the banality of evil," which seemed to trivialize Nazi crimes.

Reading *Eichmann in Jerusalem* today, however, in light of all we have since learned from and about Arendt, it is clear that these local issues were only the occasions for resentment, not the whole cause. That cause, once again, can be traced back to the "laboratory of Arendt's political thought," and to her own experience as a Jewish woman in Germany. What raised Arendt's Jewish consciousness was her recognition of Jewish helplessness, both psychological and political. But if she responded to that helplessness with an insistence on self-help, she found it hard to avoid condemning those Jews who, in her view, did not or could not help themselves. Rahel was the first of these, the members of the Jewish Councils the last: "To a Jew this role of the Jewish leaders in the destruction of their own people is undoubtedly the darkest chapter of the whole dark story," she wrote.

Arendt's need to distance herself from the Jews, and especially Jewish victims, accounts for the ironic tone that has always struck readers of *Eichmann in Jerusalem*. Arendt's attitude towards Eichmann himself is simply dismissive: her whole characterization of him as a banal bureaucrat, oblivious to the evil he does, is a way of asserting his human and intellectual inferiority. What really inflames Arendt, on the other hand, is any attempt by the Jewish witnesses to draw attention to what they suffered. "I hate, am afraid of pity, always have been," she once told McCarthy, and she mocked whatever appeared to her as an appeal for pity. "The gist of the background witnesses' testimony about conditions in the Polish ghettos, about procedures in the various death camps," she irritably wrote, "were never in dispute; on the contrary there was hardly anything in what they told that was not known before." She complained to Blücher that "the basic mistake" of the trial was "that the Jews want to pour out their sorrow to the world"—though "of course," she granted, "they have suffered more than Eichmann has."

In this and many other places, Arendt's critics saw that the pride she so effortlessly cultivated carried shame as its necessary obverse. This shame is what led a critic like Gershom

Scholem—whose upbringing was similar to Arendt's, but who left Germany for Palestine and took a Hebrew name—to accuse her of lacking "love of the Jewish people." It is a tribute to Arendt's toughness, and her self-knowledge, that she acknowledged the charge, in a deeply revealing letter included in *The Jewish Writings*. "You are quite right—I am not moved by any 'love' of this sort . . . I have never in my life 'loved' any people or collective . . . I indeed love 'only' my friends and the only kind of love I know of and believe in is the love of persons." The Heidegger correspondence confirms that Arendt indeed lived this principle. In 1950, seventeen years after they had last corresponded, Arendt and Heidegger met again, when she came to Germany to help track down stolen Jewish cultural treasures. Arendt had been publicly critical of Heidegger's behavior during his rectorship and afterward, but the renewal of their ties banished all her suspicions: "This evening and this morning are the confirmation of an entire life," she wrote him after their meeting. For the next two years, their love enjoyed a brief afterlife, as Heidegger wrote poems about her and told her things like "I wish I could run the five-fingered comb through your frizzy hair." Even when the jealousy of Heidegger's wife, Elfriede, brought this quasi-romance to an end, Arendt kept in touch with her old teacher. In the last years of his life, she served as his literary agent in America, helping to get his work translated.

Arendt's unqualified support of Heidegger helped to establish the convenient myth that his Nazi involvement had been, as she put it, a case of an unworldly man getting carried away by politics, and thus "finally a matter of indifference." Not until after her death did scholars in Germany and America demolish this notion, by tracing the profound affinities between Heidegger's thought and his reactionary milieu. It is a task that Arendt herself was equipped to perform, if her loyalty to Heidegger, and to the German tradition he represented, had not made it impossible.

o o o

Arendt's experience at the Eichmann trial confirmed her in the belief that defines her political philosophy: that there must be a rigorous separation between love, which we can only experience privately, and respect, which we earn in, and require for, our public lives. If it is true that, as Arendt once observed, "In the works of a great writer we can almost always find a consistent metaphor peculiar to him alone in which his whole work seems to come to a focus," then her thought is certainly focused on the image of distance or separation. A dignified individual existence, she believes, requires distance from others, the "interspace" she described in the Hamburg speech. Compassion is dangerous, in her view, because "not unlike love, [it] abolishes the distance, the in-between which always exists in human intercourse." What preserves that distance, on the other hand, is pride—the pride of equals that she finds exemplified in the political realm, the "public space."

This view of politics helps to explain why, in *The Human Condition* and *On Revolution*, Arendt exalts it as the highest of human activities. Politics, in her work, is not really an empirical concept—an affair of elections and legislation, still less of tax policy or Social Security reform. Everything having to do with economics, in fact, Arendt prefers to exclude from her definition of politics, relegating it to the nebulous category of "the social." Real politics is found, rather, in the deliberations of the Founders at Philadelphia, or the debates of the Athenians in their assembly. It is an affair of exceptionally talented individuals—people not unlike Hannah Arendt—arguing with one another under conditions of equality and mutual respect.

Still more revealing than Arendt's definition of politics is her explanation of why people are drawn to it in the first place. We do not enter the political world to pursue justice or create a better world. No, human beings love politics because they love to excel, and a political career is the best way to win the world's respect. In ancient Greece, she writes, "the polis was permeated by a fiercely agonal spirit, where everybody had constantly to distinguish himself from all others, to show through unique deeds or achievements that he was the best of all. The public realm, in other words, was reserved for individuality; it was the only place where men could show who they really and inexchangeably were." Arendt recognizes that most of the people of Athens, including all women and slaves, were shut out from this arena, but she accepts that her kind of politics is necessarily an aristocratic pursuit. In yet another instance of her favorite metaphor, she defends "the bitter need of the few to protect themselves against the many, or rather to protect the island of freedom they have come to inhabit against the surrounding sea of necessity."

Nothing could be more characteristic of Arendt than the longing for respect and recognition that shines through these seemingly abstract arguments. All of her experiences as a woman and a Jew, all the hard wisdom she learned from Heidegger and from Rahel, goes into her yearning for the masculine, aristocratic freedom of the Greek polis. (Richard Wolin, one of Arendt's sharpest contemporary critics, has called this yearning "polis envy.") At times, Arendt's love of the public and political, and her fear of the private and psychological, become almost neurotically intense. As she wrote to McCarthy, "the inner turmoil of the self, its *shapelessness*," must be kept under strict quarantine: "It is no less indecent, unfit to appear, than our digestive apparatus, or else our inner organs which also are hidden from visibility by the skin."

This rejection of inwardness, so constant in Arendt's work from *Rahel Varnhagen* on, is the key to what is most valuable in her legacy, and also what is most questionable. No one has argued more forcefully than Arendt that to deprive human beings of their public, political identity is to deprive them of their humanity—and not just metaphorically. In *The Origins of Totalitarianism*, she points out that the first step in the Nazis' destruction of the Jews was to make the Jews stateless, in the knowledge that people with no stake in a political community have no claim on the protection of its laws.

This is the insight that makes Arendt a thinker for our time, when failed states have again and again become the settings for mass murder. She reveals with remorseless logic why emotional appeals to "human rights" or "the international community" prove impotent in the face of a humanitarian crisis. "The Rights of Man, after all, had been defined as 'inalienable' because they were supposed to be independent of all governments," she writes in *Origins*, "but it turned out that the moment human beings lacked their own government and had to fall back upon their minimum rights, no authority was left to protect them and no institution was willing to guarantee them." This is exactly what happened in Yugoslavia and Rwanda and Darfur. Genocide is a political problem, Arendt insists, and it can only be solved politically.

Yet the supreme value Arendt places on individual pride and aristocratic distance, on intellect and excellence, also sharply restricts the human understanding that must be the basis for any confrontation with political evil, especially the evil of the Holocaust. Too much of life, and too many kinds of people, are excluded from Arendt's sympathy, which she could freely give only to those as strong as herself. If, as she wrote, "it is the desire to excel which makes men love the world," then our love for the world actually makes it harder for us to love the people who inhabit it. This is the dilemma that runs through all of Arendt's writing, demonstrating that what she observed about Marx is true of her as well: "Such fundamental and flagrant contradictions rarely occur in second-rate writers; in the work of the great authors they lead into the very center of their work."

The Interpreter:
Walter Benjamin

o o o

On December 18, 1927, at three-thirty in the morning, Walter Benjamin began writing a memorandum titled "Main Features of My First Impression of Hashish." It is characteristic of Benjamin that the first fact he thought it necessary to record was not the time he had taken the drug but the time he started writing about it. Like the books he read and the streets he wandered—like life itself—hashish was important to him less for its own sake than as a subject for interpretation.

For a writer with Benjamin's interests and allegiances, a rendezvous with hashish was inevitable. The surprising thing is that it took him until the age of thirty-five to try it. As early as 1919, he had been fascinated by Baudelaire's *Les Paradis artificiels*, in which the poet issues warnings against the drug so seductive that they sound like invitations: "You know that hashish always evokes magnificent constructions of light, glorious and splendid visions, cascades of liquid gold." Benjamin, who regarded Baudelaire as one of the central figures of the nineteenth century, admired the book's "childlike innocence and purity," but was disappointed in its lack of philosophical rigor, noting, "It will be necessary to repeat this attempt independently." The notes from his first hash-ish trance show him holding deliberately aloof from any kind of rapture. "The gates to a world of grotesquerie seem to be open-ing," he wrote. "Only, I don't wish to enter." According to Jean Selz, a friend with whom Benjamin smoked opium on several occasions, "Benjamin was a smoker who refused the initial blan-dishments of the smoke. He didn't want to yield to it too readily, for fear of weakening his powers of observation."

Over the next seven years, Benjamin participated in drug sessions as either subject or observer at least nine times, but his attitude toward drugs remained vigilantly experimental. He sel-dom took them when he was alone, and he never had his own supplier, relying on doctor friends to procure hashish, opium, and, on one occasion, mescaline. The sessions were recorded in "protocols," furnishing raw material for what Benjamin intended to be a major book on the philosophical and psycho-logical implications of drug use. When, in a letter to Gershom Scholem, his best friend from the age of twenty-three, Benja-min, then forty, listed four unwritten books that he considered "large-scale defeats"—evidence of the "ruin or catastrophe" that his career had become—the last was a "truly exceptional book about hashish."

Nearly three-quarters of a century later, a book by Walter Benjamin called *On Hashish* finally appeared in English, along-side another long-gestated work, *Berlin Childhood Around 1900*. *On Hashish* is not, however, the "truly exceptional book" he had in mind; it's a miscellany, gathering the protocols of his drug experiments, two published accounts of his experiences, and a handful of references to drugs culled from his other works. It can only begin to suggest the true importance of drug experiences for the development of Benjamin's thought.

Yet for this very reason, *On Hashish* stands in the same rela-tion to a more conventional essay on drugs as Benjamin's liter-ary essays do to conventional criticism. "You hardly feel that you have been reading criticism," Frank Kermode noted when

Illuminations, the first English-language selection of Benjamin's writings, appeared in 1968. "It requires the kind of response we are accustomed to give to works of art." *Illuminations* revealed just a few peaks from the sunken continent of Benjamin's work, but these were enough to establish him as a central figure in the history of modernism. Benjamin approached every genre as a kind of laboratory for his lifelong investigations into language, philosophy, and art, and his ideas on these subjects are so original, and so radical in their implications, that they remain profoundly challenging today.

o o o

The period of Benjamin's adulthood and achievement was 1914 to 1940, the darkest in modern European history; and if no one ever wrote criticism the way he did, it is because no other critic felt the dislocations of the time so severely. Benjamin was born in Berlin in 1892, into a prosperous Jewish family, and his expectations were formed in the halcyon period before 1914. In "A Berlin Chronicle," a series of newspaper articles that makes up the nucleus of *Berlin Childhood Around 1900*, he remembered the feeling of bourgeois security that suffused the very furniture in his family's apartment:

> Here reigned a species of things that was, no mat-
> ter how compliantly it bowed to the minor whims
> of fashion, in the main so wholly convinced of
> itself and its permanence that it took no account
> of wear, inheritance, or moves, remaining forever
> equally near to and far from its ending, which
> seemed the ending of all things.

In such a home, poverty was unimaginable: "The poor? For rich children of his generation, they lived at the back of beyond."

In time-honored fashion, Benjamin hoped to abandon the commercial milieu of his father, a successful antiques dealer, for a more prestigious career as an academic. By the time the First World War began, he was already committed to a life of scholarship and, as an opponent of the war, felt no qualms about maneuvering to get out of military service. The best source for Benjamin's life in these years, Gershom Scholem's moving yet unsentimental memoir, *Walter Benjamin: The Story of a Friendship*, records that the two of them stayed up the whole night before Benjamin's draft-board medical exam, "while Benjamin consumed vast quantities of black coffee, a practice then followed by many young men prior to their military physicals." The trick, calculated to simulate a weak heart, worked, and Benjamin was able to spend the rest of the war in Switzerland, studying for his doctorate at the University of Bern.

Scholem shared Benjamin's academic ambitions and his antiwar convictions, and their student friendship laid the groundwork for a lifetime of intellectual debate, most of which was to take place by mail. The most important issue between them, from the beginning, was Judaism, and the possibility of being a Jewish intellectual in Germany. For Scholem, an ardent Zionist who was expelled from his assimilated family for his views, the history of Jewish mysticism gradually displaced mathematics and philosophy as a focus of study. For Benjamin, however, Judaism remained more a possibility to be imagined than a life to be lived. He never mastered its religious practices or sacred texts, and, as he acknowledged to Scholem, "I have come to know living Judaism in absolutely no form other than you."

The friends' divergent attitudes toward Jewishness largely determined their subsequent careers. Neither of them entered the German university life for which they had trained. In 1923, Scholem, changing his first name from the German Gerhard to the Hebrew Gershom, emigrated to Palestine, where there was no university; he planned to support himself as a schoolteacher. As fate would have it, when the Hebrew University of Jerusalem was founded shortly afterward, he was named one of the first professors, and by the time of his death, in 1982, he had become known as the greatest modern scholar of Jewish mysticism. Benjamin, who remained closer to home, ended up straying much farther from his early academic path. Having taken his doctorate in 1919, he enrolled at the University of Frankfurt to write his *Habilitationsschrift*, the second dissertation required for teaching in a German university.

But even as he was researching the thesis, which became *The Origin of German Tragic Drama*, Benjamin suspected that it would never be approved by the tradition-bound faculty. The book, less a historical treatise than a philosophical meditation on the nature of allegory, was, he bragged to Scholem, "unmitigated chutzpah." Even worse than the possibility of being rejected, however, was the possibility of being accepted. In February 1925, as he prepared to submit the dissertation, Benjamin admitted, "I dread almost everything that would result from a positive resolution to all of this: I dread Frankfurt above all, then lectures, students, etc." He needn't have worried. Although the dissertation contains some of his most radical insights into language and literature, his examiners rejected it, admitting that they couldn't understand a single page.

In the mid-1920s, then, Benjamin's career took a sharp turn. With his parents increasingly unwilling or unable to support him, he began to earn a living as a freelance literary journalist, contributing to the culture sections of newspapers and magazines. The death of Benjamin the academic philosopher meant the birth of Benjamin the cultural critic. Harvard University Press's monumental, four-volume edition of *Selected Writings* allows the reader to chart Benjamin's change of direction and his increasing productivity, as he began to cater to the demands of the literary market. All of his writing from 1913 to 1926 fits into the first volume, which is dominated by unpublished essays on abstract topics. His first major piece of literary criticism, a long essay on Goethe's novel *Elective Affinities*, was not published until 1925. But from the mid-1920s onward, he became more and more prolific. The Harvard edition's second volume covers the seven years from 1927 to 1934, and two volumes are required for his last six years.

Much of Benjamin's early writing, though always stamped with his oblique intelligence, is the small change of journalism: travel pieces, book reviews, an article on the Berlin Food Exhibition of 1928. In addition to giving Benjamin a precarious living, such work helped him adapt his extremely dense style, formed in the harsh school of German idealist philosophy, into a more appealing literary instrument. Even so, his prose remained challenging. A friend once told him, "In great writing, the proportion between the total number of sentences and those sentences whose formulation was especially striking or pregnant was about one to thirty—whereas it was more like one to two in [your] case." ("All this is correct," Benjamin admitted.)

Benjamin's roundabout methods can be seen in his best-known literary essays, the examinations of Proust, Baudelaire, and Kafka published in *Illuminations*. These contain little of what we ordinarily expect from criticism: biographical background, information about plot and character, literary-historical comparisons. Instead, Benjamin presents his subjects enigmatically, using startling metaphors and emblems. His essay on Proust (whose works he helped translate into German) is called "The Image of Proust," and draws an implicit parallel between the novelist's method and the critic's, presenting Proust as a collector of charged images, momentary glimpses that open up passages to the buried life. "The image detaches itself from the structure of Proust's sentences as that summer day at Balbec—old, immemorial, mummified—emerged from the lace curtains under Françoise's hands," Benjamin writes. And he responds in kind, concluding his essay with the image of Proust lying in bed, his asthmatic prostration converted into heroic labor: "For the second time there rose a scaffold like Michelangelo's on which the artist, his head thrown back, painted the Creation on the ceiling

of the Sistine Chapel: the sickbed on which Marcel Proust conse-
crates the countless pages which he covered with his handwrit-
ing, holding them up in the air, to the creation of his microcosm."

Benjamin's literary criticism was too unusual and uncom-
promising to win a large audience. But his admirers included
some of the best living German writers, among them Hugo von
Hofmannsthal and Bertolt Brecht. By 1930, Benjamin was confident enough to announce that his life's ambition was to "be
considered the foremost critic of German literature."

○ ○ ○

It is not as a literary critic that Benjamin has been most influential, however, but as a pioneering cultural critic, one of the first
writers to see all the products of civilization as worthy of analysis. This is the principle that guides his most famous essay, "The
Work of Art in the Age of Mechanical Reproduction," now a
canonical text in art history, film studies, and related fields. In it
Benjamin argues that, traditionally, a painting or sculpture was
endowed with something he calls "aura," deriving from a recognition of its absolute uniqueness. That is why thousands of people
line up every day for a quick, obscured glimpse of the Mona Lisa:
not just to see it but to be in its quasi-sacred presence. In the age
of technology, Benjamin perceived, this uniqueness is diluted
by the ready availability of reproductions, which makes it possible to see a work of art without ever having seen the original.
Furthermore, in the twentieth century's characteristic art forms,
photography and film, there is no such thing as an original.

Surprisingly, Benjamin welcomed the idea of art without
aura. He reasoned that aura was a kind of aristocratic mystery,
and that its disappearance should herald a new, more democratic
art: "The social significance of film, even—and especially—in
its most positive form, is inconceivable without its destructive, cathartic side: the liquidation of the value of tradition in
the cultural heritage." This rhetoric, with its enthusiasm for

"destruction" and "liquidation," sounds distinctly odd coming from Benjamin. How, the reader wonders, did the great champion of Proust and Kafka end up decrying uniqueness and originality? How could the man who compared *In Search of Lost Time* to the Sistine ceiling also believe that "contemplative immersion" in a work of art was "a breeding ground for asocial behavior"?

The answer lies in Benjamin's exceedingly awkward embrace of Marxism. Like many other intellectuals of the time, he came to feel that only communism could save Europe from war, depression, and fascism. He visited the Soviet Union in 1926, and clung to the hope that communism would provide better for writers than capitalism had managed to do. Benjamin's personal circumstances only reinforced this judgment. Literary journalism, never a lucrative career, was an almost heroically futile one in Weimar Germany. By 1931, Benjamin confessed that "material circumstances . . . have made my existence—with no property and no steady income—a paradox, in view of which even I sometimes fall into a stupor of amazement."

And when Hitler seized power, Benjamin lost what remained of his livelihood. In March 1933 he fled Germany for France, never to return. For the rest of his life, he lived on the brink of destitution. A subsidy provided by the Institute for Social Research, itself in exile from its original base in Frankfurt, helped him scrape by. "My Communism," Benjamin said, "is a drastic, not infertile expression of the fact that the present intellectual industry finds it impossible to make room for my thinking, just as the present economic order finds it impossible to accommodate my life."

Benjamin's Marxist turn was welcomed by friends like Brecht, who regretted only that he hadn't gone far enough. Scholem, on the other hand, kept up a stream of reproaches in his letters from Palestine, thinking it nothing more than a fashionable disguise: "There is a disconcerting alienation and disjuncture between your true and alleged way of thinking." And he was infuriated by Benjamin's refusal to acknowledge how far his idiosyncratic understanding of communism deviated from Party orthodoxy. "The complete certainty I have about what would happen to your writing if it occurred to you to present it within the Communist Party is quite depressing," Scholem wrote.

Benjamin never did join the Party, though he agonized over it, just as he continually postponed his often-declared plans to learn Hebrew and move to Palestine. But his limited and private adherence to Marxist principles had significant effects on his work—effects that tended to bear out Scholem's pessimism. "The Work of Art" could not have been written without Benjamin's newfound interest in the material conditions of cultural production. Yet his masochistic insistence on putting his work at the service of the class struggle also accounts for the forced belligerence and brutalism of that essay.

The most significant casualty of Benjamin's Marxism was *The Arcades Project*, which today enjoys a reputation as one of the most famous books never written. It was the white whale of Benjamin's last years, a magnum opus of stupendous scope and originality that he found himself perpetually unable to finish. The *Passagenwerk*, as Benjamin referred to it, took its name from the *passages*, or arcades, that adorned Paris in the age of Baudelaire. These were glass-covered promenades set aside for shopping and strolling, which helped to give the city its reputation as a paradise for *flâneurs*. In the arcades of nineteenth-century Paris, Benjamin believed he had found the omphalos of the modern city, with its erotic anonymity, its phantasmagoria of fashions, its mixture of banality and enchantment.

The *passages* appealed to him, above all, because by his own day they were already going extinct, made obsolete by the department store. This gave them the charm that Benjamin found in everything discarded and superseded, all the detritus on which civilization imprints its deepest secrets. "To someone looking through piles of old letters," he wrote, "a stamp that has long been out of circulation on a torn envelope often says more than a reading of dozens of pages." In just this way, Benjamin dreamed of using the arcades to write the hidden history of the city he called, in one essay, "Paris, the Capital of the Nineteenth Century." He initially meant his arcades essay to be brief, allusive, and literary—"a fairy-play," he called it in 1928. "In any case," he assured Scholem, "it is a project that will just take a few weeks."

What transformed the essay of 1928 into the 1,000-page midden of notes, fragments, and quotations that Benjamin left behind at his death, and that was published in 1999 under the title *The Arcades Project*? Any answer would have to include Benjamin's constant tendency to procrastinate; the disordered conditions of his life in the 1930s, which made sustained research difficult; and the inherently elusive nature of what he was trying to accomplish. Above all, however, what kept him from completing the project was his Marxism. In the late thirties, when he returned to it in earnest, he was determined to recast his analysis of nineteenth-century Paris in the language of dialectical materialism. It was in support of this project that the Institute for Social Research granted Benjamin a subsidy, expecting a brilliant example of Marxist cultural criticism.

But when Benjamin started to put *The Arcades Project* into something like publishable form, sending Theodor Adorno an essay titled "The Paris of the Second Empire in Baudelaire," he was in for a shock. Although he was eager to embrace Marxist terminology, his use of it proved far too clumsy for a subtle theorist like Adorno. Instead of sharpening his vision of Paris, Marxism had settled over it like a fog, reducing Benjamin to crude clichés. (For instance, he interpreted Baudelaire's great poem about drunkenness, "The Ragpickers' Wine," as a response to the wine tax.) In a devastating letter, Adorno said that, by using "materialist categories," Benjamin had "denied yourself your boldest and most productive thoughts in a kind of precensorship." Adorno's judgment echoed Scholem's: Benjamin's Marxist vocabulary had betrayed his true insights.

This rejection, coming from a representative of Benjamin's

last remaining sponsor, was a terrible blow. The timing made it even worse: he had worked through the fall of 1938 to finish the essay, believing that war could break out at any moment. "I was in a race against the war," he told Adorno, who was then living in New York, "and in spite of all my choking fear, I felt a feeling of triumph on the day I wrapped up . . . before the end of the world (the fragility of a manuscript!)." Now he was being told that the triumph was illusory, that the Arcades Project could not be written on the terms he proposed. Even if Benjamin had lived long enough, it is doubtful that he could have completed it. The intellectual and ideological basis of the work was in ruins.

In any case, history was not to give him the chance. Despite his friends' attempts to persuade him to emigrate to England or America, Benjamin was still in Paris in the summer of 1940, when the evil he had fled in Berlin caught up with him. The fall of France set the stage for a secular martyrdom that is a large part of his legend. The exact details are disputed, but it seems that, on September 26, 1940, Benjamin was part of a group of refugees trying to cross the Franco-Spanish border at Port Bou. The Spanish border guards, perhaps out of deference to the Gestapo, did not honor their visas and turned them back. In despair and exhaustion, Benjamin took an overdose of morphine. The next morning, the guards relented, and the rest of the party escaped over the border. Only Benjamin, buried in the cemetery at Port Bou, remained as an exemplary victim—a reproach to a Europe intent on murdering its Jews, its radicals, and its best minds.

o o o

Where does hashish fit into this parable of persecuted genius? A reader who turns to *On Hashish* for a clear answer may be disappointed. Like a small-scale version of *The Arcades Project*, it is the placeholder for a book Benjamin could never finish, a ruin occupying the site where he planned a monument, and, as such, it has to be carefully interpreted. This is entirely fitting, since Benjamin himself believed that "all human knowledge, if it can be justified, must take on no other form than that of interpretation."

The most common kind of interpretation, of course, is reading, which provides a metaphor for many activities that have nothing to do with written texts: the fortune-teller "reads" palms, the astrologer "reads" the stars. The intellectual quest that defined Benjamin's work—at times, it seems, the dare that he set himself—was to find out how much of the world could be "read" in this way. In *The Arcades Project*, he made lengthy catalogues of ephemera—advertising posters, shop-window displays, clothing fashions—commenting, "Whoever understands how to read these semaphores would know in advance not only about new currents in the arts but also about new legal codes, wars, and revolutions."

The suspicion that everything in the world carries a hidden message seems to have come to Benjamin at a very young age. *Berlin Childhood Around 1900* is organized as a series of vignettes, each devoted to a thing or a place from his childhood: "The Telephone," "The Sock," "At the Corner of Steglitzer and Genthiner." The result is an eerily depopulated memoir, in which Benjamin's parents are mute presences, and friends are almost entirely absent. Benjamin told Scholem that the project contained "the most precise portrait I shall ever be able to give of myself," yet it is a portrait in which the sitter never appears, his place taken by the objects that surround him.

The effect is not just to make Benjamin seem like a lonely, wary child, though he undoubtedly was. Rather, if Benjamin luxuriates in memories of solitude, sleepiness, and sickness, it is because these unguarded states allowed him to communicate most intimately with the objects around him. "Everything in the courtyard became a sign or hint to me," he writes in the section titled "Loggias." "Many were the messages embedded in the skirmishing of the green roller blinds drawn up high, and many the ominous dispatches that I prudently left unopened in the rattling of the roll-up shutters that came thundering down at dusk."

Benjamin always hoped to turn his powers of reading to even more tempting and obscure kinds of signs—astrology fascinated him—and his willingness to indulge such ideas hints at the metaphysical, even mystical inspiration that is at the heart of all his work, especially his understanding of language. This affinity for the mystical was evident to Scholem, who described Benjamin's work as "an often puzzling juxtaposition of the two modes of thought, the metaphysical-theological and the materialistic," but it is not easy for modern readers to embrace. The theological side of Benjamin's thought remained hidden, during his lifetime and long afterward, in part because he chose to hide it. He never published the seminal 1916 essay "On Language as Such and on the Language of Man," which explicitly set forth his mystical vision of language, or later writings that show its continued hold on his imagination. Only with the publication of the *Selected Writings* did it become possible for English readers to grasp the crucial fact that the "metaphysical-theological" element of Benjamin's thought was older and more profound than the "materialistic" element.

Benjamin's essay "On Language as Such and on the Language of Man" states, "There is no event or thing in either animate or inanimate nature that does not in some way partake of language, for it is the nature of each one to communicate its mental contents." Everything in the world—stars, faces, animals, landscapes—has a meaning, and Benjamin accepts that this implies the existence of a cosmic author. "God," he declares, "made things knowable in their names." Of course, secular reason holds that human languages are purely conventional, but Benjamin would not countenance the idea that words are arbitrary: "It is no longer conceivable, as the bourgeois view of language maintains, that the word has an accidental relation to its object." Instead, he holds that every human language is really a failed and garbled translation of a divine language that speaks in things: "It is the translation of the language of things into that of man."

The vision of language that Benjamin advances here is

moving precisely because it is beyond logical proof, and because it expresses so eloquently his longing for meaning in a world that usually presents itself as mere chaos. This longing drew him, slowly and equivocally, to hashish. In a hashish trance, he hoped, it would be possible to understand the language of things more directly than in ordinary life—to experience a universe suffused with meaning.

By the time Benjamin tried drugs, he had been reading and wondering about them for years, and when the moment finally came, it proved to be a letdown, at least in the philosophical sense. This is not to say that Benjamin did not experience, and enjoy, all the usual effects. He felt mellow. "Boundless goodwill. Falling away of neurotic-obsessive anxiety complexes," he noted during his first attempt. He saw weird visions, such as "a long gallery of suits of armor with no one in them. No heads, but only flames playing around the neck openings." He even got the munchies: "I had been suddenly unable to still the pangs of hunger that overwhelmed me late one night in my room. It seemed advisable to buy a bar of chocolate."

But what Benjamin called "the great hope, desire, yearning to reach—in a state of intoxication—the new, the untouched" remained elusive. When the effects of the drugs wore off, so did the feeling of "having suddenly penetrated, with their help, that most hidden, generally most inaccessible world of surfaces." All that remained were the cryptic comments and gestures recorded in the protocols, the ludicrous corpses of what had seemed vital insights. In a session on April 18, 1931, Fritz Fränkel, a doctor who administered the drug to Benjamin, noted, "Arm and index finger are raised high in the air, without support. The raising of the arm is 'the birth of the kingdom of Armenia.'"

During another trance, Benjamin was very excited to have come up with the phrase "*Wellen schwappen—Wappen schwellen*" ("Waves splash—armorial bearings swell"), claiming that the rhyming words held the clue to a deep structural connection between waves and the designs used in heraldry. "The subject holds forth in learned fashion," Fränkel noted. "'*Quod in imaginibus, est in lingua.*'" Fränkel may have known the meaning of the Latin phrase—"Insofar as it is in images, it is in language"— but he could not have recognized how crucial the notion was to Benjamin's thought, or how tremendously significant the nonsense phrase must have appeared to him. Under the influence of hashish, he felt that names and things belonged together, that a rhyme had revealed a reality.

The tragedy, or perhaps the comedy, was that this insight, the crown of Benjamin's philosophical labor, could not survive the trance that fathered it. In the cold light of the morning after, "*Wellen schwappen—Wappen schwellen*" is a meaningless jingle, and the raising of an arm has no perceptible connection to the kingdom of Armenia. "What we are on the verge of talking about seems infinitely alluring," Benjamin wrote resignedly. "We stretch out our arms full of love, eager to embrace what we have in mind. Scarcely have we touched it, however, than it disillusions us completely. The object of our attention suddenly fades at the touch of language." Hashish, like an evil genie in a fairy tale, granted Benjamin's wish, but guaranteed that he couldn't enjoy it.

What makes *On Hashish* an important book is that Benjamin's drug experiments were not only a failure in themselves, but also shifted the ground beneath his other work, in a way that he never fully acknowledged. The allure of his thought lies in his imagination of a perfected world, in which objects would be redeemed—to use one of his favorite words—from their imprisoning silence. Borrowing from the Jewish tradition, Benjamin sometimes imagined this redemption as messianic; later in his career, he often cast it in Marxist terms, seeing redemption as revolution. He clung to these hopes more and more passionately the more terrifying the world around him became. The last sentence of his last major essay, "Theses on the Philosophy of History"—written in 1940, when Nazism seemed unstoppable— insists that even at the darkest hour redemption remains possible, that every second is "the small gateway in time through which the Messiah might enter."

Hashish, by granting a vision of this redemption in such a compromised and transient form, forces us to confront the likelihood that it was never anything more than a fantasy. If Benjamin discovered a mystic language in his hashish trance, it is because he so fervently wanted to discover it. And something similar holds true for all his messianic speculations. The beguiling complexity of his work, built out of profound insights into language, thought, art, and society, makes it tempting to ignore the difficulty of actually dwelling inside it. After all, if the world is not a text because it does not have an author, then Benjamin is not an interpreter but a poet, creating meanings rather than perceiving them. Ultimately, his strange, beautiful works are best read as fragments of a great poem—the poem of a longing that no world, and Benjamin's least of all, could possibly satisfy.

Alfred Kazin's Clamor

o o o

"As a man is, so he sees. As the eye is formed, such are its pow-ers." Alfred Kazin reveled in William Blake's words in 1944, at the age of twenty-nine, as he stood in the Huntington Library turning the pages of *The Marriage of Heaven and Hell*. When he described this epiphany in *New York Jew*, the third volume of his memoirs, Kazin clearly wanted the reader to be swept up, as he was, by the sovereignty of the Blakean self: "All is within the vaulting leaping mind of man," he continues. "All deities reside within the human breast." But to say that a man sees as he is does not necessarily mean that what he sees is true. What he sees may strike him as lovely because it is made in his own image; but what is not made in his own image he will not be able to see at all. The world, to such a self, may become a prison of mirrors, all of them reflecting the same obsessions, the same cycles of delight and disappointment.

Alfred Kazin's journals, which begin in 1933, when he was seventeen years old, and continue until 1998, the year of his death, are a monument to the literary consequences of such overpow-ering subjectivity. The self on display in these notes is magnifi-cently, ruinously consistent: the voice we hear in the first entry is recognizably the same as the one we hear in the last. It is the

same, above all, in its devout belief in the overwhelming fascination of the self. "Life calls us to nothing more than passionate
and rigorously logical (truthful) introspection," Kazin declares
weeks before his eighteenth birthday. "There is no externality
but the outpourings of the self." Thirty-seven years later Kazin
has learned that introspection can bring torment as well as rapture, but he has not desisted from it: "All this lifetime feeling, all
this long passion of the heart, all this longing—all this anger—
all this bitterness, all this love, all this seeking," he writes in 1970.
"I feel as if I were the site of many storms. Everything keeps
thundering through me."

No reader of Kazin's autobiographies could be entirely surprised by the storminess of his inner weather, as documented
with often painful candor in the *Journals*. *A Walker in the City*, his
extraordinary memoir of growing up in the Jewish tenements
of Brownsville, in Brooklyn, begins with a confession: "Every
time I go back to Brownsville . . . an instant rage comes over
me, mixed with dread and some unexpected tenderness." Rage,
dread, and tenderness are leitmotifs of the *Journals*, too—as are
Jewishness, sexual desire, and literature, the other central subjects
of *A Walker in the City*. Indeed, the great historical value of that
memoir was that it helped to dispel the nostalgia and sentimentality about the immigrant experience that the descendants of
immigrants love to foster. From the perspective of the suburbs,
the ghetto can appear as a place of warmth, but to those who
lived there, Kazin showed, it felt more like fire: "I was always
holding my breath. What I must have felt most about ourselves,
I see now, was that we ourselves were like kindling—that all the
hard-pressed pieces of ourselves and all the hard-used objects in
that kitchen were like so many slivers of wood that might go
up in flames if we came too near the white-blazing filaments in
that naked bulb. Our tension itself was fire, we ourselves were
forever burning—to live, to get down the foreboding in our
souls, to make good."

The life laid bare in the *Journals* is the fated product of this tense, anxious, ambitious childhood. To call Kazin's background parochial would be too ample: it was not a parish he called home, but a single city block. The world was divided into "the block and beyond," and "anything away from the block was good: even a school you never went to, two blocks away." The energy and the ambition of the children raised on that block boiled over into the "scalding . . . hammer blows" of handball games, in voices that "crashed against the walls like a bullet." When the wide world finally opened up, Kazin shot out of Brownsville with the same violence and recklessness. "My aggressiveness has been terrible; my lack of love and understanding has been terrible," he writes in his journal in 1944. "All my life I have lived like a bullet going through walls. I have thought only of my own progress, and in the end there has been no progress, for in my life-long terror, in my never-ending anxieties, I have lived only for myself, so that now I am left only with myself."

Reading such savage self-criticism makes the reader of Kazin's *Journals* uncomfortable, because it is hard to know how to respond: with pity, understanding, impatience? But as the journals progress and the same note of self-hatred is sounded again and again, impatience begins to get the upper hand. It is exasperating to read about a man who never seems to achieve any self-mastery or self-forgiveness—though not a fraction as exasperating as it was to be that man. In 1948: "It takes me violent efforts and ruthless self-urgings to lift myself out of that pit. . . . The chaos in my nature fills me with despair." In 1961: "At least when I write like this, and not in some pompously analytic style like the rest of this fucking notebook, I can say that I feel pain. I feel pain! I'm in pain!" In 1970: "I mustn't dwell on this—or I will take my life, I'm so unhappy." Kazin even predicted how the reader of his journals would react to them: "What will not be forgiven me by the reader of these diaries is my obstinate unhappiness. And quite right. This is what I do not forgive myself. Lord, what a disease, what sentimentality, what rhetoric! What excuse for not living!—Above all, what self-centeredness!"

This passage puts into focus one of the literary problems with Kazin's journals. It is not that Kazin is writing a journal with an eye on future publication—as his comparisons of his own diary with those of Edmund Wilson and André Gide make clear. It is, rather, that the primary audience for the journals is Kazin himself: they are a performance in which author, actor, and audience are the same person. And it is impossible to exhort and chastise oneself in print in an earnest, unselfconscious way.

Here, for instance, is Kazin in 1975: "I nevertheless cry out against all determinism of my condition, and with a free heart opt for joy, for difference, for independence, for fantasy, for love impossible. . . . To be free of my determined condition! An everlasting yea and yea again!!!!" As a proposition, this is strong, with its ardent echoes of Carlyle; as writing, it is awkward and false, because it is not the language of actual consciousness. It is the language of a man admiring himself in the act of making a speech about the beauty of joy, difference, and so on. It is, in a word, rhetoric. And this is the tone of most of Kazin's journals, whether he is in a joyful mood or a wretched one.

Kazin often seems aware that his diary is fundamentally a performance for his own benefit. Contrasting his journals with those of Edmund Wilson, which were being published in the 1960s, he writes, "I notice in all excerpts from Wilson's famous journal that they are set pieces of literary-historical description, formal portraits, essays in miniature. How nice it would be to keep a journal like that, to leave a treasure like that. But so often I turn to this notebook as if it were my private lie detector, my confession, my way of ascertaining authenticity—and recovering it—of making myself whole again." What Kazin does not want to admit is that a journal written in Wilson's style—objectively, frankly, looking outward—is superior in literary terms to a journal written for the audience of the self. Yet he clearly intuits this, as you can see from the way he lashes out defensively at Wilson: "I wonder if E.W., the literary surgeon of the culture-world, ever gets into his journals the incoherence that comes with the honest personal note with so much passion."

This kind of defensiveness is always a mark of literary failure. It is characteristic of a kind of writer who, unable to escape his ego while writing, insists that egotism is a proof of authenticity. James Agee does something similar in the tormented prose of *Let Us Now Praise Famous Men*, and it makes perfect sense that Kazin, in *New York Jew*, writes so warmly about Agee, whom he met when they both worked for Henry Luce in the 1940s: "What I loved most about him was his gift for intoxication. At any given moment he swelled up to the necessary pitch, he made everything in sight seem equally exciting." This is exactly the ideal of Kazin's own prose, too. At moments of high emotion, he "swells up," with a catch in his throat at the beauty of his own feelings:

> the riot in my heart as I saw the cables leap up to the tower, saw those great meshed triangles leap up and up, higher and still higher—Lord my Lord, when will they cease to drive me up with them in their flight?—and then, each line singing out alone the higher it came and nearer, fly flaming into the topmost eyelets of the tower.

Kazin was a seeker after, and a student of, rapture. Whenever he encounters a writer who is less self-delighting, cooler, more objective, his journals suffer painful eruptions of envious self-justification. Saul Bellow is the supreme example. In *New York Jew*, Kazin writes ambivalently about Bellow, acknowledging his genius—"He had pledged himself to a great destiny. He was going to take on more than the rest of us were"—while also criticizing his pride: "He was proud in a laconic way, like an old Jew who feels himself closer to God than anybody else. He could be unbearable in his unresting image of himself."

In the diaries, this ambivalence appears as early as 1950, when Kazin writes: "Why I do not like Saul Bellow, no—au fond, I don't; a *kalte mensch* [cold man], too full of his being a novelist to be a human being writing." Here is the same tactic

Kazin used against Wilson: the suggestion that literary perfection is somehow humanly inferior to his own hot sincerity. But the results—Bellow's books and Kazin's books—suggest that to succeed at being a human being writing, one has to make oneself something less indulgently human, more professional and disciplined: a novelist, or a memoirist, or for that matter, a critic.

It was as a critic that Kazin came to renown after the publication of *On Native Grounds*, his study of modern American literature, in 1942. He published widely, and achieved great cultural authority, over the next four decades; but it is impossible to deny that Kazin is remembered today for his autobiographies more than for his criticism. Indeed, *On Native Grounds* itself probably matters to more readers as an event in the life of Alfred Kazin and his generation of Jewish intellectuals in New York than as a book in its own right. Many young writers must have walked into the New York Public Library on 42nd Street, where Kazin wrote the book in his early twenties, and shared his dreams of glory: "Even the spacious twin reading rooms, each two blocks long, gave me a sense of the powerful amenity that I craved for my own life, a world of power in which my own people had moved about as strangers."

The nature of Kazin's posthumous reputation would probably not have surprised or displeased him. In the journals, he is often frank about his impatience with criticism, his sense that it is not his true métier. As early as 1942, while finishing *On Native Grounds*, he remarks, "I may have come to make too much of criticism—but the truth is that it no longer even begins to satisfy me. When I write criticism, I feel as if only a quarter of my mind . . . were going into it." No wonder he could make no progress on what was supposed to be his next critical work, a study of American literature called *The Western Island*, or that he did not publish another full-length critical study until *An American Procession*, a disappointing book, in 1984. More and more, he realized that what he really wanted from the great American writers was not to interpret them, but "sanctions for my own kind of search. Unless I could find that a Ryder, a Thoreau, a Whitman, a Melville had lived . . . I could not believe that what I sought so doggedly and furtively was real."

Kazin was a critic whose genius shied away from criticism. He was "bored with the objectivity I can muster as a critic . . . for such objectivity does not express itself in continuous feeling and brooding, but has limited aims and ends detached from myself." It is no wonder, then, that he measured himself so irritably against writers who were objective and unselfconscious enough to become critics of genius—Wilson and, above all, Lionel Trilling. It would not be too strong to say that Kazin was obsessed with Trilling. His complaints about him begin in 1951 ("the continuous ache about Lionel and his nervousness with me") and continue until after Trilling's death in 1975. They would culminate in the vicious portrait of Trilling in *New York Jew*, where he is portrayed as an ultracautious careerist, "intent on not diminishing his career by a single word."

At moments in the journals, however, Kazin is able to acknowledge that his running feud with Trilling was one-sided. "Trilling, the pompously respectable professor, is a character in *my* imagination of society, not a person to argue with," he notes in 1966. Indeed, he is only one of a number of writers onto whom Kazin projects his uncomfortable sense that to rise in the world, to become a member of the literary establishment, is a betrayal of his own origins, and of his class and political allegiances. In an entry in 1956, there are other examples: "The 'success-story' for America *does* blunt and dampen all one's fires by its belief in 'happiness' and fulfillment. All those fat Jews—Jason Epstein and my own Richard H[ofstadter] . . . all this represents the death not merely of 'alienation,' but of the vital and fiercely hungry intelligence. . . . We wanted to get *out* of Brownsville, the steerage— and we got into the 'American' business."

Kazin is well aware of the irony that this was written while he was on vacation in Nice, "sitting here on the balcony overlooking the sea." Indeed, the bullet speeding out of Brownsville ended up hitting some lofty targets. "John Chamberlain wrote in the *Times* this morning that I was the only new voice in criticism to come out of the thirties. Who, me?" Kazin writes in 1942. By 1959, he is having lunch with Dag Hammarskjöld at the United Nations: "The view from the 38th floor reminded me of Jesus being shown the mountains of the earth and tempted."

The allusion is a little grandiose—it is not obvious that Kazin was actually being tempted with anything more than lunch—but he is sincere in his conviction that, if he were to forget Brownsville, his right hand would lose its cunning. One May Day, the labor holiday that was celebrated fervently in socialist-communist Brownsville, the middle-aged Kazin finds himself "at a soirée, a real soirée, honest, at the Frankfurters on Park Avenue. . . . Ah nuts, ah soirée, ah poo-poo-nuts," he mutters to his journal.

You can hear in this mock petulance the comic echo of what would become one of Kazin's major preoccupations in the second half of his life: the estrangement of many of his Jewish and intellectual peers from socialism and liberalism. Much (perhaps too much) has been written about the New York intellectuals' journey from left to right, the pilgrimage that started in the Trotskyists' Alcove B in the City College cafeteria during the early 1930s. If Kazin never made that journey, it is largely because, even though he went to City, he was never part of Alcove B and what it stood for—the deft ideological infighting of the communist and ex-communist left. Kazin's interests were always primarily literary; he was a socialist by tradition and instinct, rather than a communist out of conviction and a will to power. "Socialism," he writes in *A Walker in the City*, "would be one long Friday evening around the samovar and the cut-glass bowl laden with nuts and fruits," and later, "Socialism would come to banish my loneliness."

Kazin is smiling at himself in this passage, well aware that nuts and fruits do not make a politics. As early as 1945, he recognizes in his journal that "my own belief in humanist-socialism is only a private ideal; it has no actual political meaning at the moment. But ideals are psychological goals, necessary to the health of the mind." To be on the left was for Kazin less a political philosophy than a token of identity. Naturally, this did not make his emotional investment in liberalism less intense. "It is not their fucking revolution I loved, it was the revolutionaries," he writes in 1959, striking the familiar emotional pitch. "It was not a system, any system; it was man at his bravest, at his most loving, at his most far-reaching. O brave, O more brave, O mighty hearts!"

Having invested his romantic self-image in liberalism, Kazin perceived abandonments of liberalism by his peers as an attack on his identity—just as Trilling's reserve, or Bellow's literary discipline, were implicit rebukes to his own emotionalism and subjectivity. And in politics, just as in literature, the stakes were raised by Kazin's lifelong tendency to cast all questions of identity in terms of fidelity to Jewishness. ("For Trilling I would always be 'too Jewish,' too full of my lower-class experience," he writes in *New York Jew*.)

But Kazin's intense personalization of Jewishness had the effect that he was never able to see it clearly, on its own historical and religious terms. "My autobiography will always be most deeply the autobiography of a Jew," he writes, and while he makes hundreds of attempts in the journals to define Jewishness, he is always drawing only a self-portrait. Often this means advancing the familiar idea that the real Jew is a universalist, a dissident, a moral critic, a prophet: what Kazin calls, in 1957, "the heroic isolation and eternal fightingness of the real Jews, the true Jews, the few Jews." "The Jew wears the great burden of history. . . . and it is a *prophetic* burden," he writes in 1949; the Jewish exemplars are "Yeshua [Jesus] or Marx, Simone Weil."

But few of the Jews Kazin knew growing up in Brownsville, or encountered in literary New York, were of that caliber. Thus, in another familiar turn, the failure of actually existing Jews to live up to the heroic dissidence of the "true Jews" gives rise to an impatience that is hard to distinguish from contempt.

"Every original Jew turns against the Jews—they are the earth from which his spirit tries to free itself," Kazin writes in 1951. "And shall I tell you a secret?" he says a few months later. "I don't feel like a Jew." Meeting with a group of émigré professors at the New School prompts this entry: "The German Jews—each one slightly more grotesque, more Cruikshank-looking than the other. What a race, what a group." At one point, Kazin reaches the conclusion that "Christianity alone does justice to the historic mission of the Jews—that it is only as Christians that Jews can remain Jews." For a moment in 1950, he even seems to be toying with conversion: "I, who am not a Christian, who may become one by the time this journey of reflection is finished, but strongly doubt it," he writes in an entry headed "Easter Sunday."

How seriously are we to take this fantasy of apostasy and release? Kazin's hostile statements about Jews must be taken in the context of his whole career—a career that could not have been more publicly identified with Jewishness. In the privacy of his journals, Kazin feels free to express his moments of frustration and resistance toward his Jewishness, just as he also feels free to express moments of joyous solidarity—for instance, after the Six Day War: "Every day since the Israeli victory in early June, I go to bed thinking: we are not as fit for killing as we were—we can be proud. . . . It is Israel that will keep the flame of Jewish faith alive. What does anything else matter? The Jews will hold—they cannot *but* keep faith. Nothing else matters but that God lives, and that His people know Him—in their own land."

What the reader resists at such moments is not the content of the sentiments but their theatricality. Kazin seems more interested in how it feels to enunciate a lofty sentiment than in its truth or its accuracy, or even whether he actually believes the statement that it excites him to utter. It is notable that, in all the decades of rumination about Judaism that fill the journals, we never see Kazin actually reading a Jewish text, or studying Jewish history. To give Judaism any kind of objective content—to treat it as a historical phenomenon or a body of knowledge, rather than a mystique—would limit Kazin's ability to make grandiose pronouncements about it, whether positive ("A Jew has had experiences that other people simply don't understand or wish to understand") or negative ("Christians, in my experience, are so much more complicated than Jews, so much more at home in the world").

It is not until a trip to Israel in 1970 that he begins to realize the problem: "Somewhere I had come to believe that *Jew* and my *family* were identical. . . . Has the 'Jewish experience' ever meant anything to me outside these relations-identifications?" But the realization doesn't stick: three years later, Kazin is reflecting on "how the State of Israel reminds me of myself, and how myself reminds me of the State of Israel." At such moments, the journals seem less valuable as the record of a life, or of a brilliant, passionate mind, than as a document of a failed pursuit of wisdom—the kind of self-knowledge and knowledge of the world that, ideally, is supposed to come with maturity.

Wisdom seldom comes, of course; but the best writers are those whose works communicate an understanding that may be conspicuously missing from their lives. One reason to be grateful to literature is that it grants an opportunity for self-forgetting and self-transcendence, not to still the inner clamor but to gain a saving, objective, ironic distance from it. "The task," as Kazin recognizes, "is to use our suffering and to use it so well that we can use it up." That is what he does in *A Walker in the City* and *Starting Out in the Thirties*, his enduring books. His journals are made of what's left over.

Susan Sontag's Seriousness

∘ ∘ ∘

It would be hard to find two writers with less in common than Cynthia Ozick and Camille Paglia. Ozick the owl is wise, serious, modernist, and devoted to literature; Paglia the peacock is flashy, provocative, postmodernist, and celebrates pop. Put them in a room together and they would probably have nothing to talk about. Except, perhaps, for one thing: their profoundly ambivalent feelings about Susan Sontag. For as it turns out, both Ozick and Paglia have written essays describing their own private agons with Sontag and everything she represented, especially to other women writers, in the 1960s and 1970s.

Ozick's essay, "On Discord and Desire," was written in response to Sontag's death in 2004, and it begins with a reflection on Sontag's image, as it appeared on "the back cover of my browning paperback copy of *The Benefactor*, [Sontag's] first novel published in 1963, when she was thirty: dark-haired, dark-browed, sublimely perfected in her youth." The image is an appropriate, even inevitable starting place for a consideration of Sontag, not because her image was her main achievement or primary concern, but because so much of her power as a cultural figure came from what she was seen to represent.

As Ozick sees it, when Sontag published her landmark essay

collection *Against Interpretation* in 1966, she fired the first shot in what would become the 1960s revolution in taste and standards. When Sontag declared, "In place of a hermeneutics we need an erotics of art," she issued what sounded to Ozick like a "summons to hedonism" and a "denigration of history." Sontag's name became a battle cry, which stood for "fusion rather than separation, it meant impatience with categories, it meant infinite appetite, it meant the end of the distinction between high and low." And to Ozick, who at the time was laboring away in obscurity in the Bronx, Sontag seemed to speak with all the authority of the *Zeitgeist* itself: "she was the tone of the times, she was the muse of the age, she was one with her century." When Ozick looks at that photo of Sontag, she sees the stylish barbarism of the sixties in a single alluring image.

Turning from Ozick's Sontag to Paglia's Sontag is a weird, *Rashomon*-like experience. For in "Sontag, Bloody Sontag," Paglia's slashing, self-regarding attack, what angers her most about Sontag is precisely her dull, old-fashioned seriousness. Paglia, too, begins by remembering Sontag's "glamorous dust-jacket photo," which "imprinted [her] sexual persona as a new kind of woman writer so indelibly on the mind." But by the time Paglia met her idol, when she arranged for her to speak at Bennington College—an event that turned into a memorable fiasco—she found Sontag a different person than the one she had expected.

Ironically, what infuriated her is that Sontag was not the hedonistic leveler Ozick imagined, and that Paglia herself had admired. "I grew more and more aggravated by her arch indifference to everything she had glorified in *Against Interpretation*," Paglia writes. "Sontag's calculated veering away from popular culture is my gravest charge against her." She was particularly appalled by Sontag's declaration, in a *Time* magazine profile, that she didn't own a television: "Not having a TV is tantamount to saying, 'I know nothing of the time or country in which I live,'" Paglia scoffs.

The strange thing is that Ozick and Paglia were both right about Susan Sontag. At the beginning of her career, she was a revolutionary and a hedonist and a leveler; by the end, she was an elitist and an enforcer of literary and cultural hierarchies. You can see the transformation neatly encapsulated in the paperback edition of *Against Interpretation*, which comes with an afterword Sontag wrote in 1996, on the thirtieth anniversary of the book's publication. In the title essay, the thirty-three-year-old Sontag inveighs against the mind in Blakean terms: "In a culture whose already classical dilemma is the hypertrophy of the intellect at the expense of energy and sensual capability, interpretation is the revenge of the intellect upon art. Even more. It is the revenge of the intellect upon the world. To interpret is to impoverish, to deplete the world—in order to set up a shadow world of 'meanings.'" Instead of meanings, she calls for "transparence," for "new sensory mixes," for sheer experience cut loose from the need to interpret, analyze, and moralize: "A work of art encountered as a work of art is an experience, not a statement or an answer to a question. Art is not only about something; it is something."

Yet in the afterword, the sixty-three-year-old Sontag sounds a Prufrockian note: that is not what she meant, at all. "In writing about what I was discovering," she now realizes, "I assumed the preeminence of the canonical treasures of the past. The transgressions I was applauding seemed altogether salutary, given what I took to be the unimpaired strength of the old taboos." But in fact, those taboos were like a house eaten up by termites, ready to collapse at the first push. "What I didn't understand (I was surely not the right person to understand) was that seriousness itself was in the early stages of losing credibility in the culture at large," Sontag writes in 1996. "Barbarism is one name for what was taking over. Let's use Nietzsche's term: we had entered, really entered, the age of nihilism."

In fact, a close look at the evolution of Sontag's writing shows that it did not take her half a lifetime to start regretting, or at least rethinking, *Against Interpretation*. Take, for instance, the development of her views about Leni Riefenstahl, the director whose films glorifying Nazism are among the greatest works of propaganda ever made. In *Against Interpretation*, Sontag went out of her way to praise these films on aesthetic terms: "To call Leni Riefenstahl's *The Triumph of the Will* and *The Olympiad* masterpieces is not to gloss over Nazi propaganda with aesthetic lenience. The Nazi propaganda is there. But something else is there, too, which we reject at our loss." For a Jewish writer publishing in *Partisan Review*—for decades the Bible of scrupulous antitotalitarians—this was a carefully chosen heresy. It was meant as a concrete example of Sontag's elevation of the aesthetic over the ethical, of "sensory mixes" over what she called, contemptuously, the Matthew Arnold school of moral journalism.

It was an unmistakable recantation, then, when Sontag published the essay "Fascinating Fascism," which is collected in her 1980 volume *Under the Sign of Saturn*. For in this celebrated piece, she writes thoughtfully and indignantly about the rehabilitation of Leni Riefenstahl. She exposes the way Riefenstahl rewrote her CV to minimize her profound Nazi ties, and links her late-life photographic portraits of African tribesmen to her earlier fascist glorification of the body and violent struggle. But most of all, Sontag decries the way Western intellectuals and connoisseurs have been complicit in this rehabilitation. The author of "Notes on Camp" blames this moral dereliction on "the sensibility of camp, which is unfettered by the scruples of high seriousness: and the modern sensibility relies on continuing trade-offs between the formalist approach and camp taste."

More, Sontag detects a subterranean connection between fascism, with its celebration of irrationality and community, and the New Left of the 1960s and 1970s, which valued the same things. Thus "a fair number of young people now prostrating themselves before gurus and submitting to the most grotesquely autocratic discipline are former anti-authoritarians and anti-elitists of the 1960s." By the end of "Fascinating Fascism," Sontag concludes, in a boldly elitist spirit, that when it comes to culture, *quod licet Jovi non licet bovi*:

> Art that seemed eminently worth defending ten years ago, as a minority or adversary taste, no longer seems defensible today, because the ethical and cultural issues it raises have become serious, even dangerous, in a way they were not then. The hard truth is that what is acceptable in elite culture may not be acceptable in mass culture, that tastes which pose only innocuous ethical issues as the property of a minority become corrupting when they become more established.

Indeed, it's possible to see this dilemma—the balancing of the claims of ethics with those of aesthetics—surfacing even earlier in Sontag's career. Her second collection of essays, *Styles of Radical Will*, appeared in 1969, at the height of the sixties turmoil, and probably the best-known piece in it is "What's Happening in America (1966)." This originally took the form of a response to a *Partisan Review* symposium, which served Sontag as a chance to issue a wholehearted attack on America. Most famously, she declared that "the white race is the cancer of human history; it is the white race and it alone—its ideologies and inventions—which eradicates autonomous civilizations wherever it spreads, which has upset the ecological balance of the planet, which now threatens the very existence of life itself." Here Sontag praised the lifestyle experiments she would go on to condemn in "Fascinating Fascism," sympathizing with "the gifted, visionary minority among the young" and "the complex desires of the best of them: to engage and to 'drop out': to be beautiful to look at and touch as well as to be good; to be loving and quiet as well as militant and effective—these desires make sense in our present situation."

Yet even in *Styles of Radical Will*, Sontag is clearly wrestling with her own scruples about the limits of the "new sensibility." This is especially clear in one of the book's best essays, "The Pornographic Imagination." In keeping with the program of *Against Interpretation*, Sontag sets out to argue that pornography should not be too quickly written off as a vulgar or utilitarian genre. The Marquis de Sade and *The Story of O*, she writes, have their own wisdom; they are experiments in spiritual extremity, and have something in common with the ordeals of religion. "The exemplary modern artist," she writes with aphoristic flair, "is a broker in madness."

Yet by the end of the essay, she cannot avoid the question of whether the authenticity and spiritual integrity of pornography make it proper reading, or viewing, for the average sensual man, who is not inclined to put it to such elevated or intellectual purposes. Sontag remains evasive, not yet ready to state forthrightly what she will say in "Fascinating Fascism," but already she recognizes what is at issue: "The question is not whether consciousness or whether knowledge, but the quality of the consciousness and of the knowledge. And that invites consideration of the quality or fineness of the human subject— the most problematic standard of all."

Sontag writes so exigently and intelligently about pornography that it is easy to miss the basic comedy of "The Pornographic Imagination," which is the basic paradox of all her most radical and groundbreaking work. After all, this is a writer who praises the liberating power of porn by turning it into a spiritual and intellectual experiment—that is, by draining it of any sensuality, any genuine transgressiveness. "However fierce may be the outrages the artist perpetrates upon his audience, his credentials and spiritual authority ultimately depend on the audience's sense . . . of the outrages he commits upon himself," Sontag writes, thus shifting the grounds of discussion from pleasure to "spiritual authority" and, direly enough, "credentials."

Credentials, in fact, are an important category of Sontag's thought. The ones that matter to her are not university degrees or professorships—after starting out in academia, she spent her whole career defiantly outside the academic system—but something more profound, if still capable of misuse: seriousness. Indeed, you could learn a lot about Sontag just by following the career of the word "serious" in her work. In "The Aesthetics of Silence," she notes that a writer who stops writing, such as Rimbaud, thereby earns "a certificate of unchallengeable seriousness"; silence is what happens "whenever thought reaches a certain high, excruciating order of complexity and spiritual seriousness." In her essay on Elias Canetti, "Mind as Passion," she praises the way "his work eloquently defends tension, exertion, moral and amoral seriousness." In the introduction to *Reborn*, the first volume of Sontag's diaries, her son David Rieff recounts the story of how her Oxford tutor, the philosopher Stuart Hampshire, once sighed to Sontag: "Oh, you Americans! You're so serious . . . just like the Germans." "He did not mean it as a compliment," Rieff observes, "but my mother wore it as a badge of honor."

What makes *Against Interpretation* Sontag's most important and powerful book is precisely its unconscious, unresolved ambivalence about seriousness. Ozick, taking Sontag's words at face value, saw her as launching an assault on seriousness. But if you pay as much attention to the form as to the substance of the book, it is unmistakable that this attack on seriousness was made with every trapping and intention of seriousness. A person who genuinely believes in the senses over the intellect, in erotics over hermeneutics, does not write long, erudite essays in praise of the senses and publish them in *Partisan Review*. *Against Interpretation* talks about vices in terms that make them virtues, just as Sontag would later do with pornography.

So great is the disconnect in *Against Interpretation* between what Sontag is saying and the way she is saying it, and the people she is saying it to, that this disconnect itself represents its lasting source of interest. The ideas and attitudes Sontag advances in her early work now seem utterly period—they couldn't even keep her interest for long—and the same is true of many of the works she writes about: no one today could feel as reverent toward Godard and Antonioni as Sontag was in 1966. What matters about Sontag now—and this is an evolution typical of many or most critics—is not what she said, but why she said it; not the work, but the person who produced it, and for whom it served certain psychic purposes. Page by page, Sontag's work has mostly lost its power to thrill. What survives, as Ozick and Paglia intuited, is her image, and the tortuous connections between that image and the woman who projected it.

o o o

For that story, the key texts are Sontag's journals, which contain a human drama more fascinating than anything in her essays. The first act of that drama is told in *Reborn*, the first published volume of the journals, which covers the years 1947 to 1963. The second volume, *As Consciousness Is Harnessed to Flesh: Journals and Notebooks, 1964–1980*, takes us through the years of Sontag's greatest celebrity and accomplishment. When the book opens, she is thirty-one years old and the author of a single, not particularly well-received novel, *The Benefactor*. By the time it closes, she has published *Against Interpretation*, *Styles of Radical Will*, *On Photography*, *Illness as Metaphor*, and other books; directed several films; and become famous on two continents. Here is how Sontag sums up her career standing in 1978:

> In every era, there are three teams of writers. The first team: those who have become known, gain "stature," become reference points for their contemporaries writing in the same language. (e.g. Emil Staiger, Edmund Wilson, V. S. Pritchett). The second team: international—those who become reference points for their contemporaries throughout Europe, the Americas, Japan, etc. (e.g. Benjamin). The third team: those who become

reference points for successive generations in many languages (e.g. Kafka). I'm already on the first team, on the verge of being admitted to the second—want only to play on the third.

This entry is noteworthy not only for the guilelessness of its ambition—there is something very American about the notion of literature as a series of farm teams, leading up to the major leagues—but because it is one of the few occasions in the journals when Sontag thinks in such self-conscious terms about her "standing." For the truth is that Sontag spends very little time, in the diaries as edited at any rate, worrying about her career, or about what the public thinks of her. She is far too intent on her own inner experience, on the creation of her self, to care about her image—something that might have surprised Paglia or Ozick, for whom that image seemed so carefully cultivated. And the utter sincerity of the diaries, the sense that Sontag is always able to speak honestly to and about herself, is what makes them such compelling documents.

The first volume of Sontag's diaries is more dramatic than the second, because it covers a more dramatic and formative period in her life. *Reborn* tells the story of a brilliant, enormously ambitious and self-conscious adolescent, who at the age of fifteen sets down a hundred-item reading list for herself, and collects obscure vocabulary words ("effete, noctambulous, perfervid"), and vows to live on a large scale: "I intend to do everything . . . to have one way of evaluating experience—does it cause me pleasure or pain, and I shall be very cautious about rejecting the painful—I shall anticipate pleasure everywhere and find it, too, for it is everywhere!"

The first act of *Reborn* shows Sontag just about to find herself, thanks to the independence she enjoyed at Berkeley, where she started college, and above all to the lesbian society she experienced for the first time there and in San Francisco. For while she was always hesitant to make it part of her public identity as a writer, the diaries show that Sontag knew she was a lesbian from earliest adolescence, if not before. An important part of the "everything" she wanted to do was sexual, and you can feel the excitement and release in her descriptions of her first sexual encounters: "I have always been full of lust—as I am now—but I have always been placing conceptual obstacles in my own path."

Then all at once, and with not a word of explanation in the journals, Sontag swerves off this path and gets married, at the age of just seventeen, to Philip Rieff, her teacher at the University of Chicago, where she transferred for her sophomore year. The ensuing years-long gap in the diaries is a dire signal, suggesting that marriage switched off Sontag's inner life entirely. When the journals resume, it is with a desperate cynicism about marriage that speaks volumes: "Whoever invented marriage was an ingenious tormentor. It is an institution committed to the dulling of the feelings. The whole point of marriage is repetition," Sontag writes in 1956. Even worse, she imagines showing her journals one day to her great-grandchildren: "To be presented to my great grandchildren, on my golden wedding anniversary. 'Great Grandma, you had feelings?' 'Yeh. It was a disease I acquired in adolescence. But I got over it.'"

There is nothing in the journals (as published, at any rate) about the details of Sontag's marriage to Philip Rieff, but details are hardly necessary. Without casting aspersions on Rieff's character, the reader can tell that she has made a horrible mistake, that she should never have entered into this marriage; and the journals only resume when Sontag starts to admit this to herself. This is a sign of how keeping a diary, for Sontag, was not a matter of recording the details of everyday life. The reader of her journals never learns, for example, just how she managed to make a living writing long essays on Barthes and Artaud. Rather, as she writes, "in this journal I do not just express myself more openly than I could do to any person; I create myself. The journal is a vehicle for my sense of selfhood. It represents me as emotionally and spiritually independent. Therefore (alas) it does not simply record my actual, daily life but rather—in many cases—offers an alternative to it."

The title *Reborn* was aptly chosen for the first volume of diaries by David Rieff—the son of Sontag and Philip Rieff, whose feelings about editing and publishing his mother's intimate confessions can only be imagined. For starting in the late 1950s, when Sontag left husband and son in the United States while she went to study at Oxford, she deliberately and ruthlessly gave herself a new birth—essentially, by resuming the life she had glimpsed as a teenager and then given up. We follow Sontag in France, having love affairs with women, reading and thinking and beginning to write, with some of the sense of guilty liberation that she herself must have experienced. This was emphatically a woman's liberation, and *Reborn* deserves to become a classic feminist document, for the way it shows Sontag painfully unlearning the stereotypical role of wife and helpmeet. "I'm not a good person. Say this 20 times a day. I'm not a good person. Sorry, that's the way it is," she adjures herself in 1961.

For Sontag, duty and desire clashed in an especially intricate fashion, as she shows in a diary entry from 1960: "The will. My hypostasizing the will as a separate faculty cuts into my commitment to the truth. To the extent to which I respect my will (when my will and my understanding conflict) I deny my mind. And they have so often been in conflict. This is the basic posture of my life, my fundamental Kantianism." There is a paradox in the way Sontag uses Kant's ideas and vocabulary. According to Kant, reason instructs us about what is good, and the will must be disciplined to carry out the edicts of reason. What Sontag means, however, is just the reverse: for her, the will to do "good"—to be a good wife and mother, by sacrificing her own ambitions— was what had to be resisted, and it was her reason that instructed her to do "wrong," by abandoning her marriage to follow her own path.

The sense that she had to reason herself into defying her

own will is absolutely central to Sontag's early work, especially *Against Interpretation*. Read in the light of the diaries, with knowledge of her own life and emotional state in the early 1960s, it becomes clear why Sontag argued in such intellectualized and dutiful terms against the intellect and duty. She commands the world to an "erotics of art" just as she commanded herself to be faithful to her own erotic nature; she apotheosizes experience at a time when she was in search of all the experiences she had missed. But she does all this in terms that make eroticism a discipline and experience an obligation, in language as rigorously argumentative as she could make it. As she puts it in 1965, in *As Consciousness Is Harnessed to Flesh*, she was "becoming inhuman (committing the inhuman act) in order to become humane." Following the will could only become acceptable to Sontag if the will were commanded by reason, just as Kant had it. One might say that she was a hedonist according to the categorical imperative.

Which is really to say that she was not much of a hedonist. "Not to give up on the new sensibility (Nietzsche, Wittgenstein; Cage; McLuhan) though the old one lies waiting, at hand, like the clothes in my closet each morning when I get up," she warns herself. One of the rare comic moments in *As Consciousness Is Harnessed to Flesh* comes when Sontag is in Tangiers, hanging out with Paul Bowles, and has a revelation about the counterculture. To her, the counterculture was a grand intellectual and aesthetic experiment, a matter of "new sensory mixes." But she now realizes that a large part of what struck her as its strangeness is owed simply to the fact that its adherents were stoned all the time:

> This is what the beat generation is about—from Kerouac to the Living Theatre: all the "attitudes" are easy—they're not gestures of revolt—but natural products of the drugged state-of-mind. But anyone who is with them (or reads them) who isn't stoned naturally interprets them as people with the same mind you have—only insisting on

different things. You don't realize they're somewhere else.

One can imagine Sontag getting stoned only in the same
spirit that Walter Benjamin tried drugs, in order to experiment
with consciousness. Similarly, it becomes clear in the journals
that Sontag supported the sexual revolution not because she
was at ease with eroticism, but precisely because she was not. "I
am so very much more cool, loose, adventurous in work than
in love," she admits to herself. Much of the second volume of
her journals is given over to agonized reflections on failed love
affairs, in which she reproaches herself mockingly for her sexual
incompetence: "Why can't (don't) I say: I'm going to be a sexual
champion? Ha!" Similarly, the Sontag who clued in the *Partisan Review* readership to the excitement of "happenings" can be
found writing: "I feel inauthentic at a party: Protestant-Jewish
demand for unremitting 'seriousness.'"

It was not easy to be so serious. Sontag writes movingly and
very candidly about the way her great intelligence made life and
relationships difficult for her, starting from childhood: "Always
(?) this feeling of being 'too much' for them—a creature from
another planet—so I would try to scale myself down to their size,
so that I could be apprehendable by (lovable by) them." Many
entries, clearly inspired by sessions with a therapist, show Sontag
tunneling down to her early childhood, trying to understand
how her father's early death and her difficult relationship with
her mother conditioned her adult life.

But for Sontag, intelligence and seriousness were far too
integral to her sense of self to be wished away. She is always
prepared to double down on seriousness: "Seriousness is really
a virtue for me, one of the few which I accept existentially and
will emotionally. I love being gay and forgetful, but this only
has meaning against the background imperative of seriousness,"
she writes in 1958.

And in the second volume of journals, she circles around, but never quite reaches, a revelation about "seriousness" that explains many of the flaws of her criticism. Though Sontag announced at the age of five that she was going to win the Nobel Prize, by the 1960s she was worrying, "My mind isn't good enough, isn't really first rate . . . I'm not mad enough, not obsessed enough." (Ironically, Sontag in this vein sounds exactly like Lionel Trilling in his journals—although conscientious old Trilling was Sontag's foil in *Against Interpretation*.) But it was not insufficient madness or obsession that limited Sontag's work as a critic.

Rather, it is her reverent—or, more precisely, her acquisitive—attitude toward seriousness that makes her essays so solemnly, ostentatiously intelligent. "I make an 'idol' of virtue, goodness, sanctity. I corrupt what goodness I have by lusting after it," she writes in 1970. The same could be said of her worship of seriousness: a person who is instinctively sure that she is serious does not spend so much time proving it. Irony and wit, qualities signally absent from Sontag's work, are only possible when seriousness is the premise of one's self-conception, rather than the result that must be achieved.

This explains why so much of what has been written about Sontag after her death paints her as a rather ludicrous figure. In Terry Castle's barbed elegy "Desperately Seeking Susan," or in Sigrid Nunez's short book *Sempre Susan*, Sontag often comes across as hugely self-centered and inadvertently comic—and the best way to be inadvertently comic is to always insist on being, and looking, serious. If Sontag's inner life, as revealed in the diaries, is a moving drama, to other people she evidently seemed more like Dr. Johnson—a figure of massive egotism and unconscious eccentricity. It's too bad that she had no Boswell following her around day after day to put her fully on paper; but even if she had, an outsider could have known only part of the truth about her. The more important parts are to be found in her essays, her novels, and—above all—in her diaries.

The Importance of Being Earnest:
David Foster Wallace

o o o

Today, we think of the 1920s as a golden age of American fiction. But to Edmund Wilson, looking back from the vantage point of 1944, the most striking thing about this modern generation, which he did more than any critic to foster, was its failure to reach full development. The best writers of the twenties, he wrote in "Thoughts on Being Bibliographed," had either "died prematurely . . . leaving a sad sense of work uncompleted," like F. Scott Fitzgerald, or "disconcertingly abandoned their own standards"—here the unnamed culprit is surely Ernest Hemingway, whom Wilson had helped to discover. To us, these are canonical names, predestined for Library of America cursive. So it is helpfully disconcerting to learn that, to Wilson, they seemed to have been canonized prematurely: "men of still-maturing abilities, on the verge of more important things, have suddenly turned up in the role of old masters with the best of their achievement behind them."

At the time Wilson wrote, this particular style of American literary martyrdom was on the verge of obsolescence. After the war, as the center of cultural gravity moved from London and

Paris to New York, and the American university and publishing establishments began their dramatic expansion, the situation of the American writer became very different, and in most material respects much better. Consider the major American novelists who emerged in the 1950s—Bellow, Updike, Mailer. All enjoyed longevity, consistent productivity, and public honor; the disorder of their personal lives was chronic and in some sense stimulating, rather than acute and lethal. In all these respects, they are markedly different from the great writers of the 1920s. And today's leading writers, who are more dependent on the academy for sustenance, seem still further from the old, prodigal, unhappy American career.

Except for David Foster Wallace. Wallace was exceptional in many ways—in the scale of his ambition and achievement, the affection he inspired in readers, the generational significance of his life and death. But the root of this distinction may have been his untimely, unfashionable style of Americanness. Like Sherwood Anderson, Wallace presented himself as a sensitive man at odds with a crass commercial society; like Fitzgerald, he was a collegiate prodigy (his first novel, *The Broom of the System*, started as a senior thesis at Amherst) who achieved fame as the voice of an era; like Hemingway, he was deeply concerned with traditional manliness, and with the ethics of sports and games.

And like all three, he was a self-conscious son of the Midwest. Wallace grew up in Champaign, the son of a philosophy professor at the University of Illinois; but he did not see himself as part of a relatively placeless academic caste. Instead, he fully embraced his origins in America's physical and metaphorical "heartland," and he wrote with a certain trepidation about the big cities of the East. In "A Supposedly Fun Thing I'll Never Do Again," his celebrated essay about taking a luxury cruise, he offhandedly mentions "the way we find even very basic human decency moving if we encounter it in NYC or Boston."

Wallace admitted that it was, in part, the ethnic and racial diversity of the metropolis that made it seem alien to him. "For me, public places on the U.S. East Coast are full of these nasty little moments of racist observation and then internal P.C. backlash," he confesses. As a writer who went to college and entered the literary world in the mid-1980s, during the first flush of multiculturalism and political correctness, Wallace was highly aware of his ambiguous status as a white male. "If all blacks are great dancers and athletes, and all Orientals are smart and identical and industrious, and all Jews are great makers of money and literature, wielders of a clout born of cohesion, and all Latins are great lovers and stiletto-wielders and slippers-past-borders—well then gee, what does that make all plain old American WASPs?" he asks, only half-jokingly, in an early story, "Westward the Course of Empire Takes Its Way."

That title is itself half a joke, borrowed from Berkeley's poem; yet the story, which enacts a complicated homage to and rebellion against John Barth's metafictional classic "Lost in the Funhouse," takes its directional symbolism seriously. Barth lives in and often writes about the Maryland tidewater country, on America's eastern rim. Wallace's story, which describes a group of writing students visiting rural Illinois, explicitly casts the journey west as a movement away from eastern complexity and metafictional jadedness, toward a new birth of naïveté and sentimental directness. This early in his career, Wallace already saw himself as a spokesman for "the forward simplicity of a generation for whom whatever lies behind lies there fouled, soiled, used up. East." Hemingway's Nick Adams, recuperating from war by going fishing on the Big Two-Hearted River, or Fitzgerald's Nick Carraway, returning to "my Middle West" after his corrupting sojourn among the Buchanans and Wolfsheims, would have understood Wallace perfectly.

Certainly, the body of work Wallace left behind is open to the criticism Wilson leveled at those writers—it is precocious, very uneven, at times immature. And Wallace's death by suicide, at the age of forty-six in 2008, has sealed him forever in the catalogue of tragic, "premature" American writers. Yet with

Wallace, too, the faults of his work seem inseparable from the virtues. A more disciplined, tactful writer would not have published a thousand pages of *Infinite Jest*, with all its shaggy-dog repetitions and manic elaborations and half-baked jokes. But then, a shapely, 400-page version of *Infinite Jest* would not have been a cultural sensation or a generational landmark.

Some intelligent readers have declared themselves simply allergic to Wallace's style, unable to cope with all the mannerisms and acronyms and footnotes, the boyish self-conscious earnestness, the sentences that start "And but so now" or "The improbable thing of the whole thing was that." And it's true that Wallace's style is so stylized that it teeters on the edge of self-parody, like Hemingway's. Yet reading a story like "The Depressed Person," which even at thirty pages feels too long, it is undeniable that this feeling of excess, of being trapped in a room with a very intelligent obsessive-compulsive, is exactly the sensation that Wallace wanted to convey. With Wallace, waste is of the essence of the scheme.

The most American thing about Wallace, however, is his conviction that his unhappiness is a specifically American condition. Like many classic American writers but few contemporary ones, he genuinely experienced being American as a bitter, significant fate, a problem that the writer had to unravel for the benefit of his fellow sufferers. In a late story, "The Suffering Channel," Wallace theorizes about "the single great informing conflict of the American psyche," which is "the conflict between the subjective centrality of our own lives versus our awareness of its objective insignificance." All of *Infinite Jest* can be seen as a demonstration of the thesis Wallace advances early in the novel: "American experience seems to suggest that people are virtually unlimited in their need to give themselves away, on various levels."

When Wallace wrote about how difficult it was to be an American, he specifically meant an American of his own generation—the post-sixties cohort known as "Generation X."

"Like most North Americans of his generation," Wallace writes about the teenage hero of *Infinite Jest*, "Hal tends to know way less about why he feels certain ways about the objects and pursuits he's devoted to than he does about the objects and pursuits themselves." Likewise, in "Westward," he writes, "Like many Americans of his generation in this awkwardest of post-Imperial decades . . . Sternberg is deeply ambivalent about being embodied." It is no wonder that readers born between 1965 and 1980 responded to this kind of solicitude, with its implication that they were unique, and uniquely burdened.

What is actually most American and most Generation X about these laments, of course, is their provincialism. For Wallace to find it plausible that "being embodied" or "objective insignificance" were new American problems is as sharp an indictment of American ignorance, in its way, as those polls which are always showing that half of us can't find the U.S. on a map. Except that if any young novelist knew the ancient history of such problems, it should have been Wallace. He was very widely read, and he studied philosophy in college and graduate school; his first novel plays knowingly with Wittgenstein and Derrida. In the introduction to *Fate, Time, and Language*, the posthumous edition of Wallace's senior thesis, his father James remembers reading the *Phaedo* with the fourteen-year-old David: "This was the first time I realized what a phenomenal mind David had."

That short book is both an homage to Wallace's reputation as a philosophical novelist and an attempt to solidify it. As a senior at Amherst, while working on the fiction that would become *The Broom of the System*, Wallace also produced a philosophy thesis, "Richard Taylor's 'Fatalism' and the Semantics of Physical Modality." In challenging Taylor's 1962 paper "Fatalism"—which is reproduced in the book, along with a number of other philosophers' responses to it—Wallace set out to defend our commonsense intuition of free will. This sounds like a big, novelistically fertile subject, and in his introduction, James Ryerson claims that Wallace's early training in philosophy "would play a lasting role in his work and thought, including his ideas about the purpose and possibilities of fiction."

In fact, what *Fate, Time, and Language* demonstrates is not the value of analytic philosophy for literature, but its dramatic inferiority to literature as a way of discussing the most existentially urgent problems. Wallace's paper boils down to the statement that the future can't be fixed before it happens, because it is the future and not the past. But to get to this point, he wends his way through spiny thickets of *modus ponens* and *modus tollens*, demonstrating a mastery of propositional logic so thorough as to make the idiom itself seem facile, even comic.

If there is a continuity between Wallace the undergrad philosopher and Wallace the novelist, it is not in the profundity of his ideas, but in his perfect pitch for all kinds of jargon. One section heading in the paper reads "A Formal Device for Representing and Explaining the Taylor Inequivalence: Features and Implications of the Intensional-Physical-Modality System J." The same teasing relish for professional idioms finds its way into Wallace's writing about pharmaceuticals in *Infinite Jest*, or about lexicography in the essay "Authority and American Usage," or about the tax code in *The Pale King*, his unfinished, posthumously published book.

If Wallace's sense that his own time and place is uniquely afflicted by loneliness and doubt and mortality cannot be ascribed to ignorance, however, it becomes even more significant. For then it must mean that the ways human beings have always addressed these subjects—through philosophy, religion, and literature—have simply lost potency and reality for Wallace, and for the American generation he represents.

There is a revealing exchange on this subject in *Although Of Course You End Up Becoming Yourself*, a book-length transcript of an interview with Wallace conducted by David Lipsky in 1996. Wallace has been denigrating "conventional realistic" fiction, the way "it imposes an order and sense and ease of interpretation on experience that's never there in real life." Lipsky, who is also a novelist, cogently objects that "Tolstoy's books come closer to the way life feels than anybody, and those books couldn't be more conventional." To which Wallace replies with a familiar litany: "Life now is completely different than the way it was then"; "some of it has to do with . . . MTV videos"; "life seems to strobe on and off for me, and to barrage me with input"; "I received five hundred thousand discrete bits of information today."

This kind of phenomenological presentism is itself pretty old by now—at least as old as modernism. But every generation seems fated to discover it again, and for Wallace it served a very useful purpose. It made loneliness and despair not mere existential conditions, but timely "issues"; it allowed him to think of himself as a representative man and a social commentator. In fact, one whole strand of Wallace's work is concerned with diagnosing the cultural causes of his generation's unprecedented anomie. In an influential essay, "E Unibus Pluram: Television and U.S. Fiction," he blames television—not simply in *Bowling Alone* terms, because it physically isolates people and breaks down communal ties, but for the way its massive formulaic stupidity encourages intelligent viewers to develop a defensive irony. "Irony and ridicule are entertaining and effective, and . . . at the same time they are the agents of a great despair and stasis in U.S. culture," Wallace writes.

This argument is translated into fictional terms in the early story "My Appearance," from his 1989 collection *Girl with Curious Hair*. The story concerns a middle-aged, moderately successful TV actress who is making an appearance on David Letterman's talk show. Her challenge is to find a way to communicate sincerely in the face of Letterman's sneering, withering irony, which to Wallace is the epitome of TV-bred cynicism. A friend tells her that the only way to cope is to out-Letterman Letterman: "Laugh in a way that's somehow deadpan. As if you knew from birth that everything is clichéd and hyped and empty and absurd, and that that's just where the fun is."

Wallace dreads this kind of irony, which poisons communication and makes displays of emotion look ridiculous. ("There's never been a time in serious art more hostile to melodrama," he complains to Lipsky.) He dreads it on civic grounds, of course; but he also sees cool knowingness as a deadly threat to his own literary genius, which is essentially sentimental and melodramatic. That is why Wallace is exercised by the ironic self-consciousness of postmodern fiction, in much the same way that he is by David Letterman. John Barth's "Lost in the Funhouse" can hardly be held responsible for "a great stasis and despair in U.S. culture"—for one thing, not enough people have read it. But in "Westward," Wallace offers a novella-length attack on the metafictional gamesmanship of Barth's story: "You want to get laid by somebody that keeps saying 'Here I am, laying you?' Yes? No? No. Sure you don't. I sure don't. It's a cold tease. No heart. Cruel. A story ought to lead you to bed with both hands."

o o o

Wallace is generally described as a cerebral, difficult writer, and sometimes thought of himself that way. Discussing *Infinite Jest* with Lipsky, he said, "I wanted to try to do something that was really hard and avant-garde, but that was fun enough so that it forced the reader to do the work that was required." Yet as time passes, it becomes harder to see why that novel was ever considered difficult or avant-garde. Yes, Wallace rotates through a few different narrators, and leaves some background information unclear, and uses some five-dollar words. But none of this requires more "work" than, say, a movie by David Lynch (whom Wallace admired very much). Certainly, the notorious length of *Infinite Jest* is not a gauntlet thrown to the reader. It feels, rather, like a return to the spaciousness of Dickens and Balzac, its bulk a product of repetition and detail and the multiplication of characters. These are all techniques of readerly seduction and immersion, ways of "leading you to bed with both hands."

Infinite Jest is written on the pleasure principle: that is its strength and its weakness. Wallace's sheer joy in writing is responsible for what he calls in the novel itself "the aleatory flutter of uncontrolled, metastatic growth." It is full of catalogues, stories within stories, invented idioms, and elaborate anecdotes about characters who appear only once. His use of footnotes, one of the most recognizable elements of his style, is a way of making more room for irrelevant digressions, the way a hoarder might build a second story on his house.

One footnote in *Infinite Jest* offers the filmography of an invented director, listing dozens of movies Wallace describes even though they never feature in the novel at all; it runs to eight pages of small print. Elsewhere, Wallace describes a school party at which all the students are encouraged to wear funny hats. This is supplemented by a footnote listing the kind of funny hat worn by every attendee: "Troeltsch wears an InterLace Sports baseball cap, and Keith Freer a two-horned operatic Viking helmet along with his leather vest, and Fran Unwin a fez," and so on. In the introduction to *The Pale King*, Michael Pietsch, Wallace's editor, mentions that he referred to his first drafts as "freewriting," and this term perfectly captures the self-delighting excess of much of *Infinite Jest*.

Yet *Infinite Jest* is also an attack on the pleasure principle. The main plot concerns a movie that is so entertaining it reduces everyone who sees it to a catatonic stupor. Wallace offers several installments of a dialogue between a Québécois terrorist, Marathe, whose colleagues want to acquire the movie and use it as a weapon against the United States, and an American spy, Steeply, who is trying to outwit the terrorists and find the movie first. It's typical of the novel that this dialogue is at once totally slapstick—Steeply wears ill-fitting drag, Marathe speaks mangled, Frenchified English, and the whole conversation takes place on a narrow ledge on a mountainside in the Arizona desert—and didactically earnest. Marathe argues that the only reason America fears "the Entertainment," as it's called, is that the country has lost its willpower, its character:

"Now is what has happened when a people choose
nothing over themselves to love, each one. A
U.S.A. that would die—and let its children die,
each one—for the so-called perfect Entertainment, this film. Who would die for this chance
to be fed this death of pleasure with spoons...can
such a U.S.A. hope to survive for a much longer
time? To survive as a nation of peoples? To much
less exercise dominion over other nations of other
peoples? If these are other peoples who still know
what it is to choose? Who will die for something
larger?"

This line of argument, comical as it is coming from a French
Canadian—the very idea of a dangerous Canadian is a gag, to an
American—sounds more formidable when it comes from, say,
an Islamic jihadist. (Shortly after September 11, an Afghan *muja-
hideen* was widely quoted as saying "The Americans love Pepsi
Cola, but we love death," which is more or less Marathe's point.)
Wallace sharpens the indictment of American hedonism by setting half of *Infinite Jest* in the world of twelve-step programs and
halfway houses. How much must people be suffering, Wallace
asks, if they are willing to destroy their lives and court death in
order to temporarily blot out consciousness?

The name of the movie that entertains to the point of
killing is *Infinite Jest*, and Wallace means us to see the parallel
between it and the novel, which is itself a literary overdose.
Can reading—or, more to the point, can writing—be a kind
of drug, a distraction from an otherwise insufferable existence?
Is it possible to be addicted to writing? There's no avoiding
the question in a book that is so knowledgeable and convincing about the dynamics of addiction—the way suffering leads
to excess, which compounds suffering, until it is impossible
either to go on taking Substances (Wallace's term) or to stop.

In Alcoholics Anonymous, Wallace insists, it is the most intelligent, articulate addicts who have it hardest: "They identify their whole selves with their head, and the Disease makes its command headquarters in the head."

Inevitably, we read Wallace now with the knowledge that he committed suicide, after a lifelong struggle with depression. Talking to Lipsky, he took pains to hide the facts of his illness: he insisted "I'm not biochemically depressed," and specifically denied that he took antidepressants. In fact, according to posthumous articles by D. T. Max, Jonathan Franzen, and others, Wallace took the antidepressant Nardil for almost two decades, and it was his attempt to go off the drug that precipitated his final depression and suicide. No reader of his fiction, however, could have been convinced by Wallace's denials, as Lipsky clearly wasn't. There are just too many characters in his books who share the experience of Kate Gompert, from *Infinite Jest*, whom we first meet in a mental hospital after a suicide attempt: "I wanted to just stop being conscious . . . I wanted to stop feeling this way."

What would it be like to inhabit such a suffering consciousness, without muffling it in a thousand pages of voluble prose? *Brief Interviews with Hideous Men*, the book Wallace published after *Infinite Jest*, is his devastating answer. The book consists of a number of stories, interwoven with "transcripts" of the titular interviews, from which the questions have been deleted. Both stories and interviews show that Wallace's truest subject as a writer, the one that provoked his most moving and convincing work, was the sickness of the will. Again and again, he creates characters intelligent enough to anticipate every one of their own thoughts and reactions, even the most destructive and dysfunctional, but who lack the will to change them. The maddening self-consciousness and hyperarticulacy that sometimes seem like mere tics of Wallace's prose become, in *Brief Interviews*, the absolutely faithful reflection of a consciousness that knows itself too well, and is disgusted by what it knows.

The ultimate case study here is "The Depressed Person," in

which we see how a woman's unbearable suffering—"depression's terrible unceasing agony itself, an agony that was the overriding and unendurable reality of her every black minute on earth"— makes her unbearably self-obsessed. This, in turn, renders her deeply unsympathetic, not just to the friends who abandon her, but to herself, so that self-hatred is added to unhappiness. It is a spiral or Moebius strip of misery, and a genuinely Dostoevskyan performance. Behind the Depressed Person we hear another eloquently damned soul, the Underground Man, who also suffers from the gap between reason and will, between knowing what's wrong with you and being able to repair it.

o o o

"Standard therapy [is] such a waste of time for people like us—they thought that diagnosis was the same as cure. That if you knew why, you would stop. Which is bullshit." So says Meredith Rand, one of the half-dozen IRS agents who emerge as major characters in the incomplete drafts and notes of Wallace's last novel, published as *The Pale King*. Other prominent voices in the plotless chorus include Lane Dean, Jr., who takes a job at the IRS after getting his high-school girlfriend pregnant; Claude Sylvanshine, a hapless underling whose career has stalled at a low pay-grade; Toni Ware, whose violent childhood is narrated in a florid style that reads like a parody of Cormac McCarthy; and, most significant, Chris Fogle, who describes his work as an auditor as a kind of religious vocation.

And then there is "David Wallace" himself, who addresses us directly in a few passages. *The Pale King* was apparently meant to be cast as Wallace's own "vocational memoir," a description of the year he spent working for the IRS in the mid-1980s, after being suspended from college for running a term-paper mill. Of course, the real Wallace never worked for the IRS, and it is a little dispiriting to see him still toying with metafictional tricks—all the more so when he teasingly disavows those tricks even as he plays them: "Please know that I find these sorts of cute, self-referential paradoxes irksome too—at least now that I'm over thirty I do—and that the very last thing this book is is some kind of clever metafictional titty-pincher." The awkwardness of the "David Wallace" passages in *The Pale King* are indicative of the difficulty Wallace had finding the right way to frame the subject. Indeed, it seems clear from the book as we have it that Wallace chose the IRS as a subject without knowing quite how to write about it, or what stories he wanted to tell.

Why pick such an unpromising subject, and stick with it through years of frustration? (Pietsch writes that Wallace "described working on the novel as like wrestling sheets of balsa wood in a high wind.") A clue to the answer can be found in a question Wallace asked in *Infinite Jest:* "Why is the truth usually not just un- but anti-interesting?" In that excessively interesting book, the interesting is always suspect. Substances are interesting, the Entertainment is interesting, because they distract a mind that would otherwise tear itself apart; but they only distract, they do not really fulfill or heal.

As an alternative, Wallace offers two images of genuine fulfillment: the utter athletic discipline of the young players at Enfield Tennis Academy, and the utter spiritual surrender of the recovering addicts at Ennet House. In both cases, Wallace is explicit that the key to happiness is the relinquishing of consciousness. The AA slogan is "my best thinking got me here," while at E.T.A., "the program . . . is supposedly a progression toward self-forgetting," in which the player abandons all thought of fame and victory, concentrating solely on the game itself. In both cases, serenity comes not from the frenzied quest for new sources of stimulation, but from a quasi-Buddhist acceptance of everything that occurs.

This is the Nirvana attained by Don Gately, a recovering addict who is in the hospital for a gunshot wound but refuses to accept any kind of narcotic, lest he jeopardize his sobriety. In the novel's last hundred pages, Gately overcomes his pain by recognizing that "everything unendurable was in the head, was the head not Abiding in the Present but hopping the wall and doing a recon and then returning with unendurable news you then somehow believed."

But if the interesting is the delusive, addictive *maya* of this world, then the boring and unpleasant is what is really real; and the token of mental wholeness, of adult sobriety, is the ability to cope with unrelieved boredom. That is why *The Pale King* had to be a novel about the IRS. For what is more boring and repellent than the tax code, or more notoriously inevitable? "The whole subject of tax policy and administration is dull. Massively, spectacularly dull," says "David Wallace." But he suggests that it would be a sign of weakness to ignore it simply because it is dull:

> To me, at least in retrospect, the really interesting question is why dullness proves to be such a powerful impediment to attention. . . . Maybe dullness is associated with psychic pain because something that's dull or opaque fails to provide enough stimulation to distract people from some other, deeper type of pain that is always there, if only in an ambient low-level way, and which most of us spend nearly all our time and energy trying to distract ourselves from feeling, or at least from feeling directly with our full attention.

The Pale King is Wallace's attempt to find out if fiction can sustain this kind of attention to boring, banal reality, without contracting into the solipsistic fugues of *Brief Interviews*, or expanding into the manic inventions of *Infinite Jest*. In fact, Wallace only occasionally tries to make his book itself rebarbatively dull—to enact the boredom he writes about. There are several passages of tax jargon, and a long description of a traffic jam (which doubles down on dullness by turning into a discussion of the failure of the municipal bond issue that could have expanded the jammed road). Most notably, there is a three-page section, printed in double columns like a dictionary or Bible, describing a room full of tax-form examiners at work: "Chris Fogle turns a page. Howard Cardwell turns a page. Ken Wax turns a page. Matt Redgate turns a page." This is Wallace's stab at evoking the routine that leads Lane Dean, for one, to think of his job as a foretaste of hell:

> He felt in a position to say he knew now that hell had nothing to do with fires or frozen troops. Lock a fellow in a windowless room to perform rote tasks just tricky enough to make him have to think, but still rote, tasks involving numbers that connected to nothing he'd ever see or care about, a stack of tasks that never went down, and nail a clock to the wall where he can see it, and just leave the man there to his mind's own devices.

A genuinely avant-garde or experimental writer might have tried to compose a whole novel out of those double columns. But Wallace was not that kind of writer. Too generous and warm-hearted to torment the reader, what he really wanted was to delight and instruct—above all, in his last years, to instruct. For *The Pale King* belongs in a series of late works in which Wallace was grappling with the idea of authority, and tentatively trying on the role of an authority figure. (And how terrible to have to use the word "late" for things written in his early forties.)

In 2000, Wallace covered John McCain's presidential campaign for *Rolling Stone*. The resulting essay—"Up, Simba!" in *Consider the Lobster*—celebrates a very traditional ideal of masculine stoicism and honor: "The fact is that John McCain is a genuine hero because of not what he did but what he suffered—voluntarily, for a Code. That gives him the moral authority both to utter lines about causes beyond self-interest and to expect us, even in this age of spin and lawyerly cunning, to believe he means them." Wallace found a different kind of authority in Bryan Garner, whose *Dictionary of Modern American Usage* he writes about in "Authority and American Usage." "America is in a protracted Crisis of Authority in matters of usage," he observes. But Garner, whose work Wallace praises inordinately, strikes him as a model of democratic authority, based not on coercion but on rational consent: "in the absence of unquestioned, capital-A authority in language, the reader must now be moved or persuaded to grant a dictionary its authority, freely and for what appear to be good reasons."

In the introduction to *Fate, Time, and Language*, James Ryerson suggests that Wallace was a philosophical novelist in the tradition of Voltaire and Sartre. Perhaps the best reason for denying this is that Wallace did not seem to recognize that the problem he had discovered was Kant's problem, and that his solution was Kant's solution. The only valid laws are the ones we legislate for ourselves, in accordance with the dictates of reason: this is the key to moral autonomy, and in *The Pale King*, it is the definition of adulthood.

In the words of Chris Fogle, the most significant character in the book, "If I wanted to matter—even just to myself—I would have to be less free, by deciding to choose in some kind of definite way. Even if it was nothing more than an act of will." Fogle's story seems to express Wallace's deepest intention in writing about the IRS, and his most heartfelt counsel to his readers. It is explicitly cast as a conversion testimony: once a layabout, a stoner, a self-described "wastoid," Fogle is born again as a mature, disciplined adult, a worthy heir of the father he was always disappointing.

His moment of grace comes when he accidentally stumbles into an Advanced Tax course at his college, and hears what amounts to a sermon, from a professor whom Fogle believes is a Jesuit (though he turns out not to be). Punning bluntly on the notions of "calling" and "accounting," the teacher tells the students that they are "called to account." The CPA is commercial society's indispensable man, its quiet hero: "I wish to inform you that the accounting profession to which you aspire is, in fact, heroic. . . . Enduring tedium over real time in a confined space is what real courage is."

Wallace peppers *The Pale King* with a number of surreal, invented details about the IRS, including its alleged Latin motto, *"Alicui tamen faciendum est"*—roughly, "Anyway, someone has to do it." And in this book, the ones who step up, who attend to the tedious business of life, are defiantly archaic authority figures. They are midwestern patriarchs, men in gray flannel suits ("like so many men of his generation, his body almost seemed designed to fill out and support a suit," Fogle says about his father), and earnest Christians—types that seldom appear in pop culture (or literary fiction) except as figures of fun. In one section of *The Pale King*, Lane Dean decides not to pressure his girlfriend to get an abortion, but to marry her instead, even though he doesn't love her. He makes this decision by asking, literally, what Jesus would do, and you can sense Wallace daring you to roll to your eyes.

Such nostalgia for a vanished style of religious and patriarchal authority is a familiar part of conservative political discourse. And while all the voices we hear in *The Pale King* are personae, not the author himself, Wallace takes obvious pleasure in rehearsing a number of conservative tropes, which he knows many readers will find provocative. Hostility to the 1960s has been a constant in his work, dating back to the early story "Lyndon," which displays a surprising sympathy for LBJ in his contest with antiwar protestors. In *The Pale King*, Chris Fogle's mother is a victim of the 1960s: drunk on women's lib, she impetuously divorces her dutiful husband, becomes a lesbian, and opens a feminist bookstore called Speculum Books with her lover Joyce. Once Fogle's father dies, however, she is consumed with remorse for her flightiness, and moves back into the marital home. In a vindictive touch, Joyce ends up getting married to a man and becoming a suburban housewife in Wilmette. See what happens when consciousness-raising gets out of hand?

Other characters in this polyphonic book say things like "the sixties were America's starting to decline into decadence and selfish individualism—the Me generation," and talk about the sacredness of the Constitution and the Federalist Papers. Even "David Wallace" describes the invention of rolling luggage carts as "the sort of abrupt ingenious advance that makes entrepreneurial capitalism such an exciting system—it gives people incentive to make things more efficient." Meanwhile, the Advanced Tax instructor scoffs at Karl Marx's vision of a society in which a man can "hunt in the morning, fish in the afternoon, rear cattle in the evening, criticize after dinner, just as I please." Doing just what you please, for Wallace, is the fatal freedom that leads to anomie and despair.

The problem with Wallace's cultural nostalgia is not so much the sentiment behind it, which is genuine and partly admirable, as the danger of patness, and the edge of nastiness. But while some passages of *The Pale King* feel complacent, others suggest that Wallace was aware of this danger, and intended to put his central conceit under some ironic pressure. To Chris Fogle, the IRS is "the Service," and joining it is like joining the priesthood or the Marines. But "David Wallace," who arrives at the Peoria office and is mistaken for a much higher-ranked IRS employee of the same name, gets to see that the Service is actually full of sinister bureaucratic slapstick, of the kind that Kafka evokes in *The Castle*. Again, Fogle yearns to be like his father, but Lane Dean is shown regretting his decision to assume the responsibilities of fatherhood and adulthood so soon.

All of this suggests, once again, that Wallace had not yet imagined his way to a satisfying treatment of the themes he wanted to address in *The Pale King*. Above all, he had not resolved the tension at the heart of the project, the problem of how to write an interesting book about boredom. This becomes especially clear in the last major episode in the book, when Meredith

Rand describes her experience of mental illness to a fellow auditor, Shane Drinion. Drinion is a perfect IRS employee because he is, evidently, an Asperger's type, devoid of social instincts but capable of intense, narrow focus. In one of the brief "Notes and Asides" at the end of the volume, Wallace describes Drinion as "*happy*":

> It turns out that bliss—a second-by-second joy + gratitude at the gift of being alive, conscious— lies on the other side of crushing, crushing boredom. Pay close attention to the most tedious thing you can find (tax returns, televised golf) and, in waves, a boredom like you've never known will wash over you and just about kill you. Ride these out, and it's like stepping from black and white into color. Like water after days in the desert. Constant bliss in every atom.

The way Wallace tries to dramatize this bliss is by having Drinion, at the moment of total focus, literally levitate: while listening to Meredith Rand's story, he starts to rise out of his chair. But this is "interesting" in exactly the style of *Infinite Jest*, with its unyielding liveliness and cartoon mobility—that is, it is interesting in the way *The Pale King* itself distrusts. When Wallace died, the book shows, he was still in the middle of the ordeal of purging and remaking his style. This is the kind of challenge only the best writers set themselves. One of the many things to mourn about Wallace's death is that we will never get to know the writer he was striving to become.

The Lesson of the Master:
Cynthia Ozick

∘ ∘ ∘

There is no swarming like that of Israel when once
Israel has got a start, and the scene here bristled,
at every step, with the signs and sounds, immiti-
gable, unmistakable, of a Jewry that had burst all
bounds. . . . It was as if we had been thus, in the
crowded, hustled roadway, where multiplication,
multiplication of everything, was the dominant
note, at the bottom of some vast sallow aquar-
ium in which innumerable fish, of over-developed
proboscis, were to bump together, for ever, amid
heaped spoils of the sea.

The author of this description hardly needs to be named: no
writer signs his prose quite like Henry James, and even when
confronted with the shock of the Lower East Side circa 1905,
his adjectives and clauses keep their meticulous fluency. Only
the joke about noses sounds, in its obviousness and crudity, like
a betrayal of the James we know from the novels. Indeed, the

refinement of James's prose, in this section of *The American Scene*, is integral to his argument, which is that the appearance of a "New Jerusalem" in the streets of New York is not primarily a racial or social threat, but a literary and linguistic one. "It was in the light of letters, that is in the light of our language as literature has hitherto known it, that one stared at this all-unconscious impudence of the agency of future ravage," James continues. In their very intimacy with the American language, he predicts, Jews will "torture" it out of recognition. Eventually, "we shall not know it for English—in any sense for which there is an existing literary measure."

Finally, the immigrant Jews, who have earlier been compared to fish and to "snakes or worms ... who, when cut into pieces, wriggle away contentedly," take on the image of a more dignified and threatening reptile. They are a dragon, James writes, like the one that fought St. George; and the saint, in this comparison, is played by the American man of letters, who "sits astride of the consecrated English tradition, to his mind, quite as old knighthood astride of its caparisoned charger."

Cynthia Ozick's career-long *agon* with Henry James—which reaches a kind of culmination in *Foreign Bodies*, her polemical rewriting of *The Ambassadors*—cannot be fully understood except in the light of this famous passage. Ozick may be the last in the illustrious line of writers whose complicated engagement with James helped to define, not just American Jewish fiction, but the American conception of modernism itself. For the stark, often-noted irony is that it was precisely the children and grandchildren of those immigrant Jews, with their dragonish Yiddish accents, who did most to secure James's place at the center of the modernist canon. In the 1930s, when James's alleged snobbishness and escapism made him the favorite target of both left-wing and all-American critics, it was the intellectuals at *Partisan Review* who insisted on defending the Master. They taught readers to appreciate not just his prose style, but his insights into art, society, and evil. And it was Leon Edel—an

American Jew born in 1907, just two years after James's *American Scene* trip, though not in New York—who devoted his life to writing James's biography.

Ozick, who was born in 1928 and has spent most of her life in the Bronx and environs, represents one of our last links to that mid-century New York intellectual milieu. (Her sense of having survived into a different, and worse, literary era is pervasive in her later essays.) And the chief inheritance she preserves from that earlier time is its reverence for modernism. For Ozick, modernism does not mean demotic fracture—as it did to its first, appalled or delighted audiences—but supreme authority. "Joyce, Mann, Eliot, Proust, Conrad (even with his furies): they knew," she writes. "And what they knew was that—though things fall apart—the artist is whole, consummate. At bottom, in the deepest brain, rested the supreme serenity and masterly confidence of the sovereign maker."

The sovereign of sovereigns, for Ozick, has always been the Master. Only James is immune to the obsolescence that other modernists—notably, T. S. Eliot—have undergone, she writes in "What Henry James Knew": "In the ripened Henry James, and in him almost alone, the sensation of mysteriousness does not attenuate; it thickens. As the years accumulate James becomes, more and more compellingly, our contemporary, our urgency." Yet Ozick's own relationship with James has always been a difficult one, oscillating between imitative reverence and ferocious repudiation. She has, in fact, made her mixed feelings about James one of the central myths of her work, writing about him again and again. There has seldom been a more self-conscious case of the anxiety of influence.

In the beginning, Ozick says, she was simply James's slave. She wrote her master's thesis on "Parable in Henry James," then left academia in order to write fiction that was meant to channel James's. "Gradually but compellingly," she recalls in her essay "The Lesson of the Master," "I became Henry James. . . . When I say I 'became' Henry James, you must understand this: though

I was a nearsighted twenty-two-year-old young woman infected with the commonplace intention of writing a novel, I was also the elderly bald-headed Henry James. Even without close examination, you could see the light glancing off my pate; you could see my heavy chin, my watch chain, my walking stick, my tender paunch."

This is comedy, but it is also a kind of horror—indeed, it could be a horror story by Henry James, one of his parables of mastership and impersonation. And Ozick cannot repress a sense of horror, and of abiding anger, at the toll her James-worship exacted from her. For many years, she failed to publish or even finish her projected novels; her friends outpaced her, her rivals didn't even know she existed. "All around me writers of my generation were publishing. I was not," she writes in "Henry James, Tolstoy, and My First Novel." "I held it as an article of faith that if you had not attained print by twenty-five, you were inexorably marked by a scarlet F—for Folly, for Futility, for Failure. It was a wretched and envious time." One of her best essays, "Alfred Chester's Wig," turns on the tortoise-and-hare competition between her and the now-forgotten writer Alfred Chester, her NYU classmate. In the late 1940s, Ozick writes, Chester went to Paris and "was well into the beginnings of an international reputation—he was brilliantly in the world—while I . . . had nothing of the literary life but my trips on the bus to the Westchester Square Public Library."

The climax of Ozick's early James-worship, and its fiasco, was the publication of her first novel, *Trust*, in 1966. After two decades, she had finally come out with the big, ambitious, immaculately literary novel she dreamed of—and it was inert, virtually dead on arrival. (It is, among other things, perhaps the only book published in 1966 that unselfconsciously uses the word "withal": "Even his haircut had a vaguely shaggy air, so that he emerged, withal, a wonderful bison.") A paperback edition of *Trust* is still in print, all these years later, but Ozick continues to speak of it with the defensiveness of wounded pride.

In a 2004 interview, she joked, "I will have struck a gold medal, for anybody who can give me evidence that they actually finished this book."

The failure of *Trust* also represented, for Ozick, the failure of Henry James. While writing it, she recalled, "I kept on my writing table . . . a copy of *The Ambassadors*, as a kind of talisman," but the talisman had brought bad luck. Other writers might have been silenced by such a disappointment after so many years of expectation, or at least refused to talk about it. If Ozick, on the contrary, has made it central to her personal myth, returning to it in essay and memoir, the reason is that she relishes the double irony involved. The first irony is that it was the wreck of her early worship of literature, and of James, that released the energies—the ruthless, angry, often satirical energies—of her great stories of the 1970s and 1980s. The second irony is that her Jamesian error—her attempt to *become* Henry James—was itself a supremely Jamesian error—the kind of mistake James cautioned against in some of his most famous stories.

It is out of this recognition that Ozick titled her confessional essay after *The Lesson of the Master*. That is the story of James's in which a young writer, Paul Overt, befriends a successful older writer, Henry St. George, whose best work is long behind him. The reason, St. George tells his disciple, is that he gave in to the temptations of the world—he married, had children, yearned for social status, and so had to write for money. Heeding this advice, Overt decides to give up Miss Fancourt, the woman he hopes to marry, and goes abroad for two years to finish writing his next book. When he returns, however, it is to discover that St. George, whose wife has died in the interim, has swooped in and married Miss Fancourt himself. By blindly submitting to the older writer's authority, Overt realizes, he has allowed himself to be deceived, neutered, cuckolded. The parallels with Ozick's own situation were clear to her: "Trusting in James, believing, like Paul Overt, in the overtness of the Jamesian lesson, I chose Art, and ended by blaming Henry James."

o o o

In 1971, five years after *Trust*, Ozick published *The Pagan Rabbi and Other Stories*. In the title alone, two major course corrections are announced. After investing so much effort in one massive novel, Ozick became in the next decade a writer of stories—this first collection was followed by *Bloodshed and Three Novellas* (1976) and *Levitation: Five Fictions* (1982). The shift was partly inspired, she wrote, by reading the stories of Frank O'Connor, which offered an appealing alternative to the "style both 'mandarin' and 'lapidary'" of *Trust*: "how simple, how human, how comely and homely!" Ozick's own stories are none of those things—they are complex, ghost-ridden, and allegorical—but the new genre did release her genius. Ever since, shorter or longer stories have been the mainstay of Ozick's fiction. Not until 2004's *Heir to the Glimmering World* did she produce another full-length novel.

At the same time, *The Pagan Rabbi* marked an intense new engagement with the subject of Jewishness. Even in *Trust*, Ozick was exploring Jewish subjects, especially the Holocaust, and the novel ends with a major character, Enoch Vand, taking lessons in Hebrew from a Holocaust survivor ("the number tattooed on Enoch's teacher's forearm was daily covered by phylacteries"). Starting with *The Pagan Rabbi*, however, Ozick became an emphatically Jewish writer, and in a way that was quite unusual for that golden age of American Jewish fiction. It's not just that Ozick stopped writing about characters named Enoch Vand and Nicholas Gustave Tilbeck, and started writing about characters named Kornfeld, Edelshtein, and Bleilip. Saul Bellow had done as much long before, and the influence of Bellow seems to have helped drive out the influence of James at this stage of Ozick's writing.

But Ozick is quite different from Bellow in the way she treats Jewishness in her fiction. For Bellow, Jewishness is a condition of experience: in writing about his childhood, for instance, he is inevitably writing about an immigrant Jewish world. His boldness lay in declining to see this as a literary disadvantage, in the metaphysical self-confidence that allowed him to embrace every detail of his own experience as universally significant. (This is, of course, a very American, Emersonian kind of confidence.) He was so certain he belonged to English literature that he never worried English literature might not belong to him; to return to James's metaphor, he was already St. George, so he couldn't possibly be the dragon.

With Ozick, things are different and less comfortable. Starting with *The Pagan Rabbi*, she begins to experiment with the idea that James's metaphor might actually be correct—that there really is a necessary friction between being Jewish and being an English writer. This is not, however, because the Jew is incapable of mastering pure literary English. As a living refutation of that idea, Ozick couldn't possibly entertain it herself. Indeed, in her essay "The Question of Our Speech," she pounces on another instance of James's linguistic snobbery—a speech he delivered at Bryn Mawr, lamenting the way "our quickly assimilated foreign brothers and sisters . . . dump their mountain of promiscuous material" into the American language. Ozick remarks that the novelist had, ironically, forgotten about the power of imagination, which allows immigrants to enter into a seemingly foreign literary tradition. She instances her own mother, an immigrant child who memorized "The Lady of the Lake" and never forgot it until she died.

If writing fiction is somehow forbidden to Jews, Ozick now proposes, it is not because Jews can't do it, but because they shouldn't. And they shouldn't because, seen in a certain light, literary imagination is a double sin against Jewish law: it is both a form of lying and a form of idolatry. "An idol is a thing-that-subsists-for-its-own-sake-without-a-history; significantly, that is also what a poem is," Ozick writes. She puts the idea into parable form in "The Pagan Rabbi," where a pious Jew, Isaac Kornfeld, takes his first step toward damnation simply by beginning to appreciate beauty in the natural world. From noticing brooks and flowers, he soon moves to worshiping them—that is, to paganism; and from there it is a short step to falling in love with an actual wood-nymph or dryad. Kornfeld goes so far as to have sex with this spirit—"Scripture does not forbid sodomy with the plants," he observes—before he ends up committing suicide.

A less subtle writer than Ozick might make this a clear-cut tale of obsession leading to insanity, and cast Kornfeld's suicide as a kind of self-inflicted punishment. But Ozick does not want us to see the nymph as a delusion, and, crucially, it is not Kornfeld's paganism that does him in. Rather, it is the discovery that, as much as he loves Nature's beauty, Nature can never love him back—because while his body might be pagan, his soul is incurably Jewish. Granted a vision of his soul as the dryad sees it, he finds it is "a quite ugly old man," trudging down the road holding a "huge and terrifying volume"—a tractate of the Mishnah; "His cheeks are folded like ancient flags, he reads the Law and breathes the dust." Ozick makes the portrait as repulsive, even offensive, as possible. But she does so with the sly knowledge that the Law is absolutely on her side. For her image of a pious Jew who "passes indifferent through the beauty of the field" is actually a reference to *Pirkei Avot*, the "Ethics of the Fathers": "Rabbi Yaakov would say: One who walks along a road and studies, and interrupts his studying to say, 'How beautiful is this tree!,' 'How beautiful is this ploughed field!'—the Torah considers it as if he had forfeited his life."

This idea would have been quite familiar to the Hebrew writers of the Haskalah, the Jewish Enlightenment, who agreed that traditional Jewish education led to physical ineptitude, and rebelled against it for that reason. Ozick's provocation is to reverse the terms of that judgment: for her, the ugly soul is desirable, the beautiful body reprehensible. "We are not like them," says Kornfeld's pious widow. "Their bodies are more to them than ours are to us. Our books are holy, to them their bodies are holy."

A novel, according to this puritanical logic, is a book that is really a body—not a book of the Law, but a book that replaces the Law by creating a lying, beautiful, desirable world. Ozick presses this notion to a shocking extreme in "Usurpation (Other People's Stories)," one of her best and most difficult fictions. The usurpation in question is, first, a kind of plagiarism. The story opens with the narrator, who is more or less Ozick, attending a reading by a writer who is more or less Bernard Malamud, at the 92nd Street Y. Hearing this writer read a story called "The Magic Crown"—a deliberately uncamouflaged allusion to Malamud's "The Silver Crown"—leads the narrator to feel that she could do a better job with it, that it was really meant for her.

In Ozick's version, which goes on to unfold with dreamlike illogic, it becomes a story about a crown which grants the wearer immortal literary fame. One of the writers who have worn it in the past, we learn, is Saul Tchernikhovsky, the early-twentieth-century Hebrew poet who was notorious for his literary paganism (he was the author of poems called "My Astarte" and "Before a Statue of Apollo"). In other words, Tchernikhovsky was a writer who defied the moral of "The Pagan Rabbi." He accepted that secular literature is a kind of idolatry, and therefore a sin, but in a Nietzschean spirit he made that evil his good.

His heavenly reward, Ozick writes in the last paragraph of "Usurpation," is to get everything he wished for in life: "Tchernikhovsky eats nude at the table of the nude gods, clean-shaven now, his limbs radiant, his youth restored, his sex splendidly erect. . . . Then the taciturn little Canaanite idols call him, in the language of the spheres, kike." It is the story's last word, and it is genuinely shocking, because it turns Jewish alienation into a cosmic principle. There is no escape, in this world or the next, for the Jewish writer; she is trapped between duty and desire, forever.

The catch, though, is that this despairing rejection of literature is offered in a short story. "When we enter Paradise there will be a cage for story-writers, who will be taught as follows: All that is not Law is levity," Ozick writes. But she is left in the position of the Cretan liar: to write a story whose message is that stories are frivolous is to raise the suspicion that the message is itself frivolous, because a writer who seriously believed it would not have written the story in the first place.

Sometimes Ozick tries, in her fiction and essays, to find a way out of this paradox. The most notable of these attempts is "Toward a New Yiddish," a talk she delivered in Israel in 1970. Here Ozick proposes that the only honorable course for a Jewish writer is to write in a Jewish language, and since the language of American Jews is English, English can or should become a Jewish language, a "New Yiddish." It is not hard to see that this odd suggestion, which Ozick herself later abandoned, served her at the time as a form of psychic revenge on English literature. She announces her "revulsion . . . against what is called, strangely, Western Civilization"; she declares, "I no longer read much 'literature.' I read mainly to find out . . . what it is to *think* as a Jew." Finally, she makes the wild assertion that "there have been no Jewish literary giants in Diaspora . . . there are no major works of Jewish imaginative genius written in any Gentile language, sprung out of any Gentile culture."

The statement is too obviously false to require refutation. What is important is the complex emotion that led Ozick, who certainly could have provided the necessary counter-examples, to make it in the first place. It is out of her rage and disappointment with literature—specifically, with the Anglo-American tradition of the novel, associated by her with Henry James—that she turns to Jewishness as subject and theme, identity and vindication. For other writers, Jewishness can be autobiography, sociology, religion, ethics; for Ozick, it is all these things at times, but it is primarily a way to think about, and against, literature. Which means that literature remains the master term of her imagination, even or especially when she is rejecting it.

This explains why nearly all of Ozick's best fiction is about writers and writing. She ironically alludes to this at the beginning of her story "Levitation," where she refers to "the importance of never writing about writers. Your protagonist always has to be someone *real*, with real work-in-the-world—a bureaucrat, a banker, an architect . . . otherwise you fall into solipsism, narcissism, tedium, lack of appeal-to-the-common-reader; who knew what other perils." The joke is that "Levitation" is itself a story about a pair of married writers (they are the ones who believe that you should never write about writers).

Ozick knows better. Her two masterpieces are the long stories "Envy, or Yiddish in America" and *The Messiah of Stockholm*, and both are about writers—specifically, about thwarted writers. Edelshtein, in "Envy," is an aging Yiddish poet who is left readerless by the extinction of Yiddish. Its death in Europe was a murder, the result of the Holocaust, but its death in America is more like a case of terminal neglect, as young Jews grow up to speak English instead. "What right had these boys to spit out the Yiddish that had bred them, and only for the sake of Western Civilization?" he fulminates about some young acquaintances. "Edelshtein knew the titles of their Ph.D. theses: literary boys, one was on Sir Gawain and the Green Knight, the other was on the novels of Carson McCullers."

Ozick's M.A. thesis was on Henry James, and she is writing this story in English, the usurper language. What allows her to sympathize so deeply with Edelshtein is her bitter knowledge of literary frustration, of the rage of the neglected writer at his feckless nonreaders. When Edelshtein meets a young woman who actually knows Yiddish, and begs her to translate his poems, she spits back: "It isn't a translator you're after, it's someone's soul." She's right, and Ozick's readiness to acknowledge this is what makes "Envy" so brilliantly unsentimental, despite the subject's many temptations to sentiment.

But it is in *The Messiah of Stockholm* that Ozick offers her most ingenious solution to the perceived incompatibility of Jewishness and literature. Lars Andemening, the story's protagonist, is a middling literary critic for a Swedish newspaper—another one of Ozick's frustrated writers. The form his literary longing takes, however, is not to be a great writer himself, but to be the son of one. He is convinced that he is the secret child of Bruno Schulz, a Jewish writer killed in Poland during the Holocaust. (Incidentally, Schulz, who wrote in Polish, serves all by himself to refute Ozick's earlier claim that there have been no Jewish literary geniuses "in any Gentile language.")

Lars confides his belief, which the reader is inclined to call a fantasy, to an old woman who runs a used bookstore. To Lars's shock, she introduces him to Adela, who also believes she is Schulz's child, and who seems to have the proof: she possesses the manuscript of Schulz's last, lost work, a novel called *The Messiah*. Schulz really is supposed to have written a book with that name, though it is presumably lost forever. By introducing Schulz's book into her own, Ozick gives herself the chance to re-create it in her own image—much as she did with Malamud's story in "Usurpation."

In Ozick's version, *The Messiah* is a bizarre fable, in which the town of Drohobycz—Schulz's home and the setting for his work—has been totally depopulated, its people replaced by ambulatory idols. "The streets and shops were packed and milling with all these remarkable totems of wood, stone, pottery, silver and gold." But in the absence of human beings to worship them, the idols are forlorn—until they begin to worship one another, which means sacrificing to one another: "The town was on fire, idols burning up idols in a frenzy of mutual adoration." Through the dark glass of this parable, we can see Ozick's oldest concerns at work. The empty town is a vision of the Holocaust, which really did annihilate the Jews of Drohobycz; the idols are a fantastic rebus for literature itself, which survives in a ruined world by engaging in sterile self-admiration. Yet the masterstroke in Ozick's fable is that the Messiah, when he finally comes, is *also* a book, a book that is at the same time a horribly living body:

> Its locomotion was dimly frightening, but also
> somewhat hobbled and limited: it had several

hundred winglike sails that tossed themselves either clockwise or counterclockwise, like the arms of a windmill. But these numerous "arms" were, rather, more nearly flippers—altogether flat, freckled all over with inky markings, and reminiscent, surely, of turning pages.... [W]hen examined with extreme attention... the inky markings showed themselves to be infinitely tiny and brilliantly worked drawings of those same idols that had taken hold of the town of Drohobycz. It was now clear that Drohobycz had been invaded by the characters of an unknown alphabet.

Literature, in this vision, is not the enemy of redemption. Rather, it is a mistaken, aborted apprehension of redemption, which worships the parts of a greater whole because it does not know they are meant to be only parts. It is not necessary to reject "Western civilization," or the secular literature Ozick never really did forsake; one must only refuse to idolize it, by recognizing that there is an inconceivably greater, more comprehensive reality. At the end of Ozick's fable, the book-Messiah gives birth to a bird, which proceeds to touch the idols and dissolve them. Having grown too proud, having served their purpose, the idols of the imagination are humbled and dismissed.

This extended passage, with its nightmarish atmosphere, serves as a kind of catharsis in Ozick's work. For Lars, however, the problem is to decide whether to trust its wisdom—that is, whether to believe that the manuscript Adela has shown him really is the work of Bruno Schulz. Dr. Eklund, who claims to have smuggled the manuscript out of Poland, assures Lars of its authenticity. But when Lars sees Eklund take Adela by the shoulders and put his forehead against hers, he has a sudden intuition: such an intimate gesture means that they must know each other, that they must be closer than Lars had believed. "Something had been compounded between them," he muses, and all at once he realizes that Eklund is really Adela's father—which means that Adela has no connection to Schulz, and that he is the victim of an elaborate con. Enraged, he seizes the manuscript and sets it on fire.

The scene is highly reminiscent, but not of Schulz. It is an allusion to, or a reincarnation of, two famous moments in the novels of Henry James. In *The Portrait of a Lady*, Isabel Archer sees her husband, Gilbert Osmond, remain seated in the presence of Madame Merle—a breach of etiquette from which she begins to deduce that they are lovers. And in *The Ambassadors*, Lambert Strether runs into Chad Newsome and Madame de Vionnet boating in the country, and suddenly realizes that their friendship is not, as he had been led to believe, a Platonic one. *The Ambassadors*, of course, is the book that Ozick says she kept on her desk while writing her first novel. With this allusion, Ozick's relation to Henry James comes full circle. His ghost, first adored, then feared and hated, can be readmitted to her fiction on friendly terms, now that it has been vanquished.

o o o

Ozick's novel *Foreign Bodies* is a coda to this family romance of the intellect. It often reads, in fact, like a review of themes and properties from across Ozick's body of work, giving it a slightly melancholy, almost valedictory feeling. Bea Nightingale, the novel's middle-aged, divorced, schoolteacher heroine, could be a cousin of Ruth Puttermesser, the middle-aged, unmarried, civil-servant heroine of *The Puttermesser Papers*. Bea remembers her parents' little hardware store in terms that echo "A Drug Store Eden," Ozick's memoir of her own parents' little drugstore. Alfred Chester surfaces as a minor character in the novel, complete with "yellow wig . . . wobbling on his shiny pate." One of the settings is a refugee resettlement office in Paris, on Rue des Rosiers, the main street of the Jewish quarter in the Marais; in *The Cannibal Galaxy*, the father of Joseph Brill, that novel's Franco-Jewish protagonist, has a fish shop on Rue des Rosiers. Lili, the frail but nurturing Holocaust survivor who works in the refugee office, is a version of Rosa, the mother who suckles her baby during a death march in "The Shawl." When Bea reflects that "sometimes an ambassador serves as a spy, sometimes a spy is appointed ambassador," there is a faint allusion to *Trust*: Enoch Vand is, literally, a spy who is appointed an ambassador.

And, in the end as in the beginning, there is Henry James and *The Ambassadors*. In *Foreign Bodies*, however, Ozick does not imitate or parody James so much as she turns him inside out. James's novel begins when Lambert Strether, a refined but ineffectual New England WASP, arrives in Europe to bring back young Chad Newsome, the heir to an American fortune, who has taken up with an unsuitable Frenchwoman. Ozick's begins with Bea Nightingale coming back to America, having failed to make contact with her nephew Julian in Paris, where he has similarly strayed. To drive home the point that she is writing as an anti-James, Ozick makes sure to include, on the very first page, a glaring grammatical error: "I did the best I could to track him down—tried all the places you said he might be working at." Ozick is no more likely than James to mar her prose with a dangling preposition. She means us to notice how different straight-ahead Bea is from reverberant Strether.

The differences continue with their respective targets. Chad Newsome is improved—morally, socially, aesthetically—by his life in Paris, and by his affair with Madame de Vionnet. It is because Strether sees this so vividly that he is eventually seduced away from his mission and becomes the defender of Chad's rebellion. From our first glimpse of Julian Nachtigall, on the other hand, he appears as a revolting slob: "Inner life? The boy was no better than a savage. He was surprisingly plump, even his eyelids, swollen pink and fat as petals. A random drop hung from the tip of his broad nose. The stretched nostrils dripped mucus."

Eventually, though, Julian does show improvement in Paris, enough to convince Bea that she should help him escape the power of his father, her brother Marvin. Marvin has kept the original family name, which Bea has Anglicized. In every other respect, however, he is a dedicated social climber: he goes to Princeton, marries a blue-blooded WASP, and makes a fortune in business in southern California. "How happy he would have been," Bea says, "to have been sired by a Bourbon, or even a Borgia. A Lowell or an Eliot would have done nearly as well." Marvin's sin, in other words, is to want to join the very class that Henry James always wrote about, that Chad Newsome belongs to.

When it comes to writing, Ozick is quite willing to brave James's snobbery and assert her equal rights to the English language. But Marvin's *arrivisme* is not an assertion of equality; it is a plea for acceptance, which means an admission of inferiority. It must be punished, and Ozick makes the punishment fit the crime: as Marvin flees Jewishness, his son Julian embraces it. Literally— for the Madame de Vionnet figure in *Foreign Bodies* is Lili, the survivor, whom Julian secretly marries. To Marvin, the idea of losing his American prince to a Jewish refugee is intolerable: "I know what's coming, I've seen the films like everybody else, and I can't have one of those, not in my own family," he says.

Yet Bea comes to realize that Lili is just the education Julian needs. An American, he must be educated in Jewishness; spoiled and rich, he must be educated in suffering. "Little by little he was becoming another Julian . . . he had married a woman who was teaching him the knowledge of death," Ozick writes. By the end of *Foreign Bodies*, his moral sense has been stung into wakefulness, and he even talks about studying theology. Here is Ozick's latest overturning of the Jamesian scale of values. Chad Newsome needed the love of a rich French woman in order to become a gentleman; Julian Nachtigall needs the love of a destitute Jewish woman to become, for want of a better word, a *mensch*.

Ozick is by no means blind to the implications of the fact that, in both cases, the woman is only an accessory to the moral career of a man. To see Ozick's fiction as primarily concerned with the ethics of literature and Jewish identity makes her sound, not just like a "writer's writer," but like a Jewish writer's writer—a narrow enough niche, though not for that reason an unimportant one. The truth, however, is that Ozick is just as engaged with, and sharply perceptive about, feminist questions as Jewish ones.

Ozick has been ambivalent about the development of feminism—"More and more, women are urged to think of themselves in tribal terms, as if anatomy were the same as culture," she complained in *Ms.* in 1977—but there can be no doubt that she is one of the most authentically feminist writers of her time. And her understanding of what it means to be a woman, like her understanding of what it means to be a Jew, is shaped centrally by her experience as a writer—by the allure and frustration of the literary calling. In her early story "An Education," for instance, a young woman's scholarly career is destroyed by her naïve admiration for a fraudulent male genius. In the strange, sad story "Puttermesser Paired," the middle-aged Ruth Puttermesser's attempt to model her life on George Eliot's goes disastrously awry, as she is forced to replay Eliot's sexual humiliation at the hands of a younger man. And in "Dictation," the female secretaries of Henry James and Joseph Conrad conspire to transpose passages from their employers' new books. This prank is the only way they can imagine to "leav[e] behind an immutable mark—an everlasting sign that they lived, they felt, they acted!"

It is every writer's ambition, but for many women, such a self-assertion must be made in the face of strong imperatives to helpfulness and self-effacement, not to mention the claims of marriage and children. This is surely why, whenever female schoolteachers appear in Ozick's fiction, she writes about them with an odd contempt: they represent the fate that could have claimed her, the fate of sensibility subdued to usefulness. That is what happens to Bea Nightingale, who marries Leo Coopersmith, an ambitious young composer, and becomes a teacher—temporarily, as she thinks—in order to support him. At their very first meeting, when Bea confides her ambition to Leo—"I want to make my mark in the world"—he tells her, "you're well on your way to being a run-of-the-mill high school teacher. English lit, possibly—all that sensibility." At the end of *Foreign Bodies*, when Leo, now a middle-aged Hollywood hack, finally composes a real symphony, he sends the score to Bea, and she feels triumphant: "it was a gift—a kind of gift. Leo's mind! It was the thing she had hoped for, long ago."

But if serving as a handmaiden to art is Bea's victory, it could never have satisfied Ozick. Here, too, it's possible to trace the genealogy of her passions back to Henry James, and to *The Lesson of the Master*. In that story, Paul Overt tries to argue with Henry St. George's verdict that "an artist shouldn't marry": "Not even when his wife's in sympathy with his work?" But St. George will not allow it: "Women haven't a conception of such things." The role of the woman, James suggests, is not to create beauty but to embody it, the way Miss Fancourt—the woman Overt loves and St. George marries—embodies it: "real success was to resemble *that*, to live, to bloom . . . not to have hammered out headachy fancies with a bent back at an ink-stained table." It is one more lesson of the master that Ozick had to defy in order to become a master herself.

Liberation and Liberalism:
E. M. Forster

o o o

Whenever E. M. Forster is discussed, the phrase "only con- nect" is sure to come up sooner or later. The epigraph to *Howards End*, the book he described with typical modesty as "my best novel and approaching a good novel," seems to capture the leading idea of all his work—the moral importance of connection between individuals, across the barriers of race, class, and nation. What is not as frequently remembered is that, when Forster uses the phrase in *Howards End*, he is not actually talking about this kind of social connection, but about something more elusive and private—the difficulty of connecting our ordinary, conventional personalities with our transgressive sexual desires.

"Only connect" makes its entrance shortly after Margaret Schlegel, the novel's liberal, intellectual heroine, is first kissed by Henry Wilcox, the conservative businessman she has rather sur- prisingly agreed to marry. Passion has played little part in their relationship, and though they have gotten engaged, they have not yet touched. When Wilcox suddenly embraces her, then, Margaret "was startled and nearly screamed," and though she tries to kiss "with genuine love the lips that were pressed against her own," she feels afterward that "on looking back, the incident displeased her. It was so isolated. Nothing in their previous conversation had heralded it, and worse still, no tenderness had ensued . . . he had hurried away as if ashamed." A few pages later, Margaret's reflections on this erotic incompetence lead, as often happens in Forster's fiction, into an authorial homily:

> Outwardly [Henry Wilcox] was cheerful, reliable, and brave; but within, all had reverted to chaos, ruled, so far as it was ruled at all, by an incomplete asceticism. Whether as boy, husband, or widower, he had always the sneaking belief that bodily passion is bad. . . . And it was here that Margaret hoped to help him. It did not seem so difficult. She need trouble him with no gift of her own. She would only point out the salvation that was latent in his own soul, and in the soul of every man. Only connect! That was her whole sermon. Only connect the prose and the passion, and both will be exalted, and human love will be seen at its height. Live in fragments no longer. Only connect, and the beast and the monk, robbed of the isolation that is life to either, will die.

It is not surprising that the specifically erotic dimension of "only connect" has largely been lost for today's readers. For if there is one thing that separates us from Forster, it is the twentieth-century revolution in Western sexual mores. If Forster strikes us as quaint, in a way that his contemporaries Joyce and Woolf do not, it is not simply because of his relative formal conservatism, but because he shows us, in Frank Kermode's words, "a world in which what may now seem fairly trivial sexual gestures carry a freight of irreversible significance." As Kermode goes on to note in *Concerning E. M. Forster*, a brief but illuminating critical study, "two stolen kisses are sufficient to sustain the plot of *A Room with a View*." That novel was published in 1908; fourteen years later, Joyce would show Leopold Bloom masturbating on Sandymount Strand. The First World War was clearly the dividing line between these sexual epochs, but even though Forster was not yet forty when the war ended, he published only one novel after it, *A Passage to India*. His fiction remains tethered to the Edwardian period, the twilight of the sexual *ancien régime*.

The less explicit Forster is about sex, the more sentimental he becomes, with results that are sometimes quite ludicrous. When Rickie Elliot, in *The Longest Journey*, stumbles upon Gerald and Agnes, an engaged couple, stealing a kiss, Forster describes the effect on him in terms borrowed from the overture to *Das Rheingold*:

> It was a fragment of the Tune of tunes. Nobler instruments accepted it, the clarinet protected, the brass encouraged, and it rose to the surface to the whisper of violins. In full unison was Love born, flame of the flame, flushing the dark river beneath him and the virgin snows above. His wings were infinite, his youth eternal; the sun was a jewel on his finger as he passed it in benediction over the world. Creation, no longer monotonous, acclaimed him, in widening melody, in brighter radiances. Was Love a column of fire? Was he a torrent of song? Was he greater than either—the touch of a man on a woman?

Biography may have little to tell us about why a novelist writes well, but it can sometimes be helpful in understanding why a novelist writes badly. So it is not insignificant, in reading such a purple passage, to learn that at the time he wrote it—in his mid-twenties—Forster actually did not know how men and women had sexual intercourse. This would be hard to credit if it were not Forster himself who said so. In *A Great Unrecorded History*, her biography of Forster, Wendy Moffat quotes from what he called his "Sex Diary," now in the library of King's College, Cambridge, where the novelist reviewed the landmarks in his sexual development from childhood on. As a boy, he recorded, he "learnt that there was queer stuff in the Bible, and thought that 'lying together' meant that a man placed his stomach against a woman's and that it was a crisis when he warmed her—perhaps that a child was born, but of this I cannot be sure. . . . Never connected warming operation with my sexual premonitions. This chance guess, that came so near to the truth, never developed and *not till I was 30* did I know exactly how male and female joined."

Forster turned thirty in 1909, the year he began writing *Howards End*. Yet the emphasis on sexual sincerity in that book is only the development of a theme that had been present in his fiction since his first novel, *Where Angels Fear to Tread*, which was published in 1905. In each of his first four books, Forster writes as a defender of sexual freedom and self-knowledge against the suffocating ignorance of conventional morality. Kermode writes that his fiction is almost "evangelical" in its obsession with "the choice to be made between winning salvation and backsliding," and notes that critics often relate this quality to Forster's descent from the Clapham Sect—a group of rich London evangelicals who were prominent in the early nineteenth-century campaign to end the slave trade.

Forster preserves his ancestors' concern with salvation, but he reverses their definition of it. In his fiction, Christianity is always a force for damnation, because it keeps people mired in sexual hypocrisy. (One of the reasons given for Henry Wilcox's failure to "connect," for instance, is that "the words that were read aloud on Sunday to him and to other respectable men were the words that had once kindled the souls of St. Catharine and St. Francis into a white-hot hatred of the carnal.") Salvation means having the courage to be what one is, sexually speaking—to listen to the still, small voice of attraction, which for Forster is not just a matter of appetite but of conscience. So, in *A Room with a View*, when Lucy Honeychurch breaks her engagement to Cecil Vyse in order to marry the man she is attracted to, George Emerson, she is not simply doing what she likes. Rather, she is heeding the moral imperative voiced by George's father: "Yes, for we fight for more than Love or Pleasure; there is Truth. Truth does count."

Forster speaks in the voice of Bunyan's Valiant-for-Truth, and the truth he preaches is that of the body: "love is of the body; not the body, but of the body. Ah! the misery that would be saved if we confessed that! Ah! for a little directness to liberate the soul!" The problem, reading Forster today, is that we are no longer much in need of this kind of valor. Over the last hundred years, the primacy of the body and of sexual desire has become an article of psychological, medical, and commercial faith. We have not entered paradise as a result—sexual abundance and familiarity have their discontents, though reading Forster convinces us that these are not to be compared with the discontents of scarcity and ignorance. But the sexual problems of our time are nearly as far from Forster's as from Jane Austen's. Indeed, precisely because Forster does begin to address sex openly, as Austen never does, he can seem the more dated of the two. It is possible that Samuel Butler's bold novelistic call for religious liberation, *The Way of All Flesh* (which was published posthumously in 1903, just two years before Forster's debut), speaks more directly to readers today than do Forster's comparatively timid calls for sexual liberation.

○ ○ ○

But what if the kind of sexual freedom Forster championed, in these early novels, is not really what he cared about at all? That is the thesis of *A Great Unrecorded History*, which can be read as an attempt to renew Forster's pertinence by recasting him as a fighter in a different liberation struggle, one that has not yet won complete success. This is the fight for gay liberation, and the

unrecorded history Moffat alludes to in her title is the history
of Forster's homosexuality. In her preface, Moffat quotes Chris-
topher Isherwood, shortly after Forster's death in 1970, saying
that "all those books [about Forster] have got to be re-written.
Unless you start with the fact that he was homosexual, nothing's
any good at all."

That was forty years ago, however, and it has been a long
time since Forster's sexuality was a secret. To his intimates, it
never was: starting in the 1920s, Moffat shows, Forster was part
of a thriving gay community, with friends and correspondents
across England and America. From 1930 onward, moreover, he
was in a devoted relationship with Bob Buckingham, a married
policeman, and it seems that most people who knew Forster well
enough to call him Morgan also knew Bob. Yet it is true that
Forster never "came out" in the modern sense, and people who
knew him only as a writer or public figure did not necessarily
know he was gay. Only friends who had been welcomed into
Forster's full confidence were allowed to read the manuscript of
Maurice, his only novel about homosexuality, which he finished
in 1914 but never published. In 1933, for instance, Forster allowed
the young Isherwood to read it as he sat by his side, and Moffat
writes that "the moment cemented the friendship for life."

Moffat implies that she is breaking the public silence about
Forster's sexuality. "All his long life Morgan lived in a world
imprisoned by prejudice against homosexuals," she writes.
"Almost a century ago, Forster dedicated *Maurice* to 'a happier
year.' Perhaps that time is now." But *Maurice* was published in
1971, the year after Forster died, in accordance with his instruc-
tions; in 1987 it was made into a movie, a clear sign that its subject
matter had ceased to be taboo. And the key episodes in Forster's
sexual life, as Moffat relates them in her book, were all disclosed
in P. N. Furbank's authorized *E. M. Forster: A Life* in 1977. It was
Furbank who revealed that Forster did not know "the facts of
life" until he was thirty; that his first sexual experience came
in October 1916, when he was thirty-seven, with a soldier in

Alexandria, where he was doing war service at a British army hospital; that his first love was Mohammed el Adl, an Egyptian train conductor whom he met soon after; and that the love of his life was Bob Buckingham.

Moffat's "new life of E. M. Forster" is not, then, a revelation—though she does quote directly from sources, including the "Sex Diary," that Furbank paraphrased. It is, rather, a reinterpretation, designed to draw the reader's attention to Forster's gayness and his gay legacy. Moffat is driven by a great personal fondness for Forster—she calls him "Morgan" throughout, as though insisting on retroactive intimacy, and puts herself on equally close terms with other figures in the story. ("Ben was slighter than the imposing Peter," she writes about Britten and Pears.) On the book's last page, Moffat states her claim in still stronger terms: "copying out the relevant scraps [of Forster's notebooks] by hand ... engenders a trance, a feeling of automatic writing, a fleeting fantasy of complete connection with Morgan's remarkable mind and heart."

Moffat's possessiveness is colored by a strong moral earnestness, which leads her to want to make reparation to the novelist for all the repression and unhappiness he suffered in his lifetime. This laudable impulse comes across, for instance, in the way Moffat adds an approving adjective to every sexual experience of Forster's she has occasion to mention. So, when Forster visits New York and goes cruising in Central Park, Moffat writes that it was "a glorious night of casual sex," and at another moment notes that Forster liked to "discover or arrange sexy flings on trips abroad." Was the sex really glorious that night, were the flings always satisfyingly sexy? There does not seem to be any evidence on such questions, and the reader is left feeling that Moffat wants Forster to have enjoyed himself so much that she simply asserts that he did.

This tendency becomes more problematic when Moffat interprets away the genuine ambiguity, and occasional darkness, that Forster himself acknowledged in some of his sexual feelings and relationships. In 1921, Forster spent several months in India working as secretary to Bapu Sahib, the ruler of a minor Hindu principality. One of the perquisites of his job was a sex slave, a boy named Kanaya, and Forster recorded how his total power over Kanaya corrupted him:

> I resumed sexual intercourse with him, but it was now mixed with the desire to inflict pain. It didn't hurt him to speak of, but it was bad for me, and new in me. . . . I've never had that desire with anyone else, before or after, and I wasn't trying to punish him—I knew his silly little soul was incurable. I just felt he was a slave, without rights, and I a despot whom no one could call to account.

Yet Moffat, even as she quotes this passage, hastens to palliate it: "On the other hand, it seemed grotesque to Morgan to deny consciousness or agency to Kanaya . . . just because [he wasn't] white. In the murky world of English-colonial relations wasn't skepticism that a brown man could feel affection for him simply a different sort of bigotry?" Finally, Moffat writes, "Morgan concluded that he was ill-equipped to interpret the sexual lexicon of this strange world." But there is no quotation to illustrate these anachronistic-sounding doubts about "consciousness or agency," and one is left feeling that Moffat's relativism is just a way of making Forster sound more admirable than, in this case, he was or knew himself to be.

A similar thing happens when Forster confesses that living in Egypt, as a representative of the ruling race, bred racist habits of mind. "I came inclined to be pleased and quite free from racial prejudice," he wrote, "but in 10 months I've acquired an instinctive dislike to the Arab voice, the Arab figure, the Arab way of looking or walking or pump shitting or eating or laughing or anythinging—exactly the emotion that I censured in the

Anglo-Indian towards the native. . . . It's damnable and disgraceful, and it's in me." It could not be clearer that Forster, with his typical honesty, is using himself as a case study for the very evil he was to analyze in *A Passage to India*—the way that racial privilege corrupts, even if the man who enjoys it means well.

In the novel, Forster shows this process at work in Ronnie Heaslop, the English magistrate in the Indian city of Chandrapore. When Ronnie's fiancée, Adela Quested, decides to break their engagement, Forster emphasizes that Ronnie behaves admirably, humanely: "How decent he was! He might force his opinions down her throat, but did not press her to an 'engagement,' because he believed, like herself, in the sanctity of personal relationships." Yet the whole novel is a demonstration of how the British Raj, with its racialized hierarchy, makes personal relationships impossible; and Ronnie is shown to treat the Indian Dr. Aziz, a cultivated and kindly man, with brutal contempt. Goodness in one compartment of life can coexist with violence and cruelty in another—a lesson that makes *A Passage to India* prophetic of the twentieth century's many banal evildoers.

Yet Moffat does not want Forster to incriminate himself even to this extent. What he calls racist disgust toward Arabs, she insists, was really just suppressed sexual desire: "Far from instinctive, Morgan's reaction came from careful, painful observation of these Arab men . . . watching them laugh and be separate from him inflamed his desire, and his self-loathing. . . . He hated what he did not have the courage to touch." Well, maybe—but that's not what Forster said, and not what he believed was important. He was able to sustain the difficult truth that being a victim of injustice, as a homosexual, did not make it impossible for him to practice injustice, as a white man in Egypt and India.

o o o

The important question, of course, is how Forster's sexuality, and his struggles with it and with society on account of it, should affect the way we read his work. One way of coming to grips with this question is to address the place of *Maurice* in Forster's oeuvre. For Kermode, this is not hard to do: he simply dismisses it as a bad book, beginning a discussion of Forster's fiction with the words, "Leaving aside the posthumously published and inferior *Maurice*. . . ." Conversely, to Moffat, who has almost nothing to say about Forster's writing as literature, *Maurice* is absolutely central, because it is "his only truly honest novel"—that is, the only one from which the reader can easily deduce that the author is homosexual.

This is all-important, because, Moffat says, Forster was "certain that his homosexuality was the central fact of his being." This is reductive, but there is no need to quarrel with it too much. There can be no doubt that Forster's sexuality was essential to his experience of life—everyone's is. But that is exactly the problem: everyone is sexual, and everyone is different, and so it is impossible to deduce anything very meaningful about any given person from his or her sexual orientation. Nor is it possible to deduce very much about any gay writer from the fact that he is gay. Consider that Forster belonged to the same generation as Marcel Proust, whom he admired very much, and Thomas Mann, whom he seems not to have read at all. (One of Kermode's complaints, in *Concerning E. M. Forster*, is that in *Aspects of the Novel* Forster had "remarkably little to say" about his great contemporaries.) Both of these writers wrote much more explicitly about homosexuality than Forster did, although Mann concealed his homosexuality under his image as a bourgeois paterfamilias, and Proust turned his lovers into women when he put them into his novel.

Forster never adopted this strategy, in part because, at the time he wrote his first five novels, he had not had any lovers. But there was also a principle at stake, as he wrote in his diary: "N.B. I have never tried to turn a man into a girl, as Proust did with Albertine, for this seemed derogatory to me as a writer." In other words, Forster himself shared Moffat's sense that it was not "truly honest" for a gay writer to write in a way that could lead the reader to believe he was not gay. This did not mean, apparently, that he could not write about heterosexual characters and relationships—even *A Passage to India*, the only novel Forster wrote after *Maurice*, revolves around the potential marriage of Ronnie and Adela.

But it did mean that Forster became uncomfortable with strained rhapsodies about "the touch of a man on a woman." As he grew older, he complained more than once that the impossibility of treating gay love openly in a novel had made novel-writing itself unappealing to him. After *Howards End*, he wrote of his "weariness of the only subject that I can and may treat—the love of men for women and vice versa." Near the end of his life, he reflected, "I want to love a strong young man of the lower classes and be loved by him and even hurt by him. That is my ticket, and then I have wanted to write respectable novels. No wonder they have worked out rather queer."

There is something "queer," in both Forster's sense and the contemporary sense, about Forster's "respectable" novels. At times he said that *The Longest Journey*, his second book, was the one that gave him the most pleasure to have written, "a book to my own heart. I should have thought it impossible for a writer to look back and find his works so warm and beautiful." Few readers have shared this judgment—it is probably the least read of Forster's novels—but his affection for it is understandable if it is read as his first attempt, possibly unconscious, to write about homosexuality.

The story of Rickie Elliot's moral education, like that of Lucy Honeychurch, drives home the lesson that each person must listen to his actual desires, even at the price of violating convention. But while Lucy's trial of conscience involves choosing one man over another as a husband, Rickie's is a matter of learning to despise the institution of marriage itself, and to vindicate his natural preference for intimacy with men. The dedication Forster chose for the novel is *Fratribus*—"To the brothers"—and the man Rickie finally chooses above his cold, conventional wife is his

half-brother, Stephen Wonham. But the passions and intensi-
ties of the novel only really make sense if Rickie's attraction to
men is sexual, and at moments Forster seems to say as much—so
explicitly that it is surprising neither he nor his readers apparently
noticed this subtext:

> He was thinking of the irony of friendship—so
> strong it is, and so fragile. We fly together, like
> straws in an eddy, to part in the open stream.
> Nature has no use for us: she has cut her stuff dif-
> ferently. Dutiful sons, loving husbands, responsi-
> ble fathers—these are what she wants, and if we
> are friends it must be in our spare time. Abram
> and Sarai were sorrowful, yet their seed became as
> sand of the sea, and distracts the politics of Europe
> at this moment. But a few verses of poetry is all
> that survives of David and Jonathan.

Rickie goes on to wish that "there was a society, a kind of friendship office, where the marriage of true minds could be registered"—as close to a call for gay marriage as one might find in
any novel published in 1907.

For Moffat's interpretation of Forster's life to cohere, *Maurice*
ought to be his masterpiece. After writing four "dishonest" novels, in 1913–14 he finally wrote one that was "truly honest": the
story of Maurice Hall, a conventional son of the English bourgeoisie who learns to embrace his homosexuality, despite many
social and emotional ordeals. Yet *Maurice* is actually, as Kermode
says, Forster's slightest novel—and it is not too much to say that
it is his slightest artistically because it is his most admirable eth-
ically. In writing it, Forster had a clear moral and political message in mind: "To give these people a chance—to see . . . whether
their convictions of Sin are really more than the burrs in the
social fabric that the heart and brain, working together, can pluck

out—that's why I wrote *Maurice*. . . ." For the same reason, he wrote in a "terminal note" to the manuscript, "A happy ending was imperative. I shouldn't have bothered to write otherwise. I was determined that in fiction anyway two men should fall in love and remain in it for the ever and ever that fiction allows a happy ending. . . ." And so Maurice is rewarded with the love of Alec Scudder, the gruff, handsome gamekeeper, who tells him, "And now we shan't be parted no more, and that's finished."

Yet this determination to vindicate in art the injustices of life paralyzed the very qualities that we think of as most Forsterian: the relaxed irony of his plotting, the urbanity of his moralizing, the lyricism of his prose. Compare the moral balance of *Howards End*, where the reader's sympathies are suspended between Schlegel and Wilcox until the very end, with *Maurice*'s uninflected indignation against "the middle-middle classes, whose highest desire seemed shelter—continuous shelter . . . shelter everywhere and always, until the existence of earth and sky is forgotten, shelter from poverty and disease and violence and impoliteness; and consequently from joy; God slipped this retribution in."

At the time Forster wrote *Maurice*, these were things that he urgently needed to say and that the world needed to hear. Of course, the world did not hear them—Forster said that the novel was "unpublishable until my death and England's," and until very close to his death he was right. Gide could write openly about his homosexuality in *Corydon*, in 1924, and Mann could publish *Death in Venice* in 1912, the year before Forster started *Maurice*. But France and Germany were not England. Moffat usefully reminds the reader that, as late as 1952, the great mathematician Alan Turing was sentenced to chemical castration after being found guilty of the crime of homosexuality, and committed suicide as a result. Forster lamented this extreme intolerance in *Maurice* itself: when Maurice finds that even a course of hypnotism can't "cure" him, his doctor advises him "to live in some country that has adopted the Code Napoleon . . . France or Italy, for instance. There homosexuality is no longer criminal."

In 1914, *Maurice* really was a brave assault on respectability. (When Forster had sex with a man for the first time, the code phrase he used in a letter to a friend was "parting with respectability.") But sexual mores have changed so dramatically and so quickly that today, while prejudice against homosexuals has certainly not disappeared, that very prejudice is what is not respectable. The great irony of *Maurice*, then, is that it consummates the sexual critique that animated all Forster's earlier novels, and in doing so sets the seal on that critique's obsolescence.

In a world where sexuality was imprisoned by convention, Forster's earnest attack on convention—including its extreme forms, repression and taboo—was liberating, as can be seen from the intense devotion he won from readers, especially gay readers, around the world. Moffat quotes the letter that the American painter Paul Cadmus wrote Forster after reading his essay "What I Believe": "'What I Believe' is so much what I believe too that I always read it to potential friends. . . . I am afraid I [am] not able to live up to *it*, nor to *you*." Isherwood declared, "My England is E.M.; the anti-heroic hero, with his straggly straw mustache, his light, gay, baby blue eyes and his elderly stoop."

But does Forster have the same power to inspire today? Kermode, for one, takes a much drier view of "What I Believe," which he dissects in one of the best passages of *Concerning E. M. Forster*. Forster's essay, collected in *Two Cheers for Democracy*, was written in 1939, and it is a defense of his vision of liberalism in an age of ideological total war, which he calls "an Age of Faith— the sort of epoch I used to hear praised when I was a boy." In the face of huge, warring collectivities like nation and class, Forster declares his belief in "personal relationships," the only thing "comparatively solid in a world full of violence and cruelty." He reiterates, in a dark moment, vital liberal truths: that the state exists for the individual, not vice versa; that love and loyalty are owed to individuals before abstractions; that tolerance and free speech are essential for human flourishing.

Yet there is something unsatisfactory about "What I Believe," as Kermode suggests when he observes that "the ideal citizens of a Forsterian republic would not easily be recognized as democrats." The problem is that, in elevating friendship over politics—this is the essay in which he famously wrote, "if I had to choose between betraying my country and betraying my friend, I hope I should have the guts to betray my country"—Forster is actually trying to make friendship the basis of a politics. And the result can only be a kind of aristocracy, as Forster affirms: "I believe in aristocracy. . . . Not an aristocracy of power, based upon rank and influence, but an aristocracy of the sensitive, the considerate and the plucky. Its members are to be found in all nations and classes, and all through the ages, and there is a secret understanding between them when they meet."

But to associate the liberal virtues, as Forster does here, with aristocracy and the private life is to cede democracy and the public life to the opponents of liberalism. It is to condemn liberalism to a bad conscience—Forster describes the essay as "the reflections of an individualist and a liberal, who found liberalism crumbling beneath him and at first felt ashamed." It relegates liberalism to the status of an underground movement, whose members recognize each other through "secret" signs that are too dangerous to avow—a little like the French Resistance, which did form a kind of moral aristocracy in the midst of a defeated, demoralized society. And this is perhaps the source of the problem with "What I Believe": in 1939, Forster is writing as though English liberalism were already defeated, as though he were addressing an occupied country. According to Furbank, "the outbreak of war in September 1939 left him calm though pessimistic, convinced that Britain would be defeated."

The same pessimism afflicted Forster when he came to consider the future of the novel. Moffat argues, with support from Forster himself, that the reason he stopped writing fiction was his impatience with heterosexual romance as a subject. But Forster also gave other reasons—above all, his sense that the novel was intimately connected with a social order that was doomed in

Europe. Speaking to the communist-organized International Congress of Writers, held in Paris in 1935, Forster took a certain pained satisfaction in confessing to his own obsolescence: "They may say that if there is another war writers of the individualistic and liberalizing type, like myself... will be swept away. I am sure that we shall be swept away, and I think ... that there may be another war.... This being so, my job ... is an interim job. We have just to go on tinkering with our old tools until the crash comes.... After it—if there is an after—the task of civilization will be carried on by people whose training has been different from my own."

○ ○ ○

Why, in the 1930s, did Forster make such a limited, dispirited defense of the novel and of liberalism? Was it, in part at least, because he had long since resigned himself to making similarly limited claims on behalf of homosexuals, and for himself as a homosexual? He could circulate *Maurice* in private, but not publish it; he could trust friends with the knowledge of his sexuality, but not make it a part of his public literary identity. Even in *Maurice* itself, the happy ending consists of the lovers running away to "the greenwood," a Shakespearean zone of escape and freedom. The idea that they could demand public recognition—say, by setting up house together in London—was beyond literary possibility (though Forster knew a number of established gay couples in real life). Indeed, Forster's "aristocracy," whose "members are to be found in all nations and classes, and all through the ages, and there is a secret understanding between them when they meet," could with only the slightest alteration be a description of the way gay society functioned in his time—just as, in *The Longest Journey*, his "friendship office" for the "marriage of true minds" reads as a veiled description of gay partnership.

If, as Moffat says, Forster's "homosexuality was the central fact of his being," it would make sense that the burdens imposed on his sexuality took a toll on the confidence of his claims on behalf of his politics and his writing. In each of these realms, he clung to freedom as a privilege, rather than demanding it as a right; he spoke of goodness rather than justice. But this would be, once again, to commit the error of making Forster's sexuality the sole determinant of his being. It is more accurate to reverse the proposition, to say that it was Forster's being that determined the way he thought about sexuality, no less than about politics and literature. Indeed, as Moffat shows, few gay men even in Edwardian England were as cautious, or as romantically naïve, as the young Forster. Lytton Strachey, his fellow Cambridge Apostle, thought the conclusion to *Maurice* absurd: "I should have prophesied a rupture [between Maurice and Alec] after 6 months—chiefly as a result of . . . class differences," he told Forster. He also objected to its extremely high-minded treatment of sex, which Forster euphemizes as "sharing": "I really think the whole conception of male copulation in the book rather diseased—in fact morbid and unnatural."

If there is a biographical source for Forster's bad conscience, his conviction that the civilization he cherished was doomed, it is more likely to lie in his social class than his sexuality. Like the Schlegels in *Howards End*, Forster was a *rentier*, living off a large bequest from his great-aunt. In an age when class tensions were rising and the Liberal Party was giving way to Labour, his feeling of guilt at being economically unproductive, a kind of bourgeois parasite, seems to have contaminated his view of the art he produced—as though literature and civilization, too, were bourgeois luxuries. If individualism and the novel were doomed, it was in the same way that the old country houses were doomed—they would be justly confiscated in the name of a more equitable future.

The passage that brings out this feeling most clearly is one of the most objectionable in all of Forster—the mockery of Leonard Bast's literary aspirations in *Howards End*. Kermode, who is much

more interested in Forster's class feelings than his sexual feelings, writes that "to a surprising extent one's attitude to *Howards
End* depends . . . on one's response to Bast," and he is angered by
Forster's condescension toward this self-improving clerk, who
fatefully crosses paths with the Schlegels at a Beethoven concert.
Forster treats Bast's longing for art and culture as delusional,
hopeless; he is "one of the thousands who have lost the life of the
body and failed to reach the life of the spirit." Kermode argues
that this failure is not so much Bast's as his creator's: "The sor-
did scene that Forster sets in the Bast home . . . is persuasively
wretched. But it makes no provision for other possibilities, for
relationships between men and women of this class that were
not so hopeless and so wretched." He points out that writers
of the eminence of V. S. Pritchett and Edwin Muir started life
in circumstances like Bast's, as members of the "office-boy
intelligentsia."

This is all true, and Kermode persuasively shows that Forster had his thumb on the scale against Bast—even the character's name is meant to hint at "bastard." But Forster might fairly
respond that most office boys were not Muir or Pritchett, that
thousands of men as intellectually thwarted as Bast did exist,
and that in any case this story of failure was the story he wanted
to tell. Forster's really unforgivable error is not making Bast a
failure, but saying that the nature of literature itself is opposed
to Bast's success. Here is Bast reading a page of Ruskin:

> "Let us consider a little each of these characters in
> succession, and first (for of the shafts enough has
> been said already), what is very peculiar to this
> church—its luminousness."
>
> Was there anything to be learnt from this fine
> sentence? Could he adapt it to the needs of daily
> life? Could he introduce it, with modifications,
> when he next wrote a letter to his brother, the lay
> reader? For example—

> "Let us consider a little each of these charac-
> ters in succession, and first (for of the absence of
> ventilation enough has been said already), what is
> very peculiar to this flat—its obscurity."
>
> Something told him that the modifications
> would not do; and that something, had he known
> it, was the spirit of English Prose. "My flat is dark
> as well as stuffy." Those were the words for him.

If Forster really believed that "the spirit of English Prose"
was against Leonard Bast, then he had no choice but to write with
a bad conscience, and to offer at most two cheers for democracy.
If literature is against hope, against enlightenment, against the
spread of true civilization, then it is indeed a poisoned gift. But
there is no basis for such a slander. Think of what the spirit of
English prose meant for Dickens and Hardy and Lawrence—
men who did not inherit a fortune as Forster did, but made their
fortunes, and their names and souls, by writing well. They did
not, of course, write like Ruskin, and in constructing this passage Forster chose his target well—there can indeed be something complacently poetic, something rhetorical and stuffy,
about Ruskin's prose. The problem is not that this is the spirit of
English prose, however—it's that it is, all too often, the spirit of
Forster's own prose. Here is how Forster, later in *Howards End*,
apostrophizes the English countryside:

> So tremendous is the City's trail! But the cliffs
> of Freshwater it shall never touch, and the island
> will guard the Island's purity till the end of
> time. Seen from the west, the Wight is beautiful
> beyond all laws of beauty. It is as if a fragment of
> England floated forward to greet the foreigner—
> chalk of our chalk, turf of our turf, epitome of
> what will follow. And behind the fragment lies

Southampton, hostess to the nations, and Portsmouth, a latent fire. . . .

But prose does not have to sound this way, so lullingly, contentedly parochial. It is no accident that Forster's best novel, *A Passage to India*, is the one that takes him far away from England, and puts the actual sources of England's political and economic power under closest scrutiny. It is also the book in which Forster allows himself to wonder if "personal relationships," the shibboleth of "What I Believe," are not an ultimate value, but a penultimate one. "What is the use of personal relationships when everyone brings less and less to them?" Adela Quested asks. "I feel we ought all to go back into the desert for centuries and try and get good. I want to begin at the beginning."

The metaphysical scope and urgency of this novel, the way it begins at the beginning—with the null echoes of the Marabar Caves, and the pantheist epiphanies of Professor Godbole—make it trustworthy in a way that even *Howards End* never quite is. Maybe the deepest reason Forster never wrote another novel had less to do with restrictions on which relationships he could portray, than with a growing sense of the restriction inherent in all relationships, as Adela muses: "But it has made me remember that we all must die: all these personal relations we try to live by are temporary. I used to feel death selected people, it is a notion one gets from novels, because some of the characters are usually left talking at the end. Now 'death spares no one' begins to be real."

Zadie Smith and the
Future of the Novel

o o o

One of the running jokes in *On Beauty*, Zadie Smith's third novel, is that its main character is philosophically opposed to beauty. Howard Belsey is a professor of art history at Wellington College, and like all middle-aged professors in campus novels, he is a ludicrous figure—unfaithful to his wife, disrespected by his children, and, of course, unable to finish the book he has been talking about for years. In Howard's case, the book is meant to be a demolition of Rembrandt, whose canvases he sees as key sites for the production of the Western ideology of beauty. "What we're trying to ... *interrogate* here," Howard drones in a lecture on Rembrandt's *Seated Nude*, "is the mytheme of artist as autonomous individual with privileged insight into the human. ... What are we signing up for when we speak of the 'beauty' of this 'light'?" Smith captures not just the familiar inanity of the rhetoric, but, even better, the vacancy of the students' attempts to parrot it: "I don't think you can simply just inscribe the history of painting, or even its logos, in that one word 'painting,'" one of the students replies.

Throughout this classroom vaudeville, Smith cements the

reader's antagonism to Howard and his cheap aesthetic nihilism by having us view it through the eyes of his most naïve student, Katie Armstrong, a sixteen-year-old from the Midwest who is uncomplicatedly in love with art. "She used to dream about one day attending a college class about Rembrandt with other intelligent people who loved Rembrandt and weren't ashamed to express this love," Smith writes, and she makes us indignant at Howard on Katie's behalf. Indignation turns to scorn when it turns out that Howard Belsey is just as enthralled by beauty as anyone—in his case, by the beauty of another young student, Victoria Kipps, with whom he has a disastrous affair.

Howard's downfall—by the end of the book, he loses his wife and his career—is the revenge of beauty, and in the novel's last scene, Smith forces Howard to admit defeat. He is standing before a distinguished audience, about to deliver the talk that will determine his academic future, when he realizes that he has left his speech in the car. He is forced to simply cycle through his slides, finally allowing Rembrandt's pictures to speak for themselves, after all his attempts to deface them with words. And the sheer beauty of the images, in Smith's last paragraphs, becomes a promise of redemption: in Rembrandt's portrait of his wife Hendrickje, the imperfections of the skin, "chalky whites and lively pinks," is redeemed by "the ever present human hint of yellow, intimation of what is to come." In this wonderfully designed scene, Smith delivers the traditional affirmations we look to comedy to provide: beauty, love, and art triumph over malice and division.

Readers who remember Howard Belsey will surely be surprised to open *Changing My Mind*, Smith's collection of nonfiction, and find that it contains a frontal attack on the idea of beauty in fiction. "Two Directions for the Novel," first published in 2008, is a manifesto in the form of a review of two novels, Joseph O'Neill's *Netherland* and Tom McCarthy's *Remainder*, which offer Smith an eloquent contrast, not least in their worldly careers. *Netherland* was one of the most unanimously praised novels of

2008, reached the bestseller list, and received many honors. (The paperback comes with a publicist's dream blurb, from President Obama.) *Remainder* was a *succès d'estime*, published in the United States in 2007 as a paperback original after taking, Smith tells us, "seven years to find a mainstream publisher." This information comes in the first paragraph of Smith's essay, suggesting its importance to her. Later on, we learn that McCarthy is the founder of a prankish, manifesto-issuing group called the International Necronautical Society, and that he once expelled two writers from this society for "signing with corporate publishers," thus becoming "complicit with a publishing industry whereby the 'writer' becomes merely the executor of a brief dictated by corporate market research, reasserting the certainties of middle-brow aesthetics."

It is clear that part of what draws Smith to McCarthy is this avant-garde puritanism, which seems so self-consciously anachronistic today. Smith's first novel—*White Teeth*, published in 2000, when she was twenty-four years old—met with what Philip Larkin (a frequent touchstone in her essays) called "success so huge and wholly farcical"; and ever since, she has been that rare and ambiguous thing, not just a good writer but a famous writer. There is, then, a kind of penance in the homage Smith pays to McCarthy's seven years in the wilderness, and a kind of self-suspicion in her description of O'Neill's book: "It's as if, by an act of collective prayer, we have willed it into existence."

Exactly the same thing might be said, with even more justice, of *White Teeth*, which was so eagerly welcomed in part because it said things Britons, in particular, wanted very much to hear. In that book, Smith takes some of the most envenomed and insoluble problems of contemporary life—immigration, racism, religious fundamentalism, terrorism—and turns them into premises for comedy. Any of the characters in *White Teeth* could be the protagonist in a novel of social protest: Samad Iqbal, the educated Bengali immigrant reduced to working as a waiter; Samad's son, Millat, a charismatic teenager driven by boredom and resentment to join an Islamic militant group; even the lovable sad sack Archie Jones, a native Englishman trapped at the bottom of an immutable class system.

Yet none of these figures seems threatening or truly pitiable, because they inhabit a comic universe in which conflict is inadmissible, even when it is Smith's explicit subject. Sometimes, this is because Smith actively neuters her characters with jokes: the group Millat joins is called Keepers of the Eternal and Victorious Islamic Nation, or KEVIN, which automatically prevents us from thinking of it as genuinely dangerous. (The characters are in on the joke: "We are aware that we have an acronym problem," one militant says.)

But this kind of self-conscious spoofing is actually not very frequent in *White Teeth*, and Smith's comedy is more legitimately affirmative than a mere spoof could be. Politically, Smith is consoling because she tells us that rancor and racism are things of the past—problems for the grouchy old, not the exuberantly hybridized young. It is noteworthy that, in this book about Asian and Caribbean immigrants in Britain, there is only one very minor character who is actually a racist. This is the shut-in Mr. Hamilton, whom the three children in the book—Millat and Magid, Samad's sons, and their best friend Irie, who has a white English father and a black Caribbean mother—visit as part of a school-organized charity project. When the children bring the old man groceries, he launches into a homily on the importance of dental hygiene, which leads unexpectedly to this reflection: "Clean white teeth are not always wise, are they? Par exemplum: when I was in the Congo, the only way I could identify the nigger was by the whiteness of his teeth, if you see what I mean. Horrid business. Dark as buggery, it was. And they died because of it, you see?"

This eruption of ugliness reduces the children to silence, then makes them furious and tearful. But in the novel's own terms, there is no contest between Mr. Hamilton, who makes his brief contemptible appearance and then vanishes, and the children, who are its beloved heroes. If we ask *White Teeth* the question E. M. Forster asked in *Howards End*—who is to inherit England?—there can be no doubt of Smith's answer: England belongs to Irie and Millat and Magid, and a good thing too. Not for nothing did Smith choose as the book's epigraph "The past is prologue."

Smith is so certain that racism is not a threat that she finds much of the book's comedy in the attempts of well-meaning white Britons to avoid sounding racist. One of the book's many funny set pieces involves a parents' meeting at the children's school, where Samad harasses everyone with his attempts to get more Islamic holidays added to the school calendar. The comedy, typically for Smith, comes from the fact that no one takes this religiosity seriously—even Samad's wife keeps trying to shut him up—and that the other parents are exclusively concerned with not seeming culturally insensitive. The chairwoman at the meeting—named, jokingly but emblematically, Ms. Miniver—"wanted to check that it was not her imagination, that she was not being unfair or undemocratic, or worse still *racist* (but she had read *Colour Blind*, a seminal leaflet from the Rainbow Coalition, she had scored well on the self-test), racist in ways that were so deeply ingrained and socially determining that they escaped her attention."

As this suggests, another reason why Smith is finally so consoling is generic. Embarrassment and obliviousness are comic, xenophobia and hatred are not, and so in *White Teeth* the latter are invariably translated into the former. This is not to say that Smith sets out to be funny in order to be ingratiating; on the contrary, her talent for comedy is so genuine that it transforms everything in its orbit into an occasion for laughter. Smith's is the true comic vision, in which all conflicts are really misunderstandings, and everyone deserves sympathy because no one is truly evil.

This is not the only kind of comedy—for all the comparisons to Dickens that *White Teeth* earned, Dickens is far more frightening, because more sensible of evil. But it is a kind of comedy to which English literature, in particular, has always been hospitable, and it is remarkable how often Smith sounds like or even alludes to Kingsley Amis and P. G. Wodehouse. One of the best recurring jokes in *White Teeth* is about the hoariest of setups, a pair of deaf old bores in a pub. That the bores, in this case, are domino-playing Caribbeans, rather than darts-playing Englishmen, makes much less of a difference than one might think.

White Teeth was published in 2000, and it is intriguing to wonder what might have happened if it had been delayed by a year. After September 11, 2001, it would not have been as easy to write, or read, a novel in which KEVIN is the face of Islamic terrorism. In fact, all of the troubles that *White Teeth* asks us to see as things of the past, from immigration to imperialism, began in the last decade to look like the stuff of our future. It is notable that Smith's subsequent novels gave the themes and setting of *White Teeth* a wide berth. *The Autograph Man* was a farce about celebrity-worship and the immaturity of teenage boys, and *On Beauty* relocated to an American college town. Near the beginning of the latter novel, Howard Belsey and his wife Kiki decide to have an anniversary party, even though the date of the party seems to disconcert many of the guests; it is clear that the date is supposed to be September 11, but Smith, as if on principle, never actually names it.

One of the things Smith has against *Netherland* is that it set out to be, and was praised as, "the post-9/11 novel we hoped for." "Were there calls, in 1915, for the Lusitania novel?" she asks. "In 1985, was the Bhopal novel keenly anticipated?" The questions are willfully obtuse, since the comparisons are all wrong. Ask whether there was a post-Kennedy assassination novel, or a post-Pearl Harbor novel, and you come closer to the effect of 9/11, and get the opposite answer from the one Smith intends.

But Smith does not mean to be just to *Netherland*. What she objects to is precisely that O'Neill did rise to the challenge of writing a "post-9/11 novel," through an intelligent use of the conventional novel form. Like all the best novels inspired by

September 11, *Netherland* treats the attacks themselves very obliquely, and thus avoids the painful literalism that afflicted John Updike's *Terrorist* or Don DeLillo's *Falling Man*. Briefly, it is the story of Hans van den Broek, a Dutch financier living in New York, whose wife and child leave the city after the attacks. In his loneliness, Hans joins an amateur cricket league whose other members are all South Asian and Caribbean immigrants. There he befriends Chuck Ramkissoon, a Trinidadian who dreams of building a cricket stadium in New York. This story is told in prose that is consciously poetic—O'Neill courts the comparison to F. Scott Fitzgerald—and while the lyricism can sometimes feel like much of a muchness (as in Fitzgerald), it is also very impressive and moving.

To Smith, both the story and the style of *Netherland* are objectionable, and for the same reason. It is a book in which "a community in recent crisis—the Anglo-American liberal middle class—meets a literary form in long-term crisis, the nineteenth-century tradition of lyrical realism." Hans is a rich tourist in New York, insulated by race and class from Chuck's struggles as an immigrant, which allows him (and O'Neill) to turn Chuck into a fetish of authenticity. Likewise, Smith continues, O'Neill makes a fetish of language, lavishing his powers on lyrical descriptions that prevent any sharp, unsettling encounter with the real. But this "lyrical realism" is an obsolete form, unable to capture either the social dislocations or the phenomenological reality of life in our time. "Out of a familiar love," Smith sums up, "like a lapsed High Anglican, *Netherland* holds on to the rituals and garments of transcendence, though it well knows they are empty." It could be Howard Belsey talking.

The surprisingly conventional terms in which Smith abuses *Netherland* set up one half of a binary, and *Remainder* is adduced—a little opportunistically, perhaps—to supply the other half. If the former is plush, the latter is austere; if the former is traditional, the latter is avant-garde; if the former traffics in worn-out emblems of authenticity, the latter puts authenticity itself in question. McCarthy's novel is narrated by a man, never named, who has just emerged from a coma after being involved in a mysterious accident. He receives a huge settlement, and uses the money to re-create, in real life, places and events that have lodged in his memory: first an apartment building, then a car wash, then a murder scene. These reenactments are highly literal—the narrator hires actors, builds sets, re-creates things down to the last detail—but they are also, of course, McCarthy's metaphysical gambit, involving us in questions about the nature of reality and memory, narcissism and transcendence.

To Smith, McCarthy's programmatic deconstruction of authenticity is a good antidote to O'Neill's piety about it. Lyrical realism is doubly inauthentic, in its beauty and in its received notion of the integral self. McCarthy's prose, on the other hand, is deliberately dull and matter-of-fact, and the self at the heart of his story is always already ejected from itself, trying by means of grandiose reenactments to achieve an illusory, remembered unity. In both ways, Smith casts *Remainder* as the bonfire for *Netherland*'s vanities: "it means to shake the novel out of its present complacency. It clears away a little of the deadwood, offering a glimpse of an alternate road down which the novel might, with difficulty, travel forward."

Even without going very deeply into the relative merits of these two novels, it is apparent that there is something forced— dare one say, inauthentic?—about the use Smith makes of them. Smith argues that O'Neill is a writer of the day before yesterday, a Flaubertian aesthete, while McCarthy points the way to a stripped-down, decentered future. But it is impossible to read *Remainder* without being struck by how very familiar its avant-garde gestures are. The demonstratively undemonstrative protagonist reminds us of Camus's Meursault, his phenomenological alienation of Sartre's Roquentin. Smith lauds the scene in which McCarthy's narrator is repelled by the actuality of a carrot—"this carrot . . . was more active than me: the way it bumped and wrinkled, how it crawled with grit"—but doesn't mention that it alludes to the most famous moment in *Nausea*, when Roquentin contemplates a tree's roots. This kind of anti-lyricism is, by now, its own kind of lyricism.

More misleading still is Smith's suggestion that McCarthy's coolly stylized novel has a truer grasp of the real than O'Neill's warmly stylized one. "In place of the pleasure of the rich adjective," Smith writes, "we have an imagined world in which logistical details and logical consequences are pursued with care and precision: if you were to rebuild an entire house and fill it with people reenacting actions you have chosen for them, this is exactly how it would play out. Every detail is attended to. . . ." But if you turn to the relevant section of *Remainder*, you find that McCarthy describes the "logistical details" of the reenactment this way:

> We'd receive faxes on the machine we had in our car and stuff them into the back-seat glove compartment as the driver raced us to another meeting, then forget that we'd received them and have them re-faxed or go back to the same office or the same warehouse again—so the humming in our ears was constant, a cacophony of modems and drilling and arpeggios and perpetually ringing phones. The hum, the meetings, the arrivals and departures turned into a state of mind—one that enveloped us within the project, drove us forwards, onwards, back again.

McCarthy's realism turns out to be abstract, generalized, aestheticized. If you actually did want to rebuild an entire house and fill it with reenactors, this passage would be totally useless as a guide—you would not know where to begin, much less how to finish. In fact, McCarthy has no interest in the logistical side of the reenactments, which is why he introduces a character, Naz, to serve as the narrator's factotum. Naz deals with reality, so the narrator and the novel can focus on sensation.

Reading *Netherland*, on the other hand, it is constantly clear how much actual observation and research went into O'Neill's description of parts of New York life that the average fiction reader, not to mention writer, will never see. O'Neill's description of the "2003 Annual Gala of the Association of New York Cricket Leagues" may or may not be based on a real event, but reading it, one feels that if it took place it would have been just like this: in this kind of vulgarly elegant event hall, in this remote part of Queens, with these guests of honor (a state assemblyman, a low-ranking functionary from the mayor's office), and these corporate sponsors (Air Jamaica, Red Stripe). Far from proving that lyrical realism is a fraud, the experience of reading O'Neill and McCarthy side by side suggests that it is precisely an interest in reality that enables and justifies a novelist's lyricism. It is because O'Neill is so attentive to the world that he attempts to capture it in the only way language allows—poetically.

If Smith has misread these books, however, she has done so in a way that is very suggestive about her own writerly ambitions and anxieties. In linking the (alleged) debility of the novel to the (alleged) crisis of the Anglo-American liberal middle class, Smith is making a connection that is not especially pertinent to *Netherland*. (Hans van den Broek is neither Anglo-American nor middle-class—he is a rich Dutchman.) But it is at the very heart of another writer who is much more important to Smith than Joseph O'Neill: E. M. Forster, who is the subject of another major essay in *Changing My Mind*.

When Howard Belsey, in *On Beauty*, happens to pick up a copy of *A Room With a View* that is lying around in his father's apartment, he mutters: "Forster. Can't stand Forster." Of course, Howard, with his principled suspicion of beauty and truth and humanism, would have to hate Forster, whose fiction often reads like a sermon on behalf of those very things. The joke is that the novel in which Howard exists is a sustained homage to *Howards End*. The Belseys, the academic liberals of Smith's novel, loosely correspond to Forster's Schlegels, while the Kippses—whose daughter Victoria is Howard's undoing—are versions of the conservative, businesslike Wilcoxes. At several points in *On*

Beauty, Smith offers clever and affectionate parodies of famous moments from *Howards End*: Forster's description of Beethoven's Fifth Symphony, for instance, becomes Smith's description of Mozart's Requiem.

Smith's large indebtedness to Forster, in what is probably her best and certainly her most mature novel, makes her ambivalence in the Forster essay all the more striking. "It should be obvious from the first line," Smith writes in the acknowledgments to *On Beauty*, "that this is a novel inspired by a love of E. M. Forster, to whom all my fiction is indebted, one way or the other." But in *Changing My Mind*, Smith writes that "there is something middling about Forster; he is halfway to where people want him to be." (The title of the essay is "E. M. Forster, Middle Manager.") Smith argues that this middlingness is healthy humility, rather than mediocrity: "He could sit in his own literary corner without claiming its superiority to any other." We may feel that Forster rather pales in comparison to his contemporaries—Joyce, Woolf, Eliot—but Smith gives Forster credit for acknowledging their greatness: "Forster was not Valéry, but he defended Valéry's right to be Valéry."

Defense, however, is a feeble kind of recognition, and the metaphor of rights does not really belong in literary criticism. You might defend a writer's right to be himself from a mob of book-burners or a committee of censors, but when it comes to literature itself, what matters is not that a writer has a right, but that he is right. And if the writer Smith herself most publicly identifies with is merely a middle manager—a "Notable English Novelist, common or garden variety," as she also puts it—how can she help but wonder if she herself is right enough? "There's magic and beauty in Forster, and weakness, and a little laziness, and some stupidity. He's like us," Smith sums up. It's not what any writer would choose to put on her own tombstone.

Is it any wonder, then, that in castigating the tradition of "lyrical realism"—the term she coins for O'Neill, but that describes Forster, and especially *Howards End*, quite exactly—Smith writes with the passion and injustice an artist always brings to her self-interrogations? "I have written in this tradition myself," Smith acknowledges, "and cautiously hope for its survival, but if it's to survive, lyrical realists will have to push a little harder on their subject." And what draws Smith to *Remainder*, it is fair to say, is its appearance of pushing very hard, of sacrificing beauty (and popularity) in the name of truth. The same feeling animates her tribute to David Foster Wallace, the last piece in *Changing My Mind*. "Wallace chose the path of most resistance," Smith writes, "he battled his gifts rather than simply display them, seeming to seek the solution in a principle of self-mortification."

Taken together, these essays suggest a writer engaged in a reconsideration, perhaps a refashioning, of her own techniques and values. What is troubling is that Smith seems to be denigrating exactly the qualities that made her first three books, not just popular, but also good: the abundance and inventiveness and love of the grotesque that seemed to be evolving, in *On Beauty*, into a deeper and more moving kind of comedy. In fact, *Changing My Mind* includes a memoir of Smith's late father, "Dead Man Laughing," that is perhaps the most powerful narrative writing she has yet done. In explaining her father's love of British TV and stand-up comedy, Smith creates a much darker and more affecting portrait of him than she did in *White Teeth*, where Harvey Smith was the model for Archie Jones. And the moment in this memoir when Smith "put my finger in the dust of my father"—his cremated remains have been in a Tupperware box on her desk—"and put the dust into my mouth and swallowed it," provokes the kind of dreadfully consoling laughter—"I laughed as I did it"—that her fiction has so far seldom attempted. Like the rest of *Changing My Mind*, it leaves the reader curious to see what kind of writer will emerge from Smith's crisis of literary conscience.

The Turbulence of Saul Bellow

o o o

"Have you ever visited a clothing factory, heard the sewing machines rrrrh*hhahh*rrr with the loudness in the middle of the phrase?" Saul Bellow wrote to Susan Glassman, who would become his third wife, in 1961. "I feel like that myself, like the operator sliding in the cloth. Only the machinery is internal and the seams never end." If you had to pick a single passage from Bellow's *Letters*, so richly characteristic on every page, to capture the writer's essence, this would be it. That roar is the key signature of his inner life, which he bestows on every one of his fictional surrogates. The first step in creating a character, for Bellow, is not to imagine what he looks like or what will happen to him, but to set moving the vibration, the agitation, the turbulence (there is no more Bellovian word than "turbulent") that constitutes consciousness.

It is audible in Joseph, from *Dangling Man*: "If I had as many mouths as Siva has arms and kept them going all the time, I still could not do myself justice." In Henderson: "Now I have already mentioned that there was a disturbance in my heart, a voice that spoke there and said, *I want, I want, I want!* It happened every afternoon, and when I tried to suppress it it got even stronger." In Ravelstein: "one of those large men . . . whose hands shake when there are small chores to perform. The cause was not weakness but a tremendous eager energy that shook him when it was discharged." Above all, there is Bellow's greatest creation, Moses Herzog, to whom he transferred the observation made in the letter to Glassman: "Therefore, Herzog's thoughts, like those machines in the lofts he had heard yesterday in the taxi, stopped by traffic in the garment district, plunged and thundered with endless—infinite!—hungry, electrical power, stitching fabric with inexhaustible energy."

The principle that turbulence is the elixir of fictional life is not, of course, Bellow's invention. It is one of the leitmotifs of modern fiction, starting perhaps with *Rameau's Nephew*, the influential dialogue by Denis Diderot. (It is more than a coincidence—it may even be a signal—that Bellow mentions this work in his first published novel, *Dangling Man*, and in his last, *Ravelstein*.) In that dialogue, Diderot speaks both in his own voice—as the rational, meliorist man of the Enlightenment—and in the voice of the Nephew, who overpowers the reader with torrential, brilliant rants even as he confesses to atrocious vices. To Lionel Trilling, the most authoritative critic of Bellow's generation, the dialogue was ominously significant, because it made vitality seem more appealing and authentic than morality; Rameau's nephew was the first modern antihero, the ancestor of Dostoevsky's Underground Man.

There is more than a clash of personalities at stake, then, when Trilling emerges as one of Bellow's favorite targets in the *Letters*. They were never close—not the way Bellow was close to Alfred Kazin, whom he alternately cherished and alienated in a way the *Letters* show to be typical of his best friendships. Bellow used Trilling, rather, as a living emblem of the whole way of thinking about modern literature and the modern world that he set himself against in his novels. To Trilling, the energy of modernism was subversive, anti-ethical; the famous gravity of his own style is an expression of his distrust of that energy, which he resisted precisely because it attracted him so strongly. But the wager of Bellow's fiction is that this very energy can be harnessed to affirmation—that the insatiable desire and turbulence of the modern mind can impel it to embrace existence passionately, instead of passionately criticizing it.

This idea of his calling came long before he had written anything to justify it. "Suddenly, out of base *merde*, I began to manufacture gold," Bellow wrote to a friend in 1941, at the age of twenty-six. "Thank God for such alchemical powers in the greatest feat of human engineering. It is not very much nowadays to make gardens out of literal shit but to transmute spiritual shit, that is something!" It is an early, but already characteristic, expression of what would become his great theme. "The universe itself being put into us, it calls out for scope," Henderson declares. "The eternal is bonded onto us. It calls out for its share."

This belief in the redemptive purpose of his own writing helps to explain the bitterness of Bellow's letter to Trilling in 1952, responding to an article by Diana Trilling on the state of contemporary fiction:

> Are most novels poor today? Undoubtedly. But that is like saying mutilation exists, a broken world exists. More mutilated and broken than before? That's perhaps the world's own secret. Really, things are now what they always were, and to be disappointed in them is extremely shallow. We may not be strong enough to live in the present. But to be *disappointed* in it! To identify oneself with a better past! No, no!

The personal insult is hardly veiled: if Trilling succumbs to the modern intuition that the world is "broken," it could only be because he lacks Bellow's own strength and depth of spirit. A few years later, writing to the critic Granville Hicks on the same theme, he acknowledges that contemporary novelists might appear like "lizards [who] presume to call themselves still dinosaurs. Of course, lizards are far less extinct than many men I know (like Trilling)." The final act of aggression came in 1974, when Bellow attacked Trilling in a *Harper's* essay that was based on a hasty misreading of a single chapter of *Sincerity and Authenticity*. This time Bellow himself seems to have realized that the Trilling against whom he had been making psychic warfare bore only an ambiguous relation to the actual Trilling, and wrote a preemptive apology: "You may think me silly when you read a piece I've written," he begins. "I feel guilty—no, that won't do—I feel remorseful about it." The apology didn't help, and this episode marked the final break between the novelist and the critic.

The feud with Trilling is at best a minor subplot in the *Letters*. But it is worth emphasizing as an example of the way personal relationships, for Bellow, were most intense when most representative—when a friend became a way of thinking about the world, about literature, or about himself. And when these thoughts became urgent enough, they erupted into his fiction. In thinking and feeling as he did about Trilling, one might say, Bellow was rehearsing the vociferations of Herzog against "the commonplaces of the Wasteland outlook, the cheap mental stimulants of Alienation, the cant and rant of pipsqueaks about Inauthenticity and Forlornness. I can't accept this foolish dreariness. We are talking about the whole life of mankind. The subject is too great, too deep for such weakness, cowardice. . . ."

To say that people exist for Bellow primarily as provocations for writing is close to saying that they have no autonomous existence—that he is out to use them. Not surprisingly, this charge surfaces several times in the *Letters*, when one or another of Bellow's friends find themselves portrayed in a book. The sitters for some of Bellow's best fictional portraits do not figure at all in the *Letters*—apparently the letters to Delmore Schwartz (the original of Von Humboldt Fleisher) do not survive, and Bellow himself writes that Isaac Rosenfeld (the original of Zetland) maliciously destroyed his youthful letters. "Years later, he told me one day, 'I hope you don't mind, but when we moved from the West Side' (to the Village, naturally) 'I threw away all your letters.' And he made it clear that he meant to shock me, implying that I would feel this to be a great loss to literary history."

As fellow writers, however, these figures would probably have sympathized with the use Bellow made of their lives. Things are more complicated when the friend is a not a writer—like Samuel Freifeld, one of Bellow's childhood friends, whose father served as the original of the low-rent mastermind Einhorn, in *The Adventures of Augie March*. Writing to Freifeld in 1950, before the book appeared, Bellow can't quite decide what approach to take:

> For instance, your papa and a few other relatives are very lively daily preoccupations of mine. Personages *like* them appear in *Augie March*. You don't, and needn't look for yourself (the way I have of scrambling things); someone else is in your place. Most ways you'll be pleased by this monument; it's an honorable one; and you know your pa was too rich to be held by oblivion. And you're free enough a man to be pleased rather than offended.

At first, he tries the conventional, legalistic denial: the relationship between life and art is complex, a character in a book is not the same as a real person. Yet Bellow is too honest, and too proud of what he has written, to be content with this evasion, and he finally says what he really thinks: that to be memorialized in a great book, a book by Saul Bellow, is not just a compliment but an achievement. Once Freifeld has read *Augie March* and made clear that he's not offended, Bellow shows his hand freely: "I feel that I have kept things from obscurity which should not sink and for that reason the book is as much intended for you as for myself. The personal identification is altogether warranted. If you didn't make it, I'd feel that I had missed the mark."

The letters to Freifeld—and a much later one to another friend, David Peltz, who found one of his own favorite anecdotes incorporated into *Humboldt's Gift*—demonstrate the peculiar burdens of intimacy with a writer, who, by definition, is not just an individual but a representative man. Bellow's belief that what happened to him was of general, indeed cosmic, significance could seem selfish, as he well knew: "it's my vocation to write books and I follow it with the restlessness of true egomania," he joked to his agent in 1949. The aggrieved comedy of *Herzog* comes from Moses Herzog's ever-renewed surprise that the world he believes he is serving does not appreciate his service:

> The revolutions of the twentieth century, the liberation of the masses by production, created private life but gave nothing to fill it with. This was where such as he came in. The progress of civilization—indeed, the survival of civilization—depended on the successes of Moses E. Herzog. And in treating him as she did, Madeleine injured a great project. This was, in the eyes of Moses E. Herzog, what was so grotesque and deplorable about the experience of Moses E. Herzog.

We are supposed to laugh—"Oneself is simply grotesque!" Herzog says—yet in the *Letters*, anyone who slights Bellow's own mission soon finds out that he is not actually joking. The most painful example comes in a letter to his sixteen-year-old son Gregory, the child of his first marriage, who had evidently reproached him for missing child support payments. Bellow begins by explaining that he can't afford the payments to his first wife and son because he now has to make payments to his second wife and son. One could hardly blame Gregory for finding this a tasteless excuse. But Bellow goes on to argue that his financial hardship is actually a sacrifice for the good of, yes, the progress of civilization:

> If you are, as you say, making a man of yourself you might think of the condition of another man, your father. Why does he do these things? Is he a lunatic? What's the sense of those books he writes? Obviously my unreliable financial condition is related to the fact that I write books. And you might try thinking about this in terms other than the dollar.

"The name of the game is not Social Security," Bellow tells Peltz. "The name of the game is Give All." Yet it is unbecoming of Bellow to be the one to remind his friends and relations of this fact, since he is the one who is destined to Take All. "I should think it would touch you that I was moved to put a hand on your shoulder and wanted to remember you as I took off for the moon," he writes—but of course it is Bellow who is going to the moon, Peltz who is left to wave goodbye.

The *Letters* make uncomfortable reading, at such moments, because they force the reader to sympathize with these earthbound friends. Only on returning to Bellow's novels does it become clear that Bellow's taking really was a precondition of his tremendous generosity. Everything he took from his own life, he gave to the world, to posterity. Nor is his conviction of being employed in some kind of "service" a mere alibi for literary ambition. Writing to Philip Roth in 1984, Bellow explains the profound difference between these two novelists so often bracketed together: "Still our diagrams are different, and the briefest description of the differences would be that you seem to have accepted the Freudian explanation: A writer is motivated by his desire for fame, money, and sexual opportunities. Whereas I have never taken this trinity of motives seriously."

It is not a contradiction to say that, in fact, life offered Bellow all these things on a grand scale, and that he took them; for even while taking them, he did not take them *seriously*. This is why Bellow's female characters are famously insubstantial, why the seductive Ramona of *Herzog* is almost insultingly like the seductive Renata of *Humboldt's Gift*. Sex, for Bellow, is a respite from consciousness, not an occasion for it. He knows this perfectly well himself—the *Letters* are always showing just how self-aware Bellow was, even when this took the form of recognizing what he did not want to be aware of. "I learned to organize my daily life for a single purpose," he writes to an old friend in 1980—the purpose, of course, being writing. "There *was* one other drive, the sexual one, but even that presently gave way. My erotic life was seriously affected, too, in that I diverted myself with a kind of executive indiscriminateness—without a proper interest in women."

When it comes to his proper interest, on the other hand, no degree of concentration is too much. It is no coincidence that Bellow finds a metaphor for his inner "loudness" in the noise of a sweatshop: this is the sound of work being done, the serious work of remembering and perceiving. "We have our assignments," says Artur Sammler in *Mr. Sammler's Planet*, and Bellow's assignment was the one he thrillingly summarized in "Zetland: By a Character Witness":

> A very early and truthful sense of the seizure of matter by life energies, the painful, difficult, intricate chemical-electrical transformation and organization, gorgeous, streaming with radiant colors, and all the scent and the stinking. This combination was too harsh. It whirled too much. It troubled and intimated the soul too much.

What were we here for, of all strange beings and creatures the strangest? Clear colloid eyes to see with, for a while, and see so finely, and a palpitating universe to see, and so many human messages to give and to receive.

What makes Bellow rare, possibly unique, among the great writers of the last century was this conviction that seeing had a metaphysical warrant—that perception, and the recording of perception, was not a pastime but an "assignment." To believe that writing is needful, in this way, one must believe that there is some One or some Thing that needs it; and not just metaphorically, in the way that Williams says men die for want of poetry, but actually. (Bellow's next-to-last book was called *The Actual*.) To write as Bellow does, in other words, one must believe in a kind of divinity. At the very least, one must not believe in the arbitrariness of what we see and feel, which means that one must not believe in the finality of death, which obliterates all sense-impressions.

And Bellow does not believe in death—or else, he can't resist trying to disbelieve it. Writing to Freifeld in 1956, this time to console him on his divorce, Bellow says: "I have great confidence in our power to recover from everything. Except death, of course. But who's talking about *that*! Maybe we'll recover even from death, if it comes to a pinch." Even here, Bellow's great literary tact comes through: levity is the right tone for challenging death, in an age that believes in death. For it is a way of mocking his own hope, of acknowledging what Bellow also knows, the horror of absolute finality. As he writes to John Berryman, "I feel I'd rather die myself than endure these deaths, one after another, of all my dearest friends. It wears out your heart. Eventually survival feels degrading. As long as death is our ultimate reality, it *is* degrading. Only waiting until Cyclops finds us. It is horrible!"

Here, as so often in the *Letters*, one feels what Bellow himself felt—that an actual letter is a hampered, embarrassed occasion for saying what can only really be said in a book. "I sometimes think I write books in lieu of letters and that real letters have more kindness in them, addressed as they are to one friend," Bellow writes to Sophie Wilkins, the wife of the poet Karl Shapiro, in 1989. It is another way of describing the dubious transaction in which unkindness to friends is turned into kindness to anonymous readers. Just so, what he writes briefly to Berryman, in 1963, he will write fully in the story "The Old System," published in 1968:

> One after another you gave over your dying. One by one they went. You went. Childhood, family, friendship, love were stifled in the grave. And these tears! When you wept them from the heart, you felt you justified something, understood something. But what did you understand? Again, *nothing*! It was only an intimation of understanding. A promise that mankind might—*might*, mind you—eventually, through its gift which might—*might* again—be a divine gift, comprehend why it lived. Why life, why death.

Slender as this "might" sounds, it is really the premise of all his work. But if it were merely asserted, as it is here, the idea that each human life can be ultimately comprehended and justified would not have the power it does in Bellow's fiction. What rescues it from the sterility of a proposition is the way Bellow embodies it, quite literally, in his characters. His physical descriptions are charged with metaphysical meaning, in part because they avoid the clinical, cumulative precision of Flaubertian or Nabokovian word-painting. Bellow's people appear to us, rather, like people in Dickens, as a surge of features all clamoring for attention. Like Einhorn: "he floated near the pier in the pillow striping of his suit with large belly, large old man's sex, and yellow, bald knees; his white back-hair spread on the water, yellowish, like polar bear's pelt, his vigorous foreskull, tanned and red, turned up; while his big lips uttered and his nose drove out smoke, clever and pleasurable in the warm, heavy blue of Michigan." Or Von Humboldt Fleisher: "He was thick through the shoulders but still narrow at the hips. . . . A surfaced whale beside your boat might look at you as he looked with his wide-set gray eyes. He was fine as well as thick, heavy but also light, and his face was both pale and dark."

In a lesser writer, these dichotomies might seem like too obvious a predictor of Humboldt's split personality, his manic-depression. They are convincing here because, for Bellow, the correspondence of body and soul is more than a literary conceit. It is a fundamental commitment, like his skepticism about death—and related to it, as Sammler explains:

> But this was our Walter. In black raincoat, in a cap,
> gray hair bunched before the ears; his reddish-
> swarthy teapot cheeks; his big mulberry-tinted
> lips—well, imagine the Other World; imagine
> souls there by the barrelful; imagine them sent to
> incarnation and birth with dominant qualities *ab
> initio*. . . . Eternal being makes its temporal appear-
> ance in this way.

The soul makes the flesh, which is why it can survive the flesh. And this insight is guaranteed, for Bellow, by the very vividness with which the physical world appears to him—an intensity so powerful that he could not believe it was merely subjective. This very early intuition is what led Bellow to his late enthusiasm for Rudolf Steiner, whose books are so dreadfully written that only a deep spiritual aspiration could have led a reader of Bellow's sensitivity to tolerate them. Some of the most extraordinary pages in the *Letters* are addressed to Owen Barfield, Steiner's English interpreter, whom Bellow elected as a mentor in the 1970s. When editors or friends slight his work, Bellow's wrath is fearful; but to Barfield he humbly writes, "I didn't mention *Humboldt's Gift* to you because I thought you weren't greatly interested in novels. I thought it might even displease you."

Clearly, Barfield was to represent the Religious Man to Bellow's Aesthetic Man; the novelist wanted to believe that the Steinerian sage could somehow prove the doctrines he himself could only dramatize. "For that is the truth of it—that we all know, God, that we know, that we know, we know, we know," he writes in the last sentence of *Mr. Sammler's Planet.* Real knowledge does not sound like that, so desperate and imploring. But certainty, Bellow knew, was not his assignment. "To be really good, among the best, one must get hold of a kind of Tolstoyan normalcy which no one can challenge," he wrote to Edward Shils. "I don't believe I can expect that now. I think what I have is relatively good poise in the midst of abnormalities."

In Bellow's century, that poise was perhaps the only credible form of wisdom. Certainly, it was enough to make him the kind of novelist that readers do not just admire but rely on. The letters tell an old story, that writers are hard to love in real life; but when it comes to his work, no writer is more deserving than Bellow of the kind of love he expressed for John Cheever: "You were engaged, as a writer should be, in transforming yourself. When I read your collected stories I was moved to see the transformation taking place on the printed page. There's nothing that counts really except this transforming action of the soul. I loved you for this."

Proust Between *Halachah*
and *Aggadah*

o o o

Chaim Nachman Bialik is often thought of as a celebrant of *aggadah*, the imaginative lore and legend that plays such an important role in rabbinic literature. He was, after all, the editor of the anthology *Sefer Ha-Aggadah*, and in his poem "To the Aggadah" he describes it as a resource for the imaginative renewal of Jewish culture. It is noteworthy, then, that in his famous 1916 essay "Halachah and Aggadah," Bialik mounted an equally strong defense of *halachah*, Jewish law and legal reasoning. This is not because he finds *halachah* more appealing or lovable than *aggadah*. "*Halachah* wears a frown, *aggadah* a smile," the essay begins. "The one is pedantic, severe, unbending—all justice; the other is accommodating, lenient, pliable—all mercy."

Yet Bialik denies that law and legend can really be separated in this way. They are, he writes, "two sides of a single shield." Indeed, the essay goes on to reconceive *halachah* itself as a kind of aestheticism—an art form whose material was the body, physical and social, of the Jewish people. "*Halachah* is, no less than *aggadah*, a creative process," Bialik insists. "It is the supreme form of art—the art of life and of living. Its medium is the living man, with all his impulses; its instrument is education, individual, social, and national; its product is a continuous chain of goodly life and action."

Later in the essay, Bialik suggests that the energies which other peoples devoted to the creation of concrete works of art—what he calls "works of marble to delight men's senses"—were devoted by the Jews to the fashioning of the national character. "I do not decide whose work is better," Bialik concludes, "but I think that both are works of creative art, ideas raised from the potential to the actual by the creative spirit of man." Shabbat, he insists, is a greater artwork than the Cathedral of Notre-Dame, and Shabbat is the product of *halachah*:

> There are one hundred and fifty-seven double pages in [the Talmud's] Tractate Shabbat, and one hundred and five in Eruvin, and in both there is next to no aggadah; for the most part they consist of discussions of the minutiae of the thirty-nine kinds of work and their branches, and on the limits within which it is permissible to carry on the Sabbath.... What weariness of the flesh! What waste of good wits on every trifling point! But when I turn over those pages and see the various groups of Tannaim and Amoraim at their work, I say to myself that these whom I see are in very truth artists of life in the throes of creation.... Every one of those men did his own part of the task according to his own bent and inclination, and all of them were bowed before an overmastering higher will.

There is, however, a doubtful ambiguity in the phrase "higher will." For observant Jews, that will is God's, and that is the reason why it must be obeyed. For Bialik, it can be conceived only as a kind of spirit of history, working through the individual to create a collective idea. What Bialik is doing, in fact, is a highly typical modernist maneuver: he is attempting to make art a source of metaphysical value, in a way that religion used to be. But it is by no means clear that art is powerful enough to compel the adherence to law, and the intellectual creativity, characteristic of traditional Judaism. Once you start to treat *halachah* as *aggadah*, law as literature, it loses the force that made it *halachah* in the first place.

There will only ever be a few people in each generation for whom literature has the force of law—for whom, as Bialik puts it, "real art is like Torah." In Bialik's generation, one of those few was surely Marcel Proust. The two writers are not often thought of together, but they were near-contemporaries—Bialik was born in 1873, Proust in 1871. And Proust's novel, *In Search of Lost Time*, is among many other things the story of an artist coming to realize his vocation—a vocation he describes in religious terms, as an ethical and absolute duty.

Proust's greatest statement of this theme comes in the famous passage in *The Captive* describing the death of Bergotte, the writer who has exerted a deep influence on the novel's unnamed Narrator. Once a writer dies, Proust wonders, what does it matter whether he wrote well or badly, since he will never know the fate of his works in this world? What he is grappling with is the disparity between the artist's sense of commitment, which is absolute and infinite, and the finite, transitory nature of all human achievement. In other words, Proust is asking a religious question, and he ends up giving what is essentially a religious answer:

> He was dead. Dead forever? Who can say? Certainly, experiments in spiritualism offer us no more proof than the dogmas of religion that the soul survives death. All we can say is that everything is arranged in this life as though we

entered it carrying a burden of obligations...
which seem to have no sanction in our present
life, seem to belong to a different life, a world
based on kindness, scrupulousness, self-sacrifice,
a world entirely different from this one and
which we leave in order to be born on this earth,
before perhaps returning there to live once again
beneath the sway of those unknown laws which
we obeyed because we bore their precepts in our
hearts, not knowing whose hand had traced them
there—those laws to which every profound work
of the intellect brings us nearer and which are
invisible only—if then!—to fools.

Even as Proust explicitly rejects religion, he invokes a metaphysics: specifically, the Platonic scheme of a life that preexists
this one, which we spend in the company of pure Ideas and for
which we long unceasingly in this fallen world. The Idea serves
Proust in the same way that *halachah* serves Bialik: both are
attempts to reconstitute the kind of absolute authority which is
missing from the secular world. And both are invoked, as they
have to be, only hypothetically. For Bialik, we must live as if we
believed *halachah* were divine, in order to create a noble national
life; for Proust, we must live as if we believed in a world "entirely
different from this one," in order to create a noble work of art.
The similarities are as important as the differences. For both of
these are modernist artists, and both are performing the modernist leap of faith, which attempts to make art itself an independent
source of value.

What separates the two, of course, is the kind of metaphor
they employ. Bialik is using a Jewish metaphor, and what he looks
for is a collective Jewish redemption; Proust is using a Greek
metaphor, and what he looks for is the individual salvation of
the artist. And it is hard not to suppose that this difference helps

to explain the difference in the reputations of these two writers. Each has achieved the kind of reward he hoped for: Bialik became the national poet of a Jewish state, Proust became the international novelist of the modern world.

○ ○ ○

Yet it is possible to see Proust's, too, as an archetypally Jewish story. His father, Adrien Proust, was a French Catholic, and Proust was baptized and raised a Catholic, and always considered himself one. But his mother, Jeanne Weil, was the descendant of German Jews, originally from Württemberg. It was Proust's great-grandfather, Baruch Weil, who first moved the family to France, during the Napoleonic period, when he came to Paris to become a successful manufacturer of porcelain. As any reader of Proust knows, it was his mother who was his closest companion throughout his life, and the deepest emotional and intellectual influence on him. He also resembled her physically, which explains why his friends often referred to his "Persian" or "Assyrian" looks—literary euphemisms for Jewish.

And the more you examine Proust's social background and friendships, the clearer it becomes that he moved in a milieu that was extensively, if not exclusively, Jewish. This fact is reflected in *Swann's Way*, where the Narrator notes:

> It is true that my grandfather made out that, whenever I formed a strong attachment to any one of my friends and brought him home with me, that friend was invariably a Jew; to which he would not have objected on principle—indeed his own friend Swann was of Jewish extraction— had he not found that the Jews whom I chose as friends were not usually of the best type. And so whenever I brought a new friend home my grandfather seldom failed to start humming the

"O, God of our fathers" from *La Juive*, singing the
tune alone, of course, to an um-ti-tum-ti-tum,
tra la; but I used to be afraid that my friend would
recognize it and be able to reconstruct the words.

It is not especially clear why the Narrator, who is never said
to be Jewish, should have so many Jewish friends. But it makes
perfect sense that Proust, from an assimilated half-Jewish family,
should have had so many friends at *lycée* who were from identical backgrounds—including Jacques Bizet and Daniel Halévy,
both of whom were grandsons of the composer of the opera *La
Juive*, Fromental Halévy. It was Jacques Bizet's mother—born
Geneviève Halévy, she would end up as Mme. Émile Straus—
who introduced Proust to the society and salon world that he
would end up writing about so penetratingly. Mme. Straus was
a partial model for the Duchesse de Guermantes, the dazzling
society hostess whose wit is her greatest charm: thus, as Proust's
biographer Jean-Yves Tadié writes, the Guermantes wit was
really "the Halévy wit, which Marcel had heard ever since he
was an adolescent."

Later in life, Proust's great love, the composer Reynaldo
Hahn, was also the son of mixed Jewish and Catholic parents.
And the magazine where he published some of his earliest stories, *La Revue blanche*, was largely produced by Jews, including
the future Socialist prime minister Léon Blum. At a time when,
Tadié notes, the Jewish population of France was some 86,000,
out of a total of 40 million, it is clear that Proust's milieu was
highly unrepresentative of France as a whole. But it was absolutely typical of an assimilated Jewish *haute bourgeoisie* that clung
to one another even as they shed their connections with the past.

The significance of these facts is more than biographical. For
any reader of *In Search of Lost Time* knows that Jews and Jewishness are one of the recurrent themes of the book. For Proust, Jews
in the high society of the Third Republic occupy a peculiar role:

they are in it but never truly of it, and the advent of the Dreyfus Affair midway through the novel emphasizes how deep the barriers to acceptance remain. The great example of this is Charles Swann, whose Jewish ancestry does not stop him from becoming a friend of the Prince of Wales and a member of the Jockey Club. Yet when the Dreyfus Affair starts to divide France, Swann finds himself driven, as though by atavism, to take Dreyfus's side, thus putting himself at odds with most of his friends and jeopardizing his unique place in society.

Swann, we learn in passing late in the novel, had one Jewish grandparent—enough to mark him out permanently from the aristocracy, but not enough to shape his character in ways that would make him repellent to them. It is very different with the other main Jewish character, the Narrator's lifelong friend, Bloch. The Narrator first meets Bloch when they are students, and he is impressed by his friend's ostentatiously sophisticated literary judgments. But Proust the writer never ceases to make clear what the Narrator doesn't seem to realize: that Bloch is in every way a repulsive person, in ways that fit anti-Semitic caricature like a glove. The product of a close-knit Jewish family, he has all the vices of the Jewish social climber, struggling to assimilate to French society—he is pretentious, ill-bred, pushy, and insecure. The portrait of Bloch is so unremittingly awful that it is never quite clear why the Narrator should want to be his friend in the first place.

It is tempting to read Bloch as Proust's projection and exorcism of all the negative traits that his own Jewishness seemed to threaten him with. Yet this bald psychological assessment is complicated, as it always must be, by the cunning and teasing self-awareness of Proust the novelist. For if we are about to claim with triumph, or even indignation, that Proust has concealed his fears about his own Jewishness by transferring them to Bloch, we are faced with the fact that the chief item in the novel's indictment of Bloch is precisely his own concealment of his Jewishness.

This is demonstrated in a painful scene in *The Guermantes*

Way. We are in the drawing room of Mme. de Villeparisis, where Bloch has been tempting fate by constantly bringing up the Dreyfus Affair. Finally, a nobleman puts him in his place:

> "Forgive me, Monsieur, if I don't discuss the Dreyfus case with you; it is a subject which, on principle, I never mention except among Japhetics [that is, Christians, as opposed to Semitic Jews]." Everyone smiled, except Bloch, not that he was not himself in the habit of making sarcastic references to his Jewish origin, to that side of his ancestry which came from somewhere near Sinai. But instead of one of these remarks (doubtless because he did not have one ready) the trigger of his inner mechanism brought to Bloch's lips something quite different. And all one heard was: "But how on earth did you know? Who told you?" as though he had been the son of a convict. Whereas, given his name, which had not exactly a Christian sound, and his face, his surprise argued a certain naivety.

This is the ultimate humiliation for Bloch, but not for the reason he thinks. He is embarrassed because he is identified as a Jew; we are even more embarrassed for him because he was deluded enough to think that he might pass for a Christian. All the sacrifices of self-respect that he has made in pursuit of assimilation have done nothing but strip him of his dignity. And it is Proust, who in the course of this very novel so completely conceals his own Jewish ancestry, who has created this unforgettable scene of false consciousness and self-delusion.

The novel, one might say, lays out two paths for Jews seeking to assimilate to French society. One is the path of Swann and, implicitly, of the Narrator: to be truly exceptional, so innately gracious (and, not incidentally, so rich) as to win a provisional acceptance which is always capable of being revoked. The other is the path of Bloch, which is to say, of the Jew who is not exceptional: this is the path of prolonged humiliation and submission, to the point of denying one's own origins. Hannah Arendt, in the pages of *The Origins of Totalitarianism* devoted to Proust, wrote ferociously about the danger that this focus on the "exception Jew" posed to Jews in general.

What is not canvassed in the novel, except perhaps inadvertently, is a third possibility. That possibility can be glimpsed in the comic scenes where Bloch heavily drops the name of Sir Rufus Israels, a Rothschild-like figure who, to the Blochs, represents an unimaginable peak of power and influence. The joke, as always at Bloch's expense, is that the people he is trying to impress with this connection—which is itself half-invented— think of Rufus Israels as distinctly déclassé.

But could there be, the reader wonders, a Jewish society in which the Israels would occupy a peak position, analogous to the one the Guermantes occupy in French society? This is really a proximate way of asking: could there be a way to express and satisfy, without renouncing one's Jewishness, the desires for status, prestige, and achievement that drive all the characters in *In Search of Lost Time*, as they drive all of us in real life? This question is closely connected to the question about Proust as a Jewish writer. For Proust's Narrator, literature and culture are inevitably and exclusively French and European literature and culture: his intellectual points of reference are Racine and Giotto, just as his social points of reference are the Guermantes. In such circumstances, there is no reason for a writer such as Proust to insist on, or even remember, the Jewish half of his identity. Jewishness is a void, a past, a condition, when the goal of life and art is to be unconditioned and self-created. In just the same way, there is no benefit for Bloch in acknowledging his Jewishness, when everything he wants in life—recognition, honor, grace—is seen as the possession of French aristocrats.

And it is not necessary to single out Proust in this regard; it is a recurring issue for European Jewish writers and artists. Walter Benjamin, who translated some of *In Search of Lost Time* into German, was the author of one of the classic essays on the novelist, "The Image of Proust." In that essay, he praises Proust's "intransigent French spirit," and says that "since the spiritual exercises of Loyola there has hardly been a more radical attempt at self-absorption." The terms, the coordinates, of judgment and reference are once again exclusively Christian and French. Nowhere in the essay itself is there an acknowledgment that Benjamin is a Jewish critic considering a part-Jewish writer, that both of them are but a few generations removed from the same kind of traditional German Jewish life, and that this situation might well account for some of their beliefs and attitudes—for instance, the metaphysical worship of Art, which for several generations of European Jews seemed to be the one realm where the emancipation that failed in actual European politics could be said to obtain.

One response to this situation might be offered by Bialik's message in "Halachah and Aggadah." Bialik, writing in Odessa for a Hebrew- and Yiddish-speaking audience, belonged to the very kind of Jewish society that Benjamin and Proust had left behind. Yet as his essay shows, he too was anxious about the ability of twentieth-century Jews to forge a meaningful connection with their own past. In adjuring Jewish writers to make use of the Talmud, he was insisting that a literature could have modern form and Jewish content—a combination that for Proust would have seemed impossible or nonsensical.

It is hard to imagine Proust paging through Tractate Shabbat in search of inspiration. Yet there is a fundamental agreement between Proust and Bialik about the ethics of art, and the proper relation of art to life. Remember that Bialik, in affirming the value of *halachah*, argued that the creation of a goodly and godly way of life, an ethical way of being, was just as much an artistic task as the creation of Notre-Dame. And he saw this elevation of life over art as a specifically Jewish value. "Our concern," he writes, "is with halachah as a concrete and definite form of actual life, of a life which is not in the clouds, which does not depend on vague feeling and beautiful phrases alone, but has physical reality and physical beauty." Just as *aggadah* is for the sake of *halachah*, so art is for the sake of life.

Proust is easy to think of as an aesthete: after all, so much of his novel is devoted to luxurious descriptions of seascapes and hawthorn bushes, and of invented novels and violin sonatas. Yet he always insists that for him, too, art is not a final value, but a penultimate value. It is valuable to the extent that it preserves and grants a richer form of experience, of life. He reserves his greatest scorn for the kind of people he calls "celibates of art"— those who loudly proclaim their addiction to music, for instance, and go to hear the same piece performed eight times, precisely because they do not have a true, vital experience of the music they are hearing.

The distinction comes to a point in a significant scene late in the novel, in *Time Regained*, when the Narrator encounters the Baron de Charlus on the streets of Paris during World War I. In the course of their conversation about the war and its effects, Charlus complains that the great French cathedrals—the very ones invoked by Bialik as masterpieces of art—are threatened by the fighting. He deplores the loss of "all that mixture of art and still-living history that was France," and says that if the Cathedral of Amiens is lost, with it will go "the loftiest affirmation of faith and energy ever made."

The Narrator has been fulsome in his praise and description of several cathedrals over the long course of the novel, so it is rather surprising when he dissents from Charlus's complaint:

> "You mean its symbol, Monsieur," I interrupted.
> "And I adore certain symbols no less than you do.
> But it would be absurd to sacrifice to the symbol
> the reality that it symbolizes. Cathedrals are to be
> adored until the day when, to preserve them, it

would be necessary to deny the truths that they
teach. . . . Do not sacrifice men to stones whose
beauty comes precisely from their having for a
moment given fixed form to human truths."

Couldn't this elevation of "human truths" above works of art
be seen as Proust's own decision for *halachah* over *aggadah*—for
life and experience over monument and symbol? Indeed, reading
this passage in conjunction with Bialik's praise of Shabbat, I'm
reminded of the way the rabbis deduce the thirty-nine *melachot*,
the categories of labor forbidden on Shabbat, from the activities
of the Israelites when they built the Tabernacle in the desert.
The Tabernacle, of course, was a kind of building, a splendid
and magnificent one—the Notre-Dame or Amiens Cathedral
of the Israelites. After the Roman destruction of the Temple in
Jerusalem, in the year 70, there could be no such building at the
heart of Jewish life. Instead, just as Bialik says, the structure was
made dynamic: it remained a work of art, only its medium was
no longer wood and cloth, but a set of practices, a way of life. It
went, Bialik might say, from *aggadah* to *halachah*. There is something about Proust that suggests he would have understood and
approved this transformation. He, too, believed that what we do
and feel is more important than what we build and make—or,
rather, that our creations are important only to the extent that
they memorialize and preserve our experience.

o o o

It's no wonder that the question of Proust's Jewishness, and
Jewishness in Proust, still has the power to excite strong feeling among Jews today, since it touches on the very questions
of belonging and identity, culture and heritage, that continue
to define Jewish life. The strength of these feelings can be seen
in a book like *Proust Among the Nations*, by Jacqueline Rose. In

her reading of *In Search of Lost Time*, Rose makes much of a conversation between the Narrator and the Baron de Charlus, just after Bloch's humiliation at Mme de Villeparisis' party. Charlus insists on referring to Bloch as a "foreigner," despite the Narrator's insistence that he is French. He then goes on to apply this view of Jewish foreignness to the Dreyfus Affair, holding that Dreyfus should in fact be found innocent of the charge of treason: "I believe the newspapers say that Dreyfus has committed a crime against his country ... the crime is non-existent. This compatriot of your friend would have committed a crime if he had betrayed Judea, but what has he to do with France? ... Your Dreyfus might rather be convicted of a breach of the laws of hospitality."

For Rose, this speech is a pure demonstration of the logic of anti-Semitism: Jews are irreducibly foreign, alien to the body of France, and therefore deserve elimination. And she shows that Charlus's logic was stated almost word for word by the leading anti-Semite Édouard Drumont during the Dreyfus Affair. The logic of otherness is, for Rose, already the logic of expulsion and—to use a word loaded with contemporary political resonance—partition. That is why the lesson she draws from the Dreyfus Affair is the need to oppose any kind of national partition and separation, which she sees as strictly an artifact of language: "The Jew is only what he is," she writes, "stands distinct from the rest of the culture and from everybody else within it—because of the illusions we entertain about the permanence of words."

The word makes the Jew. It is from this point of view that Rose understands Charlus's venomous reference to "some great festival in the Temple, a circumcision, or some Hebrew chants." These are, she writes, "epithets which hand over the Jew to a degraded, parodic form of ancestral belonging: Temple, circumcision and the Hebrew tongue." "Barely concealed beneath these fantasies," she writes, "there is, of course, a logic of expulsion." This is a strange and telling moment in Rose's argument, for of

course, from another point of view, there is nothing degraded
or parodic about Temple, circumcision, or the Hebrew tongue.
These are, in fact, essential components of Jewishness. Charlus
only has the power to turn them into "epithets" if he is addressing someone—like Bloch, or the Narrator, or perhaps certain
readers—for whom they represent a parochial past which it is
necessary to flee in order to achieve full recognition, full humanity. Otherwise, they would be no more insulting than if Bloch
were to speak of Charlus—who is presented as an extremely
pious Catholic—as being involved with baptism or Latin chants.

What is at stake here is the difference between Jewishness as
an identity and Jewishness as a mere predicate. If it is true that
"the word makes the Jew," then the power to define Jewishness
will always be held by the anti-Semite, or at least by the non-
Jewish world. If, on the other hand, the Jew is made by more than
his name—if he is constituted by tradition, text, belief, nation-
hood, culture, or any of the other components of identity—then
it is the Jew who has the power to define and apply his name.

This very debate has played out, fascinatingly and a bit ominously, in the work of Alain Badiou. Badiou presents in formal,
philosophical language the same idea that Rose advances through
her reading of Proust: the idea that the word "Jew" is only a predicate, or, better, that it should be only a predicate. In a series of
articles collected in his book *Polemics*, Badiou argues that there
are two opposed meanings concealed in the word Jew. One is
the Jew as defined by community, tradition, and politics—one
might say, as defined by himself. To Badiou, as to Rose, this is
a corrupt and implicitly oppressive use of the word, because it
allows Jewishness to be a positive identity, and positive identity
is the source of ethnic violence and partition—notably, though
not only, in Israel and Palestine.

He describes this "bad" Jewishness, in a rather Charlusian
spirit, as "bolstered by the tripod of the Shoah, the State of Israel,
and the Talmudic Tradition—the SIT." This is Charlusian in part
because of its aggressive crankishness, but more because Badiou

assumes that these things, which indeed are at the core of Jewishness, are somehow sinister and discreditable. His own mission, he says, is "liberating the word Jew from the triplet SIT": that is, of giving "Jew" a new definition which has nothing to do with the ones Jews give it. For Badiou, a good Jew is precisely one who opposes all the other Jews, because he breaks with his own form of ethnic particularism in the name of an absolute universalism. Or, as Badiou writes: "from the apostle Paul to Trotsky, including Spinoza, Marx and Freud, Jewish communitarianism has only underpinned creative universalism in so far as there have been new points of rupture with it." He goes on to add that "it is clear that today's equivalent of Paul's religious rupture with established Judaism . . . is a subjective rupture with the State of Israel."

What goes unspoken, but not perhaps unintended, is the fact that Paul's rupture with Judaism did not lead him to an absolute universalism; it led him to Christianity, that is, another particularism that was hostile to Jewish particularism. (The same is true of Marx's and Trotsky's communism.) The lesson here is that there is no such thing as a concrete universal—or, perhaps, that every concrete identity has an equal claim to participate in universal human identity. That is why, when Bloch sought to shed his Jewishness in the belief that French society was absolute society, or when a post-Jewish writer like Proust paid no attention to Jewish culture on the grounds that French culture was absolute culture, they were only putting a greater distance between themselves and the goal they posited.

"Thinking of the key, each confirms a prison," T. S. Eliot wrote—and there is a certain irony to quoting Eliot in this context. Where Bloch and Rose and Badiou meet is in their belief that there is a key—assimilation, emancipation, universalism—which will release the Jew from Jewishness. That there is no key does not mean that the Jew is locked in a prison. It means he is in a place that he can leave as often as he wants, but to which he always eventually returns—which is another definition of a home.

Rocket and Lightship

o o o

Nor rescue, only rocket and lightship, shone

—G. M. HOPKINS, "The Wreck of the Deutschland"

The only copy of Catullus's poems to survive from antiquity was discovered in the Middle Ages, plugging a hole in a wine barrel. One of two morals can be drawn from this fact. Either pure chance determines what survives, from which it follows that eventually every work will lose its gamble and be forgotten; or else every worthy work is registered in the eye of God, the way books are registered for copyright, so that its material fate is irrelevant. The first conclusion, which is rationally inevitable, would in time lead anyone to stop writing; anyone who continues to write somehow believes a version of the second. But surely a God who was able to preserve all human works could also preserve all human intentions—indeed, He could deduce the work from its intention far more perfectly than the writer can produce it. Thus a writer with perfect trust would not have to do any work, but simply confide his intentions and aspirations to God. His effort, the pains he takes, are the precise measure of his lack of trust.

o o o

Writers are necessarily ambivalent about any kind of recognition—honors, prizes, simple praise—because they are ambivalent about their relationship to the present. The first audience that a writer wants to please is the past—the dead writers who led him to want to write in the first place. Forced to admit that this is impossible, he displaces his hope onto the future, the posterity whose judgment he will never know. That leaves the present as the only audible judge of his work. But the present is made up of precisely the people whom the writer cannot live among, which is why he subtracts himself from the actual world in order to deposit a version of himself in his writing. The approbation of the living is thus meaningful to a writer only insofar as he can convince himself that it is a proxy for the approbation of the past or the future—insofar as it becomes metaphorical.

o o o

How little of ourselves we give even to the writers we love best, compared to what they asked and expected of us. Genuine admiration and gratitude for a writer's work is very intermittent; usually, we think only about ourselves and how we can use what we're reading. But this must be considered a legitimate technique of self-defense, since if we opened ourselves to all the just demands for attention made by the dead, we would be totally overwhelmed, placed permanently in the wrong. For dead writers are like gods who are always hungry, no matter how many sacrifices they inhale.

o o o

The nineteenth-century Viennese music critic Eduard Hanslick declared that he would rather see the music of Bach and Palestrina lost forever than Brahms's *German Requiem*. This is naturally scoffed at today—but isn't that because we have lost the experience of having the artists of our own time speak to us and for us so perfectly? To be equally appreciative of the art of every era, we must be equidistant from every era, including the present: this means being estranged from our own works, and so in a way from ourselves. It would be only fair, then, if the artworks of our time fail to reach posterity. If even the artist's contemporaries don't feel fiercely protective of him, why should the future?

o o o

Writing generates more writing—not in any metaphysical sense, but empirically. The writing a writer produces will inspire more writing in scholars, biographers, critics; over time, more and more of the writer's acquaintances and surroundings will eventually be illuminated by being written about. We know more about Franz Kafka's coworkers or Virginia Woolf's servants than about thousands of people who, during their lifetimes, would have sneered at clerks and servants; illustriousness does not light people up for posterity nearly as much as proximity to a writer. And this is not because of the inherent interest of the people surrounding a writer, or even of the writer herself, but simply because it is so much easier to write about someone who has already been written about. When you introduce a grain of salt into a beaker of supersaturated fluid, it crystallizes instantly in all directions, revealing structures that were hidden before. So with lives in history: they are invisible because there are too many of them, and it's impossible to pick any one place to start recording them, until the presence of a writer sets the process arbitrarily in motion.

o o o

Just as a musical tone contains its own overtones, resonating even on frequencies far removed from it in the scale, so every kind of mind contains every other, though in muted, attenuated form. Literature would be impossible otherwise.

o o o

At the Metropolitan Museum, there is a re-creation of the Gubbio Studiolo, the workspace where Federico da Montefeltro, the fifteenth-century general and quasi-gangster, pursued his intellectual studies. Seeing the great beauty, seriousness, and lavishness of this room is painful, because it is a reminder that Montefeltro really did exist, that such honor really was paid to the intellect, that the "Renaissance type" is not just a fiction but once flourished. It drives home the immense contrast with the present, when it is certain that no such space would be created by a rich or powerful man for the same purpose.

This kind of pain is what we sublimate and forget when we read about Montefeltro in Pound's *Cantos*. To write about the great, to turn them into literature, is to make them subordinate to the reader: the reader can complacently regard himself as the heir to all the ages, because he preserves in imagination what no longer exists in fact. From there, it is a short step to convincing oneself that human perfection never really exists in fact, that all greatness is ultimately for the sake of the reader, who possesses it in imagination. What this implies is that the historical passion is rooted in resentment: reading is a way of gaining mastery over people and things that would be too painful to confront in reality, because they are so unmistakably superior to us.

o o o

One can actually get angry at the writers of the past for being so secretive about basic, intimate parts of human life. Jane Austen menstruated—why not Elizabeth Bennet? Think of all the writers who fussed with chamber pots, and not a single character does. Omitting this side of life is a betrayal of us, their posterity, by falsifying the record of themselves that writers undertake to leave; they create the illusion that they were bodiless, angelic. We know the past from literature only the way astronomers know distant galaxies: not directly, but by correcting for what we know to be distortions.

o o o

Stefan Zweig writes in his memoirs that when he published a feuilleton on the front page of the *Neue Freie Presse*, as a teenager, he felt that he had conquered the world. Nothing is more enviable than a literary culture small and integrated enough to offer that kind of success—the Augustan poets in their clubs writing to and about one another, or the New York intellectuals battling in *Partisan Review*. Yet there is also something contemptible about a literary ambition that admits of being satisfied so readily, or at all. Real greatness is defined, for us, by its unappeasability—as with Kafka, who loved literature so much that he wanted to destroy all his writing.

○ ○ ○

Every writer needs a fireplace. On publication day, an author should burn a copy of his book, to acknowledge that what he accomplished is negligible compared to what he imagined and intended. Only this kind of burnt offering might be acceptable to the Muse he has let down.

○ ○ ○

Literature claims to be a record of human existence through time; it is the only way we have to understand what people used to be like. But this is a basic mistake, if not a fraud, since in fact it only reflects the experience of writers—and writers are innately unrepresentative, precisely because they see life through and for writing. Literature tells us nothing, really, about what most people's lives are like or have ever been like. If it has a memorial purpose, it is more like that of an altar at which priests continue to light a fire, generation after generation, even though it gives no heat and very little light.

○ ○ ○

Pound's goal was to "write nothing that we might not say actually in life." But this is backwards, for nothing memorable is ever said, it is always written; only sometimes it is not written down, but written in the mind so quickly that it can be produced as speech. In speech, the mind is on the moment, the subject, the interlocutor; in writing, the mind is on these and also always on the self, and the appearance the self and its language are making. Speech is an action, writing an act (as in "putting on an act"), whose audience is always primarily oneself. To become memorable or brilliant, language needs to be fertilized by egotism.

◦ ◦ ◦

All forms of writing are only valid, maybe only comprehensible, as forms of self-expression. Even philosophy, even history, never say anything true about the world, only about the writer's experience of being in the world. Some sensibilities require the illusion of objectivity in order to get their version of the truth spoken: if the metaphysician realized he was only talking about himself, not about reality, he would be unable to say what he needs to say.

◦ ◦ ◦

Literature presents itself to us today as a museum of perished affects. Belief in God, courtly love, honor, and so forth: we can recognize that people once felt these things, but we can't feel them ourselves. Perhaps this anesthesia will be what future ages see as characteristic of our literature.

◦ ◦ ◦

In Memoriam R.W. Most suicides are a refusal of communication, or else a communication made in a language we protect ourselves against by declining to understand it. But for the suicide we know as a writer, her death becomes a continuation of the self-expression in her work, and may even be her most successful act of communication: we know exactly what she means by it.

◦ ◦ ◦

Writerly vanity is like a vicious dog chained up outside the house. You try to starve and neglect the dog into silence, but sometimes he becomes so clamorous that he must be fed if you're going to be able to ignore him again.

◦ ◦ ◦

Literature operates on the premise that humanity can be transcendent. But it now looks increasingly likely that humanity can only be transcended, that is, left behind. Like all culture, literature is a matter of directing the will inward, to create an inner life; this was a necessity for most of human history, when the conditions of outer life could not be changed. But the future is going to be defined by the ever-more-successful direction of the will outward, in the form of technology and power, which are now genuinely able to transform the conditions of life. In this sense, culture is an obsolete technology, a sunk cost that we keep adding to only because we lack the courage to write it off.

° ° °

Our understanding of history is distorted by the universal tendency to identify only with the protagonists of the past—kings, heroes, nobles, the rich, the exceptionally gifted or fated. When we read history or novels, we always imagine ourselves in the position of the protagonist, the position of agency; not remembering that we ourselves, had we lived then, would not have had the remotest chance of being protagonists, but would have lived in the outer darkness into which the light of narrative never penetrates.

° ° °

The unadmitted reason why traditional readers are hostile to e-books is that we still hold the superstitious idea that a book is like a soul, and that every soul should have its own body. The condensation of millions of books on a single device, or their evaporation in a data cloud, seems to presage what is destined to happen to our souls, to the coming end of selfhood, even of embodiment. If this sounds fanciful, imagine what a lover of handwritten codices might have thought in 1450 about the rise of print. Manuscripts, he would protest, were once rare, precious, hard to create, dedicated to holy or venerable subjects; print would make them cheap, derivative, profane, and easily disposable. And didn't exactly this happen to human beings in the age of print, which was the modern age?

° ° °

A writer begins writing, in adolescence, as a detour away from life that is supposed to return him to the main road of life further on, at a better stage. Writing is seen as a shortcut, through isolation, to the communication and connection that are unavailable in reality. Only gradually does it become clear that the detour is really a fork in the road: as the writer continues to write, he moves further away from life, from the communion with other people that writing was meant to provide. Eventually, the main road can no longer be seen, but he keeps on writing: because of spite, because he is unfit for anything else and can't go back, and because of the unbanishable hope that maybe the next turn in the road will bring him back to life.

∘ ∘ ∘

Bentham: "Pushpin is as good as poetry." In fact, pushpin is better, because it confesses its insignificance from the start. The pushpin player will never know the shame of realizing that he has built his life on the delusion that he is better than the poet.

∘ ∘ ∘

Today, finding a good used bookstore is like finding Friday's footprint—evidence of a fellowship that is ordinarily invisible.

∘ ∘ ∘

The crisis of literature, in contrast with the confidence of the sciences, is a crisis of memory and transmission. The creation of works of art is only a valid way to spend a life if those works are preserved—if they are made exceptions to the general oblivion that nature designed for us. But the sciences do not require this kind of exceptional preservation. They make use of intellect in a way that imitates nature, because the progress of science both incorporates and obliterates each contributor, in the same way that the progenitor is both incorporated and forgotten in his descendants. For the artist, the creation of a work of genius is an alternative to parenthood; for the scientist, it is an imitation of parenthood. This helps to explain the shame of the artist in the face of the scientist, which is that of the celibate in the face of the progenitor, the unnatural in the face of nature.

∘ ∘ ∘

Writers used to write for posterity—that is, for people essentially like us in the future. Now the only future we can imagine, the only plausible alternative to extinction, is made up of beings that will understand us wholly differently, and much better, than we can understand ourselves. The readers of the future will be anthropologists in the sense that we are ornithologists, studying creatures of a different and lesser species. Today, the writer's aspiration is not to communicate with such readers, the way past writers communicate with us, but to leave a body of evidence for the future to interpret.

o o o

The hallmark of a writer's late style—for instance, in Philip Roth's annual production of short, indifferently written novels—is the abandonment of the attempt to triumph over death objectively, by creating a work whose nature is superior to death. No longer believing in this possibility, the aging artist is left to triumph over death subjectively, by writing perpetually in order to keep the thought of oblivion out of his mind. In retrospect, then, even his greatest works take on this air of subjectivity: art begins to look like a method of whistling past the graveyard.

o o o

Writing, not philosophy, is the true practice of death—it translates the self into words as a rehearsal for the time when the self disappears and words are all that remain. A writer has succeeded if, when we read his obituary, we are surprised to learn that he was still alive.

o o o

The line of nihilism and despair in modern literature, from Leopardi to Beckett, asks to be taken as a true diagnosis of humanity during this period. But it is no coincidence that this was also the time when the writer lost his connection with the public, thanks to the increasing restriction and specialization of literature. Perhaps the sense we find in such writers that all human activity is cosmically pointless is simply the symptom of this isolation—as when an animal kept in a cage, far from its kind, pines away and languishes. To be immersed in the human world so deeply that one can't see outside it, so as to question the validity or purpose of the whole—that is the natural state

of man. The miserable doubts that occur to the writer withdrawn from the world are not to be answered, but dealt with
as symptoms, requiring the therapy of reimmersion.

о о о

No true universal statements can safely be made about human
beings or human nature; it is only permissible to make such
assertions hypothetically, or metaphorically. This realization is
what gives birth to literature, a realm where anything can be
expressed because it is essentially without consequence. But we
can never stop imagining the secret mastery we would gain if
this artistic power could be surreptitiously reintroduced into the
actual world: the combination of imaginative freedom and actual
power would be a kind of magic. This helps to explain the special
mystique that attaches to artists of the real like Marx and Freud.
By stating their metaphors about humankind as if they were scientific laws, they seem to gain magical powers, and promise them
to their adherents. Such intellectual mages lose their authority
once we remember that power can only be gained over the physical, and over man insofar as he is physical; the truth about the
spirit can only be demonstrated in works of the spirit.

о о о

An axiom of the novel is that people whose lives are devoted to
the competition for status—the bourgeois, the philistines—are
inferior to those who devote themselves to the realization of an
aesthetic or ethical ideal. The very fact of being a novel reader
is the badge of this distinction: to be a reader, in this sense, is
really to be a writer of one's life, to try to shape one's life in
the image of the values promoted by what one reads. Yet the
proud reader should remember that the pursuit of outward status
and the pursuit of inward perfection can both be understood as
ways of imposing direction, and therefore narrative, on a life.
Both status and goodness are useful for this purpose because both
are fundamentally unachievable: it will always be possible, and
therefore necessary, to become "higher" or "better" than one is.
These ways of imposing meaning on life are more similar to each

other than either one is to the horrible vacancy of the vast majority of lives, which are composed simply of endless repetition.
Compared to the peasant, the bourgeois is a kind of artist—and
the artist is a kind of bourgeois.

o o o

People used to wish that life could be as it is in books—that it
could have the beauty, drama, and shapeliness that writers gave
it. Today, by contrast, we hope desperately that life is not really
the way our writers portray it; in other words, we hope that
writers are not representative men and women, but unfit beings
whose perceptions are filtered through their unhealth. It is necessary to hope this, because if life were as it appears in our literature it would be unlivable. Thus Flaubert's pious sigh, *"Ils sont
dans le vrai"*—because if the writer's life were the true one, life
would be unworthy of being continued. Biographies of writers
who went mad or committed suicide are popular because they
offer reassurance on this point.

o o o

The statesman always has contempt for the historian, and understandably so: how can you compare a professor to a president? But
with the passage of only a few decades, it becomes clear that the
great man acted and suffered only for the sake of the historians.
The writer is superior to the man of action as the owner of a toy
is superior to the one who made it.

o o o

"Whereof one cannot speak, thereof one must be silent." On
the contrary: it is what we cannot speak of, what we cannot
point to and scientifically describe, that we speak about most and
best, and always have. What can be wholly comprehended and
demonstrated is "trivial" in the sense that mathematicians use
the word: even if it is very hard to understand, once understood
it does not provoke further discourse, does not point anywhere.
But authentic speech and writing are always productive of more
speech and writing—indeed, that is the point of discourse, not
to describe reality but to avoid silence.

Acknowledgments

Grateful acknowledgment is made to the publications in which these essays first appeared, usually in a somewhat different form:

City Journal: "Francis Fukuyama and the Beginning of History"

Jewish Review of Books: "Proust Between *Halachah* and *Aggadah*"

New Republic: "Art over Biology," "Up from Cynicism: Peter Sloterdijk," "The Deadly Jester: Slavoj Žižek," "Alfred Kazin's Clamor," "The Importance of Being Earnest: David Foster Wallace," "The Lesson of the Master: Cynthia Ozick," "Liberation and Liberalism: E. M. Forster," "Zadie Smith and the Future of the Novel"

The New Yorker: "Under the Volcano: Giacomo Leopardi," "Beware of Pity: Hannah Arendt," "The Interpreter: Walter Benjamin"

New York Times Book Review: "Still the Good War?"

Poetry: "Rocket and Lightship"

Tablet: "Susan Sontag's Seriousness"

Times Literary Supplement: "The Turbulence of Saul Bellow"

World Affairs: "The Last Men: Houellebecq, Sebald, McEwan"

I am especially grateful to Leon Wieseltier, literary editor of the *New Republic*, and Alana Newhouse, editor of *Tablet*, for their friendship and steadfast support.